M000170394

ADVANCE PRAISE

"This book is a road map for creating more humane workplaces. Josh Bersin gives us unusually clear and compelling directions to make people the heart and soul of organizations."
—**ADAM GRANT, #1** *New York Times* **bestselling author of** *THINK AGAIN* **and host of the TED podcast** *WorkLife*

"A must-read primer for business leaders considering how and why to build a people-centered business. *Irresistible* is an essential book and an opportunity to learn from one of the best."
—**ARIANNA HUFFINGTON, Founder and CEO, Thrive**

"For too long, businesses have been claiming that people are their most important resource. *Irresistible* offers an array of smart insights and shrewd advice to—finally!—turn that idea into action."
—**DANIEL H. PINK, #1** *New York Times* **bestselling author of** *The Power of Regret, Drive,* **and** *To Sell Is Human*

"If you want the secrets of maintaining a workforce of fulfilled, engaged, and loyal teams, read this book—now."
—**KATHLEEN HOGAN, Chief People Officer, Microsoft**

"Josh, with his reporter's background and analyst's instinct, is terrific at describing practices that affect people. The seven themes offer an outstanding view of emerging practices that will shape employee-focused organizations."
—**DAVE ULRICH, Rensis Likert Professor, Ross School of Business, University of Michigan Partner, The RBL Group**

"I have been following Josh's work for years and not long ago had the chance to teach executives alongside him. He has always taught me a great deal. And now I see some of that so beautifully encapsulated and extended in *Irresistible*. This is a book to absorb."
—**RICH LYONS, Former Dean, Haas School of Business, and Chief Innovation and Entrepreneurship Officer, UC Berkeley**

"As organizations struggle to attract and retain talent, irresistible companies will be the only ones to prevail—and creating an irresistible company starts with unlocking your employees' full potential."

—**JILL POPELKA, President, SAP SuccessFactors**

"This book is an illustration of my strong belief that 'great people make great companies.' With his unique and vast experience, Josh is helping all leaders and HR teams turn company culture, management approaches, and work models into a competitive advantage."

—**OLIVIER BLUM, Executive Vice President, Energy Management Business, Schneider Electric**

irresistible

irresistible

THE SEVEN SECRETS OF THE WORLD'S MOST ENDURING,
EMPLOYEE-FOCUSED ORGANIZATIONS

by Josh Bersin

IDEAPRESS
PUBLISHING

WASHINGTON, D.C.

IDEAPRESS
PUBLISHING

Copyright © 2022 by Josh Bersin

All rights reserved. No part of this book may be used or reproduced in any manner without written permission from the publisher, except in the context of reviews.

Published in the United States by Ideapress Publishing.

Ideapress Publishing | www.ideapresspublishing.com

All trademarks are the property of their respective companies.

Interior Design by Leff Communications
Cover Design: Ideapress

Cataloging-in-Publication Data is on file with the Library of Congress.

ISBN: 978-1-64687-110-0

Special Sales
Ideapress Books are available at a special discount for bulk purchases for sales promotions and premiums, or for use in corporate training programs. Special editions, including personalized covers, a custom foreword, corporate imprints, and bonus content, are also available.

1 2 3 4 5 6 7 8 9 10

DEDICATION

I dedicate this book to my loving wife, Heidi, who inspires me in all that I do, and to all my friends and associates in the human resources profession around the world.

contents

preface 1

introduction 3

1 **teams, not hierarchy** 7
    THE INNOVATION: AGILE PRINCIPLES AT THE CORE 21
    HOW TO GET STARTED 28
    HOW TO GET IT RIGHT 28

2 **work, not jobs** 43
    THE SHIFT: WORK, NOT JOBS 44
    THE CHALLENGE: DEVELOPING NEW WAYS TO HIRE 62
    THE INNOVATION: SELECT TO FIT 65
    HOW TO GET STARTED 67
    HOW TO GET IT RIGHT 68

3 **coach, not boss** 77
    THE SHIFT: COACH, NOT BOSS 78
    THE PROBLEM: PERFORMANCE MANAGEMENT IS BROKEN 85
    THE INNOVATION: CONTINUOUS PERFORMANCE MANAGEMENT 87
    HOW TO GET STARTED 90
    HOW TO GET IT RIGHT 91

4 **culture, not rules** 107

THE SHIFT: CULTURE, NOT RULES 108

HOW TO GET STARTED 130

HOW TO GET IT RIGHT 131

5 **growth, not promotion** 137

THE INNOVATION: ALWAYS LEARNING, ALWAYS GROWING 151

HOW TO GET STARTED 153

HOW TO GET IT RIGHT 154

6 **purpose, not profits** 165

THE SHIFT: PURPOSE, NOT PROFITS 166

HOW TO GET STARTED 179

HOW TO GET IT RIGHT 180

7 **employee experience, not output** 185

THE PROBLEM: TECHNOLOGY FRIEND...OR FOE? 191

THE INNOVATION: A NEW BREED OF TOOLS IS COMING 192

HOW TO GET STARTED 196

HOW TO GET IT RIGHT 197

conclusion 199

a final note on the pandemic 201

appendix 1: about organizational endurance 203

appendix 2: finding irresistible companies using data 211

endnotes 213

index 237

preface

You're a CEO, manager, executive, or HR leader in your company, and you want your company, your team, and your department to be fantastic. In fact, you'd like your company to be so great people consider it "irresistible." They can't wait to come to work in the morning, whether that's in the office, at home, or on the road. They love to tell their friends who they work for. And they never want to leave.

Isn't this what work should be all about—finding a job at a company with a mission that makes you feel purposeful and fulfilled? Finding a manager who really cares and helps but who also stays out of the way? And finding a company that teaches you things; looks after its employees, its customers, and its communities; cares for the planet; and does great things for the world?

That company is irresistible.

Is it even possible to create such a place?

I think it is. And I'm going to show you how.

introduction

Today's world of work is filled with paradoxes.

The economy is growing, but it's harder to hire than ever.

Companies spend billions on benefits and perks, yet employee anxiety and stress are at an all-time high.

Artificial intelligence, robotics, and automation are everywhere, yet we work more hours and get less sleep.

We can reach others in seconds from anywhere, but we feel isolated and lonely, particularly when working from home in today's flexible work environment.

What in the world is going on?

During the past 25 years, I've devoted my life to studying these issues. As a research analyst, I've led more than 100 studies of corporate talent, leadership, and HR practices and talked with thousands of employers, consultants, and software vendors.

What I see now is clear: our economy is in the third inning of a revolutionary change in the way businesses are run. We are in the middle of redefining the principles of management and even the role of businesses as environmental stewards and champions of diversity and inclusion. The way we define jobs, the way we organize our teams, the role of leaders, and the way we pay people are transforming.

And the result? Lots of worries about recruiting frontline workers, the role of hybrid work, employee wellbeing, and creating a sense of trust. Can an outside force fix all these problems? Absolutely not—the foundation of transformation lies in management: how we manage, organize, and empower our people.

One could argue that these are economic issues driven by the change in the economy—that if we grow the economy, reduce taxes, and create more jobs, these problems will go away. Well, I really disagree. As Jonathan Sacks describes eloquently in his book *Morality*, no amount of GDP growth can solve the problems we face today.[1] The solutions all come down to management.

While a small number of "hyperwinning" companies are rocketing ahead in revenue and profits, many businesses struggle to keep pace. While we as employees live longer than ever, our companies die at record-breaking rates. The average age of an S&P 500 company is less than 18 years, compared to 61 years in 1958. In 2027, three-quarters of S&P 500 companies will have disappeared.[2]

What should we do to fix this? Well, there are lots of experiments going on. The entire pandemic has seen a series of new ideas being tested on workers at all levels. This is not a new phenomenon: people have been tweaking the "employee experience" for decades. I can tell you that some of these experiments are working and others are not—and I am pretty sure I know why.

Driven by a series of lightning-fast changes in technology, globalization, and social consciousness around the world, the rules of business have changed, resulting in an extraordinarily profound rethinking of where, how, when, and even why people work today.

A failure to appreciate this transformation will culminate in an organization that is, well, resistible. I'm offering the opposite in this book: seven management principles that will truly make your company irresistible—more focused, purposeful, and aligned. Your company will become more agile, more responsive, and more profitable. But even better, your employees, customers, and other stakeholders will be drawn to your company like magnets.

Why use the word "irresistible" to describe my goal? Quite simply because the essential theme of this book is to unleash the power of the human spirit. Each individual, at every level of your company, is capable of doing more important and more valuable things than ever before. If you make your company irresistible, these individuals will contribute, innovate, and grow. If you fall behind and your people feel frustrated, uneasy, unhealthy, or disconnected, they will slow you down, get in the way, and undermine your company in ways you may not be aware of.

In this book, I am going to reveal seven secrets of the most employee-focused organizations across the world. These are essentially fundamental management values: strategies and philosophies that embrace the power of every individual. They leverage the need for speed, the technologies of today, flexible work arrangements in the new hybrid workspace, and the social and cultural issues of our time. Each embodies an evolution of management thinking with a vision for a higher performing, more engaged organization ahead.

But let me warn you, this is not as easy as it sounds. You can't just copy the programs or innovations of others. In my studies of more than 5,000 companies from around the world, under 10 percent are irresistible today. These are not young companies, tech companies, or companies in any particular industry—they're companies that understand these seven principles and work on them day after day, quarter after quarter, and year after year.

Now is your chance to join them.

Let's get started.

1

···

teams, not hierarchy

"Form ever follows function."

LOUIS SULLIVAN, ARCHITECT, 1896

For hundreds of years, a time-tested system of management stood firm—the hierarchy. Founders built companies and hired and organized employees into top-down order. It was safe, rewarding, and predictable. Each individual had a boss; there was a functional and predictable career plan; and business executives would organize, measure, and manage themselves into these functional hierarchical units. Most companies are still managed this way.[3]

The traditional functional hierarchy dates back to the Industrial Revolution. During the turn of the century, as the United States shifted from an agrarian to an industrial economy, businesses needed a way to scale, so companies invented systems of management, functional specialization, and hierarchy. Masses of untrained people were moving to urban centers from farms with little to no experience working in large organizations. Management and labor were strictly segregated. Detailed job descriptions told employees exactly what was required, and bosses made sure they completed their tasks.

It all made sense—back when industrial scale was key. But as soon as the game shifted to speed and innovation and the workforce became dominated by service workers, these structural constructs held businesses back. Not only do hierarchies slow down decision-making, but they also hurt people's aspirations. Employees might not feel able to achieve their full potential when there are dozens of layers on top of them. Enter the idea of agency. Today's efforts to better engage employees are rooted in the need to help people achieve their individual aspirations.

Winning strategies have shifted from seeking industrial scale to seeking what John Hagel and John Brown call "scalable learning,"[4] because we live in a world where time to market and speed of iteration win. While your company may have a strong brand, distribution network, or customer base, a competitor can quickly build a better mousetrap and reach your customers through an app, cloud subscription software offering, or other digital experience. If you don't learn quickly, your scale becomes a disadvantage.

Some organizations continue to retain their hierarchies, compelled by a perceived need to protect executive power, positions, and careers. This is increasingly not the case at irresistible companies.

Business and service delivery models are changing faster than ever. We sell products and services in a digital way, forcing us to organize around customer segments, services, delivery centers, and innovation units that design new features. And we need to iterate quickly: we don't have time to traverse the hierarchy every time we want to make a decision.

We are all in the service business. The way I like to think of it, a digital business is not one that builds a lot of apps; it's a business that meets customers where they are. This means letting people click, view, order, and interact with you instantaneously, creating a need for services teams that have immediate access to data, are highly skilled and engaged, and have the tools and productive environment to respond quickly.

How did we get here? It's actually quite simple: technology crept up on us. It changed the business landscape, and we are still trying to adapt.

We have phones that can read our facial expressions, interpret the sentiments behind our spoken words, and instantly share personal information with anyone in the world. Households have Amazon or Google listening devices and smart thermostats, cars, and security systems that wirelessly transmit data to homeowners.

We as consumers adapt to technology quickly. Walk down any street and you'll see people reading news on their phones, conducting video calls, buying or selling products on apps, or using electronic maps to find a location. Meta (previously Facebook), Google, Apple, and Amazon have become trillion-dollar companies because they have learned how to tap into the human desire to connect, to be discovered, and to gratify our own egos.

Today's new business drivers—speed, agility, engagement, and empowerment—have created a new organization model, one I call the "network of teams." Fundamental to this definition are two ideas: first, that teams are the center of work; and, second, that the company operates as a network (not as a hierarchy).

While most organization charts have not changed much over the years, with cascading controls not far removed from yesteryear's hierarchies, in reality, people work in cross-functional teams. There are design teams, sales teams, business unit teams, manufacturing teams, and dozens of other different cross-functional teams. I can assure you it's possible to formalize, manage, and organize this way—with tremendous scale, power, and employee success—in a flexible work environment.

Teams make sense for many reasons: they are more engaging, they are quick to form and disband, and over time they generate camaraderie and trust. Just as sports teams operate with clear roles and values, business teams can do the same. In today's irresistible companies, teams are multidisciplinary and demographically diverse, clearly defined and measured, and supported with artifacts, measurement tools, and infrastructure to perform successfully.

Think about what CEOs want most of all. They ask, "How fast can we innovate? How do we reduce our time to market? What's the quickest way to solve customer problems? What can we do to reduce cost?" Teams solve these problems.

"In the industrial era, management was very much [centered] around command and control," said Janice Semper, senior advisor and executive coach at Boston Consulting Group.[5] "When you come into the digital era, leading others takes on a completely different set of behaviors and mindsets. It's really about, how [do] you provide context for teams, how do you coach, how do you inspire them, how do you put the right team in place, [...] develop them, and give them the room to grow?"

Why do small teams work well? When people operate in small, empowered groups, they gain a sense of trust. In small teams, employees get to know one another and feel a sense of collective ownership, enabling them to design things faster, serve customers better, and iterate more quickly. Amazon, known as a ruthless competitor, operates this way. Teams form, they grow, they take advantage of shared services, and, if they fail, they go away. It's all part of the design. (Incidentally, academic studies show that the optimum team size is between four and five,[6] but this varies by project.)

In a world of perpetual disruption, the *2021 Deloitte Global Human Capital Trends* report cites teams and teaming as a survival strategy. "Teaming [during the pandemic] became a life raft for talent and organizational strategies [...] because teams are built for adaptability rather than predictability and stability," the report states.[7]

Teams learn and adapt faster than individual workers by challenging each team member to come up with more creative ideas. As organizations shift their focus to learning, they will increase their reliance on teams to navigate uncertainty and generate growth.

We know that a strong team outperforms a strong individual. Look at any sports league to see how a losing team becomes a winning team when the right coach comes along. My local Golden State Warriors basketball team is a good example: while each player is amazing in his own right, he is essentially equivalent to top players in other teams. It is the way the team works together that has helped put the Warriors in the National Basketball Association (NBA) championship match four times in the last five years, which they won three times.

An irresistible company knows this. It facilitates and supports people moving from project to project, from team to team, and from office to home. It lets people bring their A games—their skills and capabilities—anywhere they are most needed. Employees connect through technical and professional networks to build skills rapidly through peer coaching, project experience, and senior technical support. Leaders succeed through making connections and winning "followership" rather than through power and tenure. People are evaluated based on their contributions to the team, not rigid performance goals and once-a-year reviews.

During the global coronavirus pandemic (which I call "The Big Reset"), teams came together at speed. While many companies thought they would go out of business in the early months, in only a few quarters teams were redesigning work, redesigning customer service, and redesigning offerings. Employees solved problems in days or weeks, compared to the traditional lengthy processes to gain buy-in and to agree on solutions in a hierarchical structure.

Teams at PepsiCo, for example, developed a virtual onboarding program in four weeks that might have taken six months in the past.[8] The problem was simple—enable new employees to onboard virtually while offices were closed. The team agreed on the focus of the project in hours, focusing on speed first, followed by iterative improvements drawn from pulse surveys and open feedback. A highly organized central listening team ensured all input was continually analyzed. This agile approach is common among start-up software companies but rare in large global corporations.

Other forward-looking companies like Taj Hotels, Microsoft, Unilever, Telstra, Amazon, General Motors (GM), Cleveland Clinic, ING Group,

Cisco, Google, and ANZ Bank are training people for team leadership in today's highly flexible, dispersed environment, resulting in growth, innovation, and renewed employee passion. The practice is spreading.

WHAT IS A TEAM? WHAT IS A NETWORK OF TEAMS?

These sound like simple questions, but they're important. Let me begin with a definition:

> *A team is a highly interdependent group of people that comes together in a physical or virtual setting to plan work, solve problems, make decisions, and review progress toward a specific goal.*

This definition leaves room for many different types of teams. A team of nurses that runs an emergency room is completely different from a team of engineers remotely building a new software product using online tools. They have a few common characteristics:

· Teams have a clear mission or goal; they are not just an institutionalized group or department.

· Teams are dependent on each member, not a collection of single workers.

· Teams can form, endure a long time, and be disbanded easily.

· Teams have a leader, who may or may not be a manager.

· Teams are demographically diverse and multifunctional; they may include design, operations, engineering, staff, administration, and other roles.

Unlike a functional hierarchy (in which people are grouped by function, or the type of work they do), teams form to achieve a result—so their loyalty is to the *mission, not to the leader.* Leaders oversee teams, coordinate roles, stay cognizant of everyone's feelings, and handle communication. In a software company that provides file storage, for example, a team might be responsible for the mobile application that displays and manages photos. It could have engineers, designers, a project manager, and a manager. The manager would make sure the team coordinates with other teams.

A network of teams means that teams operate in groups, although not necessarily in a hierarchical way. Teams can be combined into squads, tribes, and chapters, as they are in agile software development teams, depending on their dependency on others or the constituencies they serve.

Generally, a squad is a team of fewer than 10 people, with a product owner responsible for the team's output and its overall success with its customers. A tribe is a grouping of squads, pulled together into a larger program or project. So, if you're a bank branch, the loan department may be a squad and the branch itself may be a tribe. Tribes may have as many as 150 people, keeping the size around the size of the Dunbar number—the maximum number of people that can know each other well in an organization.[9]

At ING, for example, the local-branch bank function is a tribe, and customer service, operations, and other functions are also tribes. As previously stated, tribes are not necessarily hierarchical but are instead more like affinity groups or teams of teams. They bring squads together to coordinate more closely with adjacent squads.

In IT departments, teams frequently work on software implementations or on the development of new systems. They are often part of a tribe of teams implementing other applications, which means they can coordinate their decisions.

There are two other groupings in the agile model. A chapter is a group of people with the same role. So, within a bank, there may be salespeople in each squad who share ideas and solutions across the tribe. This system lets all the sales, marketing, or operations staff across tribes work together within the branch.

The last grouping in the agile model is a guild, which is essentially a grouping of people across the whole company who have a common interest. For example, all first-line managers may make up the first-line management guild, since they all need training and help with supervision. Or all the graphic designers in the company could be a guild, since they want to share tools, designs, and color schemes.

As you reconsider this structural model, many other practices become clear.

First, teams must be aligned by the organizational culture and a set of team practices companies often formalize. Liberty Mutual Insurance, for example, built an entire management system to facilitate teams, originally called the Liberty Management System (LMS).[10] It specifies how teams are formed, how teams operate, how they measure themselves, and how they communicate with others.

LMS offers a common way of working across the global enterprise, from planning how to deliver value for customers and engaging people to improve how they work by sharing best practices, to continuously improving to compete in a constantly changing marketplace.

At Atlassian, Google, W. L. Gore, UnitedHealth Group, and other companies, a group within HR is dedicated to coaching teams, training team leaders, and building tools to make teams more productive. (Atlassian became famous for its ShipIt hackathons, in which employees are encouraged to drop their normal work for 24 hours to spend time on a creative project of their choosing. Today, the Atlassian Team Playbook gives teams exercises and guides to learn how to work well together.[11])

Second, a network of teams reduces hierarchy, eliminating a lot of the up-and-down communication that wastes time. In most functional hierarchies, middle managers exist to "get in the middle" of decisions and arbitrate priorities and budgets. Within a circle, on the other hand, a team will make decisions, while the team leader maintains alignment with the network of teams in an open and transparent way. The team values people by skill, not by role; for example, one executive told me they reduced the number of levels in the company from 40 to 9 as they mobilized into teams.

This is not an uncommon practice. In the Iraq War, for example, General Stanley McChrystal appointed liaison officers to make sure teams were coordinated. These officers were individuals with particularly strong relationship skills who provided coordinated intelligence to make sure teams would connect and receive correct real-time information. Similarly, team-centric companies use tools such as objectives and key results (OKRs, described in greater detail later), transparent goals, and whiteboards (both virtual and real) to make sure everyone knows what other teams are working on.

To maintain functional expertise, individuals are loyal to their function as well as to their team and are promoted based on experience, skills, reputation, and relationships—not based on hierarchy within the team. The team itself is flat. In most software companies, for example, designers report to their project leaders and also to a chief of design or head of design for career direction, development, and standards.

Third, in a network of teams, people easily move from team to team. As a project is formed or completed, there is a team start-up process and a team shutdown process. At W. L. Gore, Cisco, Meta, SAP, and Unilever, people work on multiple teams at once, and they have coaches, career advisors, or managers to help them decide which teams to join over time. People are sought out to join teams based on their reputation and skills, which encourages them to focus on expertise, not on politics, to succeed.

Fourth, there must be people, infrastructure, and a culture focused on information-sharing and collective intelligence across teams. Such communication often takes place through short, daily standup meetings; information portals; and squad or tribe leaders who make sure teams are coordinated and aware. Meetings focus on coordination and information-sharing, leaving detailed decisions to the teams themselves.

....

: BREAKOUT: TEAM INTELLIGENCE SYSTEMS

: The U.S. Army built an AI-based intelligence system to help fighting
: teams gain real-time information during the Iraq War. The system, as it
: was described by one of its architects, could give you useful information;
: for example, it might say, "The third house on this block is likely to have a
: terrorist inside based on activity 10 minutes ago." This technology essen-
: tially shares intelligence between teams in real time. In sales, marketing,
: and other functions, we can build similar systems using new tools such
: as Microsoft Teams, Slack, and Workplace from Meta.

....

Finally, companies optimize teams based on the project, mission, goals, and individuals involved. A well-run team has a clear lifespan, allows employees to perform at their best, supports and helps team members grow, and gives employees a sense of empowerment, progress, and independence. Teams are held accountable for their goals, and when they start to fail, they can be easily adjusted or disbanded.

Teams generally fall into several distinct types (see Figure 1.1).

How are companies making the shift from hierarchies to teams? At Southwest Airlines, the flight crew is the team and the pilot is the leader. Each crew has the responsibility and the authority to promote safety, timely travel, and the happiness of its passengers. This structure not only drives financial performance; it also makes for more engaged employees. Southwest remains one of the most profitable airlines, with a Glassdoor rating 18 percent above its peers.[12]

Ritz Carlton creates teams around each individual property. A general manager leads each property and organizes employees into hospitality teams, services teams, finance teams, and others. The company prides itself on empowerment and training, famous for its credo, "We are ladies and gentlemen serving ladies and gentlemen." This services-team approach delivers some of the highest levels of employee and customer engagement in the industry.[13]

FIGURE 1.1: TYPICAL TYPES OF TEAMS

TEAM TYPE	WHAT IT DOES	HOW IT FUNCTIONS	OUTPUT AND GOALS
DESIGN	Designs products, software, or other services	May use agile practices for creative and often technical purposes	New products, systems, designs, applications, and modules
MANUFAC-TURING	Manages manu-facturing processes and equipment	Divides work based on processes while main-taining quality, safety, and productivity	Process output, quality, safety, efficiency, and resource utilization
SERVICE DELIVERY	Serves internal or external stake-holders	Defines customer needs and organizes around quality, scale, and ethos of service	Service quality, speed, customer feedback, and continuous im-provement
SALES AND MARKETING	Develops cam-paigns, serves customers, closes deals, and develops brand awareness and leads	Segments the market, organizes to serve customers or market priorities, and com-municates and sells to clients or prospects	Revenue, leads, brand, market share, and public relations
FINANCE, OPERATIONS, AND MONI-TORING	Monitors operations, performs financial analysis, and mea-sures work to ensure it is on track and on budget	Defines metrics, devel-ops models, and helps "operationalize" and monitor work to help team leaders improve their performance	Output per dollar, budget compliance, profitability, produc-tivity, and a variety of other measures
INFRASTRUC-TURE	Develops and sup-ports infrastructure and microservices other teams need to succeed	Manages facilities, technology services, security, data, and other services that make all other teams more effective	Constant under-standing of what holds teams back and development of new tools and models to help teams succeed

SOURCE: THE JOSH BERSIN COMPANY, 2021

Unilever's emphasis on agile teams was instrumental in shifting its business profile to serve a surging demand for hygiene products at the beginning of the pandemic. "Having studied what was happening in China in the last months of 2019, we were able to shift nearly 30 percent of products to clean faces and hands in March [2020] in less than three weeks," said Jeroen Wels, Unilever executive vice president of human resources.[14]

To do this, Unilever employees who formerly served the needs of customers such as restaurants and hotels that had been sidelined by the pandemic—employees whose jobs had essentially become obsolete—were shifted to serve more robust markets. By the end of April 2020, the tasks of more than 9,000 employees were repurposed to serve higher-growth markets.

"The transition from the sales and marketing of food products to hygiene solutions ultimately showed just how agile we could be," said Wels. "Our team approach gave us the priority-setting we needed to reallocate resources from businesses that closed down to increasing the supply of products that were in high demand."

One of the keys to strong teams is their inclusive and multifunctional nature. Teams need a leader, and they also need designers, builders, implementers, and operators. The teams previously described do very different things, but the fundamental structure is the same: every team has a leader who coordinates instead of manages, employees are assigned to teams that need their skills, people are empowered to make decisions and take action, and teams are given clear goals through which they establish metrics and operational rules.

This structure is logical in theory, but what happens in practice? People work on more than one team at a time. Lori Goler, head of people at Meta, told me that people often work on many different development teams at the same time. When I asked how the company decided who works on what team, she said, "It's really up to the individual, and of course they talk about it with their manager."[15] The company's culture enables teams to form rapidly and easily.

When people are given the freedom to join teams and projects that excite them, the results are amazing. Barry Murphy, global learning lead at Airbnb, said that growth and change put a strain on organizations, making it critical to get organizational design right: "It's almost like you need to build a scaffolding to support people, instead of imposing a structure that holds them back."[16] Or as Dom Price, work futurist at Atlassian, said, his remit is "to design an environment where people are able to do the best work of their life every day. That's when people love their jobs."[17]

AN ICONIC HISTORY: REDUCING HIERARCHY AT IBM

In the 1980s, IBM was a global powerhouse of technologies. The company manufactured chips, systems, operating system software, applications, and all the networking hardware and software to bring it together. In a way, IBM was the entire IT industry in those days because you could buy everything you needed to run your data center from one company.

The company was organized into product business units, with products sold by a global network of sales organizations and specialists. At the time, IBM was the dominant provider of most IT solutions, so it was extremely hierarchical.

Of course, we all know what happened. In the 1970s and 1980s, computers started to become commodities, and companies such as Intel and Microsoft—and, later, Dell and Compaq—managed to build machines that were as powerful and useful as those made by IBM. Its huge margins on proprietary systems disappeared quickly, but the company was in denial.

IBM's top-down hierarchical structure got in the way. I know this because I had a front-row seat, having taken a job in a product sales unit at IBM in 1982. A few years later, I was selling IBM computers to the University of California, Berkeley, and regularly sat down in the computer science department to talk with the people building Unix, Sendmail, and much of the technology on the internet today. These guys were buying equipment from weird companies such as Sun, Apollo, Silicon Graphics, and Digital Equipment.

I was furious that my beloved employer, IBM, had such a hard time keeping up. It was an example of a company optimized for scalable efficiency and not speed of learning. IBM just learned too slowly.

Even though IBM did suffer in the 1980s and early 1990s, the company was still very smart. In fact, I believe IBM actually unlocked the secret of teams well before the agile software revolution even started.

In the 1970s, according to the 1975 book *The Mythical Man-Month* by Fred Brooks, an IBM executive,[18] the company had large software development teams building operating systems, databases, and networking platforms for the large, centralized mainframe computers used by banks, insurance companies, and other big businesses. Many teams worked out of the Santa Theresa Laboratory, an idyllic setting in San Jose, California, which looked like a modern tech company campus. The teams were tightly linked to the hardware teams so that whenever a new line of mainframes or communications hardware was released, enabling software was ready.

However, the software teams were quite large, and the products were monolithic. Major new releases of products came out every 18 to 36 months. As the book describes in detail, Brooks discovered that as products became more complex, the schedules became slower and slower. After carefully studying the activities of the organization, he realized that adding more people to a project did not speed it up—it actually *slowed projects down.*

The industrial concept of scale did not work. One of the biggest obstacles the teams faced, according to Brooks, was the need for people to communicate with each other. If two engineers needed to talk with each other for the project to proceed, adding more people bogged down the project until eventually it showed no progress at all.

Brooks believed the best way to foster software development was to shift from a "hog-butchering model" (each team member cuts away at the problem) to a "surgical team model" (an expert takes the lead in solving the problem, and others provide whatever support is needed). As a result, he redesigned software development around small, expert-focused teams, with a clearly defined support staff to help.

Brooks found that the optimal team included one engineer, one copilot, a documentation person, an administrator, a tester, and someone to build tools that made everyone more productive. This team structure allowed each individual to do the work they specialized in while sharing in the project's success.

Brooks's pioneering analysis 45 years ago and the implementation of his ideas led to today's focus on teams. Since then, the technology industry has continued to guide our broader understanding of which organizational design works best at a time when speed, not scale, is the competitive imperative.

the innovation: agile principles at the core

The next major evolution took place in 2001, when a team of software engineers led by John Kern, an aerospace engineer, pooled experiences to write the Manifesto for Agile Software Development, commonly known as the "agile manifesto."[19]

Agile has been a groundbreaking business innovation. Originally applied to software, it represents a new philosophy for work, one that can be leveraged throughout nearly every industry.

Kern's founding team started with the understanding that complex software systems are impossible to specify in advance.[20] Rather than using the old waterfall approach to design, where progress flows in one direction, agile focuses on building software models quickly, testing them early, and getting feedback rapidly as they grow. But agile's impact extends well beyond software because it is a set of principles about how people work best together. In other words, it's actually a culture, not just an organization model.

Visit software teams that use agile, and you'll hear a great deal of talk about culture. The focus is on empowering the individual; building a small, well-defined team; ensuring the team makes progress every day; and focusing on design, collaboration, and feedback. The entire process relies on keeping things simple and on forcing the team constantly to reduce clutter, to eliminate features that are not needed, and to concentrate on the core mission.

To see agile in practice, I spent time with the engineering leads at Pivotal Labs (now part of VMware), one of the first companies to provide cloud-platform hosting and consulting services. The experience reinforced to me that the best software teams in the world consist of three important people: a business lead (product manager or business owner), an engineer (a software developer), and a designer (someone who designs user experiences or interfaces).

As Joe Militello, former chief people officer of Pivotal, explained, "We start with a clear customer problem, we design a solution quickly, we prototype it, and we show it to a set of customers. We immediately find that 80 percent of the [prototype] is not correct, but the core 20 percent is working well, so we throw away what doesn't work and focus on the core. Then we do it again."[21]

PRINCIPLES OF THE AGILE MANIFESTO

1 Satisfy customers with early and continuous delivery of valuable software.

2 Welcome changing requirements, even in late development.

3 Deliver working software frequently (in weeks rather than in months).

4 Businesspeople and developers should cooperate closely and daily.

5 Build projects around motivated individuals, who should be trusted.

6 Face-to-face conversation is the best form of communication (colocation).

7 Working software is the primary measure of progress.

8 Develop sustainably to maintain a constant pace.

9 Pay continuous attention to technical excellence and design.

10 Simplicity—the art of maximizing the amount of work not done—is essential.

11 The best architectures, requirements, and designs emerge from self-organizing teams.

12 Regularly, the team reflects on how to become more effective and adjusts accordingly.

SOURCE: AGILE ALLIANCE, 2022

Eric Ries's *Lean Startup* and many other books on agile software development speak of the power of working toward an MVP—a minimum viable product—learning fast, then iterating with speed.[22] In six-week sprints, a team can address issues quickly, test solutions, learn, and iterate again. General Electric (GE) has institutionalized this approach throughout the company, and GE Digital, a business now with more than $1 billion in sales, is running its entire organization using agile teams.[23]

These ideas of design-centered engineering, rapid iteration, swift feedback, dynamic shifting of resources, and continuous skills development have become a new standard in business, a standard way of thinking in almost everything we do. Agile engages people in ways that are inspiring. I've visited dozens of teams using agile methodologies, and I can easily feel the energy and sense of empowerment in the room.

Think about how your company conducts sales, marketing, IT, HR, or almost any other process in the business. Do you start small, design carefully, experiment, and iterate quickly? Or do you spend months and years in design and specification using the waterfall approach to build a solution and then roll it out using a series of long, complex betas?

I recently met with Google's senior HR team and talked with them about the Google culture. What are the things that make it unique? One of the HR leaders made it clear: they have a culture of experimentation, iteration, and continuous change. They design solutions, test them, and product-manage them all the time. This model of work (and HR) is what irresistible companies do.

I'm certainly not arguing that agile works for everything. Building a nuclear submarine or a complex energy system cannot tolerate failures at any step. But even if an organization's work is all "mission critical," the ideas of small teams, collaboration, continued pace, and trust have now become hallmarks of modern teamwork. Other aspects of agile are surely appropriate for your organization.

BREAKOUT: IBM USES AGILE IN HR

Diane Gherson, the recently retired CHRO of IBM, frequently told me how powerful the agile model had become for HR. When a new project arose (such as a revised process for addressing employee grievances), she assigned an agile team of HR specialists, line leaders, and software engineers to build a prototype solution. She pioneered solutions for cognitive coaching and pay advisement, along with dozens of other tools that continue to transform IBM.

HOW DO WE MAKE TEAMS WORK AT SCALE?

Can work be rewarding and long-lasting in a network in which people switch teams frequently? Yes, but it requires a little rethinking of the problem.

High-performing teams, whether in business, in sports, or in the military, share some common characteristics. They are exciting and fun; they empower and energize people; they thrive on purpose and mission; and they have a unique combination of leadership, clarity of roles, and self-determination.

Here are some key characteristics of effective teams.

INSTILLING AUTONOMY, MASTERY, AND PURPOSE

People are most engaged when they feel a sense of ownership in their work, they are working in the right jobs, and they are clear on the team's goals. In *Drive*, Daniel Pink explains that "autonomy, mastery, and purpose" are critical to motivation.[24] They empower and energize people, creating teams that thrive and deliver results.

PROVIDING AN ABILITY TO SEE PROGRESS

Teresa Amabile of Harvard analyzed the work notes of more than 100,000 employees and found that one of the most valued aspects of work is to "make progress every day."[25] She describes this energizing process as our "inner work life," one where positive feedback on work fuels happiness, productivity, and better thinking. Managers of teams help remove barriers to progress, maintain clear goals, and provide ongoing support.

CREATING AN ENVIRONMENT OF SAFETY AND TRUST

Google's Project Oxygen team,[26] which spent a year studying performance appraisals and employee notes, concluded that great teams are built on trust, a sense of openness and freedom, and letting people do the work they love—and that they are led by managers who act as coaches, experts, and partners.[27] Google turned these findings into a set of rules for team leaders, teaching them to be open, to set clear and ambitious goals, and to focus on results:

1   Psychological safety: Can we take risks on this team without feeling insecure or embarrassed?

2   Dependability: Can we count on each other to do high-quality work on time?

3   Structure and clarity: Are goals, roles, and execution plans on our team clear?

4   Meaning of work: Are we working on something that is personally important for each of us?

5   Impact of work: Do we fundamentally believe that the work we're doing matters?[28]

FORMING THEIR OWN WORK PRACTICES

High-performing teams develop their own unique work practices. Psychologist Bruce Tuckman developed the concept of "forming, norming, storming, [and] performing."[29] He essentially proved that there are four stages to developing a team and that over time teams develop trust and work rules, build processes for feedback and improvement, and work out the role of the leader. The concept of job crafting, where the job is changed by the person (and not the other way around), is essential here.

INCLUDING DEEP KNOWLEDGE OF THE ORGANIZATION

Michael Arena, the former head of talent management at GM and current vice president of talent and development at Amazon Web Services, found that the most important factor in a team's success was its internal relationships and its knowledge of how the rest of the company works.[30] In other words, teams must not only be productive internally but also understand how their work fits into the overall structure.

DEVELOPING AN ORGANIZATIONAL CULTURE THAT SUPPORTS PERFORMANCE

Harvard professor Boris Groysberg has found that superstars in one organization (for instance, investment bankers who far exceeded their goals) did not necessarily succeed when they moved to a new company.[31] Their earlier excellence appears to have depended heavily on general and proprietary resources, organizational culture, networks, and colleagues at their old firm. In other words, culture really matters, and people who may not perform well on one team may thrive on another—forcing organizations of the future to be very focused on work and team culture.

CREATING A CULTURE OF FEEDBACK

Great teams know each other, talk to each other, and give each other feedback. When someone fails to perform, others tell the person in a constructive way. Many new tools now facilitate this, and shared goal and communication systems such Trello and Slack make this easy to do online. Continuous performance management, which I discuss later, further eases this process.

BUILDING A CLEAR SENSE OF PURPOSE

Amazon develops a sense of purpose by asking every team to write its press release before starting a project or initiative.[32] The press release must describe the team's eventual output and how they accomplished their goal, forcing the team to clarify its purpose and talk about how they want to work.

how to get started

Discuss these questions with your own leaders and teams:

1 Are we able to build cross-functional teams quickly when we need to solve problems? Why not, and what gets in our way? Culture? Rewards? Management?

2 Do our teams talk with each other and share information so they don't duplicate solutions or work at cross-purposes? Why or why not?

3 Do we have any standard tools to help teams form and work together? Do we have a set of practices, tools, or systems to help new leaders create and manage teams?

4 Can people in our organization move from organization to organization without peril or risk? Is talent mobility rewarded, or is it considered a risky move? Why or why not?

5 Can we identify the highest-performing teams and understand what they have in common that low-performing teams don't? Do we have any standards or practices we can share?

6 Will our leadership let go of their power and ownership to let teams flourish and grow, with specialists as leaders? Are they incentivized to support such structures? Why or why not?

how to get it right

While academic research reveals some of the characteristics of effective teams and frameworks, companies must also pay attention to the human side of the equation.

PHYSICAL AND VIRTUAL PROXIMITY:
WORKING FACE-TO-FACE

Highly engaged teams need face time, whether in the physical office or in video conferences. As companies continue to adjust to more flexible working arrangements, the need to cultivate relationships is front and center.

Prior to the outset of the pandemic, leaders believed only 45 percent of the workforce could productively adapt to remote work performed on a purely virtual basis, according to a study on workplace flexibility by Mercer.[33] COVID-19 shattered that belief, the HR consulting firm asserts. Today, more than 90 percent of employers suggest that productivity has stayed the same or improved, with 82 percent of companies planning to implement flexible working at greater scale.

Other studies of what has been called "the world's biggest-ever workplace experiment" have confirmed this. A 2020 Boston Consulting Group survey of 12,000 employees found that 75 percent of respondents had maintained or improved their productivity.[34]

Research by the Pew Research Center in December 2020 arrived at similar findings: of the 71 percent of Americans working from home most of the time, 87 percent had excellent tools to attend to their tasks and felt they were as engaged in their work as much as they were in the office.[35]

For the most part, the massive workplace experiment has been a surprising success, opening the eyes of more employers to the virtues of flexible work arrangements. Even before the pandemic, more than 8 in 10 companies had either implemented or planned to implement a flexible working environment.[36] The pandemic accelerated this implementation. PepsiCo's talent management head, Sachin Jain, led the company's response to COVID-19. He told me, "We accomplished in two to three months something we'd been talking about for years but had never gotten around to doing."[37]

Other companies are being pressured to do the same. Consulting firm EY's *Work Reimagined Employee Survey* found that more than half (54 percent) of more than 16,000 employees surveyed around the world would consider ending their current employment if they were not afforded flexibility in where and when they work.[38]

Companies such as Telstra, the Australian telecommunications giant, have fully committed to a flexible work strategy. Telstra has built its work strategy upon its 2018 transformation, which flattened its complex, silo-based management structure and reduced the number of management roles by 25 percent.

"Agile teams served a critical purpose in our transformation," said Alex Badenoch, Telstra group executive of transformation, communications, and people.[39] "We broke up the fiefdoms run by senior leaders and brought together cross-functional teams to take a more customer-centric approach, reducing costs and time to market. Altogether, we removed three to four layers within every part of the business, reducing close to 20 percent of the direct workforce and [50 percent of] third-party resources. Roughly 30 percent of the company has now shifted into full-scale agile."

Taking this approach in 2018 and 2019 prepared Telstra for the enormous upheaval in work that followed. "It gave us a massive advantage when the pandemic hit, as we had already instilled a culture of flexibility, with the office-oriented workforce permitted to work from home two days per week," Badenoch told me. "As they shifted to full-time remote work, we had no impairment in productivity."

Nevertheless, HR must not overlook the pitfalls of remote work. The Mercer workplace flexibility study discovered that employees in 2020 worked an average of 3 hours longer each day; more than 4 in 10 (41 percent) suffered increased pain in their shoulders, backs, or wrists; and 64 percent of employers experienced increased use of their behavioral health services by employees.

At Telstra, Badenoch said the company ramped up its mental health services for remote-work employees. "Most importantly, we instituted a practice of daily livestreams to find out how people were dealing with kids studying at home or perhaps caring for elderly parents," she said. "We also instituted a series of pulse surveys to do the same thing. And we announced publicly that we would help customers that were having trouble paying their bills through a financial hardship program we created. Doing that instilled pride throughout the organization."

Flexible virtual and on-site work is the future; the challenge for employers is one of balance. What does all this mean for your organization? Manage your team like a sports team. Make sure people know each other; focus on open and regular communication; and get people physically together on a regular basis. Let people do the work they love where they do it best. (More on this later.)

This is the credo at Microsoft, which embraces the opportunities inherent in a flexible workspace. "Work from home is now the permanent standard, with physical appearances at offices optional, except for essential on-site roles," said Kathleen Hogan, Microsoft executive vice president and chief people officer.[40] "Hybrid workspaces were happening already because of digital transformation; now they're happening more quickly, though technology will never be a replacement for human-to-human contact, when needed."

GREAT TEAMS ARE SMALL

Most studies of agile teams show that the optimum size is eight people or fewer. Why? Small teams get things done easily and quickly, communication is easy, and people get to know each other. This gives team members a sense of progress, which improves performance, engagement, and productivity. Amazon's Jeff Bezos calls this the "two pizza rule"—if it takes more than two pizzas to feed a team for lunch, the team is too big.[41]

Many neurological studies explain this phenomenon. Anthropologist Robin Dunbar developed what he calls the Dunbar number, which shows that the human mind can only store around 150 personal rela-tionships at a time.[42] Anatomical evidence shows that we are wired to work in smaller groups.

COORDINATION: REMOVE SILOS BETWEEN TEAMS

While small teams are optimal, we have to keep them coordinated. Do you want each team to optimize its design and delivery goals without considering the company's overall strategy? Of course not. This is why it's also important to build shared goals, communication, and "super teams" that coordinate the teams.

In *The Silo Effect*, Gillian Tett observes that great organizations have teams that optimize individual performance and also coordinate their work together.[43] When this does not happen, silos can generate massive risk. Her research showed, for example, that the firemen who bravely saved lives in the World Trade Center during the attacks of Septem-ber 11, 2001, were "semi-detached from everyone else." As a result, their walkie-talkies did not communicate with other emergency services, and far too many people died from poor coordination.

In product companies, teams have to coordinate to build integrated sys-tems. For example, Sony pioneered the original portable music device, the Walkman, yet the company lost the market to Apple because of its slowness to respond to challenges. What did Sony do wrong? The Walk-man team did not coordinate its efforts with the rest of Sony's enter-tainment products. At the time, it felt right to speed development with a "skunk works" approach, creating small, experimental teams within the larger organization. But as we know now, Apple's integrated model won the market, and the Walkman is now a museum curiosity.

ORGANIZING AND NETWORKING TEAMS

How do we give teams independence while also coordinating their efforts? As the Sony example shows, team success is based on two driv-ers: the productivity of the team itself and its ability to align with the rest of the organization. In some ways, though, these drivers pull against each other.

Every team wants to move fast and innovate directly with its customers. But how can we ensure that a team leverages other technology and expertise in your company? How can you prevent one team from duplicating or competing with another group? And how can we make sure one team's efforts contribute to a larger market or to revenue goals?

My research shows that the "network effect" of coordination is more important than one may think. While there are many stories of skunk works that reinvented products, organizational relationships are key in most companies. As he led talent at GM, Michael Arena found that the single biggest predictor of successful innovation was not engineering talent or customer focus but rather how well the entrepreneurial pockets of innovation within the company were unleashed.[44]

As part of CEO Mary Barra's agenda to develop an aligned, top-down, bottom-up culture of innovation at GM, Arena headed up a giant initiative called GM2020. Leveraging design-thinking methodologies, he engaged 90 employees at the bottom of the company to "build small fires of bottom-up energy that would connect with the top-down strategy in a lattice-like framework."[45]

The 90 employees were divided into small teams that competed in a hackathon to design unique prototypes for GM's Tahoe sports utility vehicle (SUV) using cardboard and 3D design software. The sky was the limit as long as the prototype helped the driver or enhanced the driving experience. The teams then trotted out their innovations in front of a select group of 30 middle managers who served as the connective tissue between the top-down and bottom-up initiatives.

In 2020, the new Tahoe featured the winner's invention—a sliding console with a center slot for a person to store a purse. "Through the use of agile teams, we found a way to facilitate discovery events and put them out into the world," Arena said.

Michael told me that he discovered the most successful innovations were those that leveraged other parts of the organization, especially the work of the people closest to the product or the customer.

Here are some examples of how to organize teams for success.

First, teams can be grouped around customers. If the organization is trying to build customer-centric solutions that might vary from customer to customer, it may create a design team, a service team, and a sales team oriented around one customer. In product-focused companies such as Apple, Samsung, IBM, SAP, and HP where product integration is a primary value proposition, teams might be organized around a product or product family. At Dell, for example, teams are oriented around lines of products, and they have responsibility for management, manufacturing, design, engineering, and sales in those teams.[46]

In banks, teams are often organized around geographic or customer segments. Most banks have private wealth management businesses that include their own sales and marketing teams, so even a distributed group can cluster its efforts around a customer or customer segment.

In the pharmaceutical industry, many companies have moved away from the traditional hierarchies of sciences toward teams centered on products or specific diseases. These teams are multidisciplinary and include many scientific and manufacturing disciplines. In fact, some pharma companies even cluster their scientists around organs or body systems.

During the global hunt for COVID-19 vaccines and treatments in 2020, several drug companies and academic institutions combined different parts of their organizations to create teams focused on novel therapies. For example, GlaxoSmithKline contributed researchers developing its immune-response adjuvant technology to a team of researchers at Sanofi S.A. who had developed the COVID-19 S protein, a key ingredient in COVID-19 vaccines.

Teams are very prominent in healthcare delivery as well. Cleveland Clinic, a pioneer in healthcare management, recently redesigned service delivery to improve patient outcomes.[47] After studying the tasks involved in diagnosing a patient and in determining the right combination of treatments, the Clinic recognized that specialist roles needed to become more flexible in order to provide ongoing care in a fast, effective, and efficient way. Nurses became "care managers" (another hybrid job), and all medical staff members are now trained in care and case management to broaden their skills beyond their technical specialties.

Cleveland Clinic also added a series of agile practices, tools, and measurements to provide continuous improvement. The Mayo Clinic then followed suit with similar adjustments, as have other healthcare providers around the world. In nearly every case I studied, employee engagement has risen as jobs have become more dynamic and as the healthcare industry has more heavily cross-trained its people.

One of the biggest changes in a team-centric business structure is that it no longer allows managers to run large departments like kings reigning over their kingdoms. Of course, in every company there are still general managers, senior executives, product-line owners, finance executives, sales executives, and others. But these people are not departmental kings; they are coordinators, facilitators, and coaches of teams. This fundamental shift leads to greater engagement by empowering team members and creating a sense of meaning and purpose in the organization.

ORGANIZING TEAMS AT SCALE: THE SPOTIFY AND ING MODELS

Seasoned agile practitioners have built entire models to promote team independence alongside coordination. One particularly innovative approach was pioneered at Spotify[48] and is now being used at scale at ING Bank.

In the Spotify model, each team or squad consists of eight people or fewer. The squad sits together physically in a pod with whiteboards and other tools to share their work. Each squad is an autonomous group that sets its own goals and long-term mission aligned with the overall organization. Examples of this mission might include "make Spotify the best place to discover music" or "build a scalable toolset for infrastructure testing." The squad then works to meet its short-term goals every quarter.

As leaders at Spotify put it, squads are very motivating because teams have autonomy.[49] They can make decisions locally without bureaucracy or overhead, and people get to know each other because they work together every day.

To maintain coordination, Spotify makes squads "loosely coupled but tightly aligned," similar to a jazz band in which the instruments operate independently but work together to make great music.

The problem Spotify and other organizations are solving is simple but profound: How should companies balance the desire for autonomy with the need for coordination?

Much of this is based on the new management practice of giving people guidance without micromanaging them. The hallmarks of this practice include efforts to share information and create a straightforward, feedback-rich culture. Companies with teams organized in this way generally employ a combination of the following practices, with some variation:

- Sprint projects done in four- to six-week segments, which let people finish work on a regular basis and feel a sense of progress

- Standup meetings every day: 15 minutes a day during which everyone shares what they are doing, giving everyone a chance to talk and feel like part of the team

- Shared whiteboards (using tools such as Trello and Asana) where people can visually see what others are doing

- A system to manage microtasks, which forces teams to build user "stories" that describe the experiences teams are trying to create

- Collaboration and messaging systems (Slack, Microsoft Teams, Workplace from Meta, HipChat, etc.) where people can quickly ask each other questions and share information

- Physical pods where people spend face time together so people can easily reach out and talk with one another

- Clearly defined roles to delineate tasks in a fair, well-organized way

- Cross-squad movement, in which people move from pod to pod or squad to squad over time, learning how to work together and gaining a shared culture

- Feedback tools and coaching, enabling people to raise issues and make sure problems are resolved quickly

Figure 1.2 shows how alignment and autonomy fit together. Low alignment and autonomy lead to confusion, disengagement, and poor results. In a high alignment but low autonomy culture, such as the military, people do what they're told but often not much more. At companies with low alignment and high autonomy, such as in many consulting firms, people do what's best for their team but don't always share critical information. The gold standard is the high alignment, high autonomy organization, in which leaders give people clear goals and direction but let squads decide how the work gets done.

FIGURE 1.2: HOW ALIGNMENT AND AUTONOMY INTERSECT WITHIN COMPANIES

	LOW AUTONOMY	HIGH AUTONOMY
HIGH ALIGNMENT	"I order you to build this bridge."	"We need to cross the river—can you guys figure out how?"
LOW ALIGNMENT	"We're confused about how to get from this side to the other."	"I hope someone is working on the river problem."

SOURCE: THE JOSH BERSIN COMPANY, 2021

Squads, by their very nature, are multidisciplinary. Unlike the functional hierarchy of the industrial age, they are self-sufficient groups. They have everything they need to fulfill their missions.

Consider a squad designed to focus on redesigning the mortgage-application process in a bank. That squad would need a legal specialist, a retail bank manager, an IT professional, and probably someone who understands design, legal, and financial systems. This group of experts could come together, design this process, test it, and then own it as it gets rolled out. Each may report to their own functional organization, but for the purpose of designing this new process, they all work together.

Such multifunctional teams became common during the COVID-19 pandemic. I talked with dozens of companies that built squads to develop remote-work, hybrid-work, and back-to-work programs for employees. These teams included IT, HR, facilities, safety, and legal professionals working together.

Despite the advantages of multifunctional teams, two obvious problems come to mind. First, how are squads grouped so they are most closely aligned with other squads with which they must coordinate? Second, how does someone assigned to a squad get access to information and tools when a squad's projects cross other squads' boundaries?

The answer is tribes and chapters.

A tribe is a grouping of squads brought together to share information and coordinate results because of a common project, geography, function, or business goal. At ING, for example, the local branch bank is a tribe, and the customer service, operations, and other functions are also tribes. Tribes are not necessarily hierarchical and are instead more like affinity groups or teams of teams. They bring squads together to coordinate more closely with adjacent squads.

At ING, tribes have fewer than 150 people. The tribe's leader sets priorities, keeps squads coordinated with other tribes, and helps make decisions that affect the entire group. In some ways, a tribe leader is a general manager, so he or she must have superb domain expertise, strong relationship skills, and excellent capabilities to develop followership.

A chapter is a functional group (such as engineering, design, or marketing) that ties together people with similar jobs across tribes and circles.

If you're having a hard time visualizing this, think about the military. In each ship there is a communications and navigation team, a propulsion team, and a variety of gun and attack teams. These teams are made up of specialists, each of which are members of their own respective chapters across tribes. Yet even though members of a team belong to different chapters, teams still work together to complete the mission.

For example, in software development each squad has a designer. But we want these designers to use common design tools and elements. At Atlassian, the head of design brings the design team together to set standards, to develop and share tools, and to ensure the team is developing and improving itself. And at ING, the chapter lead is the "boss" of that function, in a role similar to, for example, the vice president of engineering in a traditional model.

The final important part of this model is the agile coach, who coaches individuals and squads, builds tools, and serves as the learning and development (L&D) leader to help everyone learn how to work together. Companies like Telstra, Deutsche Telekom, and others invest heavily in agile coaches to help these teams form, develop processes, and work together.

THE AGILE MODEL WORKS: IT ENGAGES AND EMPOWERS PEOPLE

I review all this detail for a simple reason: redesigning an organization's structure around a network of teams yields tremendous results, including that magical, elusive goal of employee engagement. For this model to succeed, people must feel valued, they must believe their work matters, and they must be well managed and organized, with minimum bureaucracy and maximum autonomy for teams.

I've visited companies like Atlassian, ING, Telstra, and Meta and felt the energy, activity, and sense of growth. Employees at these companies feel empowered, aligned, and productive.

As ANZ Bank CEO Shayne Elliott put it, when companies shift to networks of teams, "very quickly the way of work changes."[50] Instead of specialized departments, "you organize yourself around customer outcomes. That might be about being the best bank for people who buy and own a home. So what are the skills we need there? [T]he hierarchy disappears very quickly. That has big implications for how we pay people, how we reward them."

Agile works across industries. The model is proven, as Darrell Rigby, Jeff Sutherland, and Hirotaka Takeuchi elaborate for the *Harvard Business Review*:

> *National Public Radio employs agile methods to create new programming. John Deere uses them to develop new machines, and Saab to produce new fighter jets. Intronis, a leader in cloud backup services, uses them in marketing. C.H. Robinson, a global third-party logistics provider, applies them in human resources. Mission Bell Winery uses them for everything from wine production to warehousing to running its senior leadership group. And GE relies on them to speed a much-publicized transition from 20th-century conglomerate to 21st-century "digital industrial company."*[51]

Telstra embraced agile from top to bottom, and Alex Badenoch led the entire transformation. She told me that while the first few years were rough, today Telstra has higher engagement than ever. People no longer look for promotions every time they take on a new project—they trust the company to reward them for "work, not jobs."[52] (More on this in the next chapter.)

In the end, it all comes back to people. Lori Goler of Meta told me, "[W]hen people tell me they want to work at Facebook because of the opportunity, I sense a red flag [. . .] We want people who are passionate about building things and want to join Facebook so they can touch billions of people with their work."[53] The difference is critical. A network of teams requires people who are self-motivated, passionate, and excited about their ability to have an impact. I think all humans seek this kind of work. The key is to give them an environment that makes it possible.

work, not jobs

"The only way to do great work is to love what you do."

STEVE JOBS, FORMER CHAIRMAN, CEO, AND COFOUNDER OF APPLE, 2005

How's this for a light bulb moment? In 2017, General Electric (GE) faced the monumental task of inspecting data files nearly 80 gigabytes in size (that's equivalent to about 40 movies streamed through Netflix) generated by super-powerful engines. Instead of gnashing their teeth about how to reduce processing time internally, GE sourced external talent to solve the problem.

This crowdsourcing platform, called GE Fuse, attracted 40 entries in less than eight weeks and found viable solutions from three prizewinners in India and Virginia. "This is another way of being innovative; it was born out of a desire to try to get to solutions in a multitude of different ways," says GE Fuse community leader Amelia Gandara.[54] "You can find start-ups to invest in; you can innovate internally. This is an opportunity to be able to innovate with an external community."

GE's experiment demonstrates a fundamental truth about talent today: "Work" is happening everywhere in the world, regardless of whether one has an actual "job." This chapter will help you understand how work fit for purpose creates fluidity and how to achieve it.

the shift: work, not jobs

In 2020, 59 million employable Americans worked in part-time, contingent, gig, or other forms of freelance work assignments, an increase from the 53 million Americans doing the same in 2014.[55] And a recent study found that almost two-thirds of all younger workers now have "side hustles" to complement their full-time jobs.[56]

Why are so many people falling out of the nine-to-five routine? Some are caretakers and have multiple responsibilities; some are underskilled and cannot find full-time work (a particularly tragic fact, given the fact that most employers have many unfilled roles); some have medical or other restrictions; some want to make extra money and are doing gig work to supplement their income; and some simply prefer to be independent.

Many people simply cannot, will not, or choose not to work full-time. In fact, according to a 2020 survey by global employment website Monster, in light of the pandemic's impact on work, an astonishing 92 percent of respondents said they felt now was a good time to look into the gig economy, with 57 percent expressing interest in temporary gig work to stay afloat while between jobs.[57] (More recently, in the fall of 2021, the "quit rate," the rate at which people voluntarily leave their current job, hit an all-time high.)

So, what do these people do? They don't just sit around and watch TV; they do project work, they do contract work, they set up consulting arrangements, or they start businesses and build something new. In other words, much of the world is actively involved in work, regardless of whether or not people have traditional jobs.

The bottom line is this: we have moved from an economy where your employer defines your career to one where your skills, experience, and ambition drive success. Formal job descriptions and hierarchies are going away, and internal job marketplaces are becoming increasingly common. It's time to focus on the work, not the job, to manage, lead, and build a career.

THE RECENT PAST: THE OLD WAY

First, let's look at the old way of work.

In almost every company, organization charts are hierarchical. These hierarchies have two paths for getting ahead: professional and managerial—and, in most companies, the professional path stops at a lower level. So naturally, in the past, most of us (like me, working at Exxon and IBM) reached the conclusion that to really get ahead, we had to go into management.

This path was always limited by mathematics. The span of control (number of employees per manager) in most companies is at least 6:1 (and it is going up to 10:1 in many organizations), so if you want to go up the management side of the pyramid, the competition gets fierce fast. In many companies, you have to wait for someone to retire, which makes it even more frustrating. What's more, we have lots of old-fashioned, artificial tools to weed out the people who go in this direction.

What governs this process in traditional companies? The answer is succession management, which used to be called "replacement planning" in the hierarchical management systems of the 20th century. In the early 1900s, when people were less healthy, top leaders and CEOs would simply die or fall ill, and the company needed to replace them fast. So, they built a tool called the "replacement list." Just like the command-and-control delegatory structure of management, the replacement list derived from the military, specifically from World War 1, when soldiers killed in the trenches were replaced by other soldiers on a replacement list.

This replacement process evolved into succession management, and companies such as GE, General Motors (GM), and other industrial leaders in the early- to mid-1900s built tools to decide who would replace whom. The most popular is the famous nine-box grid, which is shown in Figure 2.1.

FIGURE 2.1: THE NINE-BOX GRID

	APPROPRIATELY PLACED	POTENTIAL TO GROW ONE LEVEL	POTENTIAL TO GROW TWO OR MORE LEVELS
HIGH PERFORMER	Retain as high-performing specialist	Push to move upward	Groom for senior management
SOLID PERFORMER	Develop to move to specialist	Push for more substantive job at same level	Coach for job performance improvement
LOW PERFORMER	Consider exit or reassignment	Manage carefully	May be in wrong job or need coaching

SOURCE: THE JOSH BERSIN COMPANY, 2021

The nine-box grid evaluates individuals based on two axes: performance on the vertical and potential on the horizontal. It essentially assumes that people move "up" in some way and that these vertical progressions are typically associated with management.

When I first saw a nine-box grid, I was puzzled. How do we define "potential"? Is it the potential to do more work? The potential to become a better specialist? The potential to be a manager?

Well, in the traditional world of HR, potential was defined as "being able to move up two or more levels in the company." This always seemed silly to me. How do we know if someone can move up if we don't know what they're good at doing? I may be capable of moving up two levels as a technical specialist but not as a manager. So, "potential" really means the undefined, fuzzy idea of "management potential."

For those of us who are late bloomers—I didn't have my first true management role until I was in my 40s—we may not ever go into management. We may just stick to our professional role and grow through levels of responsibility, experience, and enjoyment—and get left behind in pay. Well, this entire philosophy of leadership is now becoming obsolete.

IT NEVER REALLY WORKED AS DESIGNED

As it turns out, the hierarchical career model never really worked as designed.

As companies develop new products, shut down divisions, digitally transform the enterprise, and adopt flexible work strategies, people find that their jobs have to change. Consequently, the up-or-out model fails at its core: what if your manager simply doesn't leave? Remember that this model of career growth goes back to the World War I replacement charts, so it really doesn't apply in a dynamic, changing business.

Today, nine-box grids are only used for senior executives. More and more companies adopt what I call the "talent marketplace" model. In other words, people move all over the company to find new opportunities or projects, and they learn and grow along the way.

Think about all the career options we truly have:

1   A new lateral assignment

2   A stretch assignment (try your boss's job for a while)

3   An external assignment (work at another company or at an overseas division for a year)

4   A developmental assignment (fill a brand-new job function to learn the business better)

5   An internship at another company or department (try it out)

6   A project or gig work

7   A job swap

8   And many more

Many companies have learned that job swaps with external companies are immensely valuable. Procter & Gamble (P&G), for example, has been doing job swaps with Google so that the consumer-products-focused P&G employees can learn about tech and the tech-focused Google employees can learn about consumer marketing.[58] This kind of dynamism has to be built into your company. (It's now often called "talent mobility.")

In fact, we've done research on almost every practice of HR, and internal mobility is now one of the most important management strategies of all. People who move from one function to another (from HR to sales, from sales to marketing, and from finance to operations) always outperform their peers.

By the way, internal mobility is harder than you think. If people are not incented to hire from within (and this is a whole cultural story I'll explain later), it's often hard to change roles, departments, geographies, or divisions. I recently met with executives from one of the most successful telecommunications companies in India and asked them about this issue, and they told me that "the best way to change jobs here is to quit and reapply." This may be ridiculous to hear, but it's true more often than you may think.

ALL THIS HAS TO CHANGE: WE NEED TO ENGINEER FOR WORK, NOT JOBS

The more that companies let go of the old architecture, the better—and it's actually starting to happen. In our most recent research, we discovered that 57 percent of companies are redesigning their career models and that 83 percent expect to have some type of "open career" marketplace in their company within the next five years.[59] And while almost all companies promote people upward in the company, two-thirds admit that they will often give people promotions without necessarily forcing them to move up a level.

Think about your company as a giant consulting firm. In a consulting firm, people are always working on projects. When a project starts, it's staffed up, and when it's completed, people are evaluated for that project and move on to the next one.

Let me use Deloitte as an example. When I left the firm in 2018, the company had only seven real job levels, each generic in name (such as consultant, manager, and senior manager). As new ideas hatch, leaders (called partners) recruit people with these generic titles to join multifunctional project teams. The project takes form, it launches, and it succeeds. Then, after a period of time (sometimes after a quarter, sometimes after many years), these individuals move on to new projects. Team members are evaluated by a peer and a managerial recognition system, and their skills and reputations build up over time.

The consulting firm even treats management this way. Client partners who know the firm well move into management roles through a peer-review process. They gain three to five years of management experience, and then they often go back to being client partners. Very few managers are institutionalized in their jobs, giving the company tremendous dynamism and flexibility. (What if at any point in time you could work for your manager and, later, your manager could work for you? Creates quite a sense of trust, fairness, and respect, doesn't it?)

This is happening all over business. Ingersoll Rand has collapsed 8,000 job titles into 800 roles to make them more generic and thereby promote fluidity. Procter & Gamble is doing the same, and so has PayPal. Hewlett Packard Enterprise (HPE) did something similar, too.

HPE's chief HR officer Tracy Keogh told me she did away with job titles like "VP [vice president], director, senior director, etc."[60] Now if you want a new job at the company, you apply because you like the work—not because you get a fancy title. (Yelp has done the same thing.) This is yet another component of the future of work.

Almost every company has a complex, bureaucratic job architecture, and it just gets in the way. Think about how much excess energy people waste thinking about their job title and the next level in their career: How does that really contribute to getting things done?

HOW PEOPLE LAND IN THE RIGHT ROLE

In a company organized as a network, business managers, designers, and engineers work together on projects, and team leaders select teammates based on skills, reputation, relationships, and followership. Individuals have career and personal goals, so they seek out projects and work based on their interests and desires. The project manager or leader's goal is to find these people, build a team that fits, and manage the project so everyone feels they can succeed. The team decides who is responsible for what work, and while some people have functional specialties, the actual jobs may vary from team to team.

Over time, as teams grow or change, people move from team to team. And today, as more AI-driven HR platforms come to market, we have systems to recommend an employee's next project, role, or position.

When I talk with executives about their business challenges, they typically tell me they want to innovate, develop more integrated teams, or drive competitive performance. And they always point out a need for an increase in skills.

But when I ask them why these problems are hard to address, we often find that job architecture is in the way. Individuals are afraid to change jobs without a promotion, professionals in one function are not sure if they should move to a different function, and individual teams and groups are biased and afraid to bring in people from the outside.

Let me give you another example. A well-known financial technology (fintech) company fell behind its competitors as innovators such as Venmo and Stripe came to market. I met with the senior leadership team, and I could see how frustrated they were. The new CEO was hired to focus on innovation, and he embarked on a series of communications about creativity and invention.

Yet the HR team was incredibly frustrated. Despite the constant communication, people were afraid to try something new. The HR team told me people simply would not embark on new projects unless they could get promoted. In other words, the company was not rewarding work but rather was rewarding position and tenure.

We found that this company had grown rapidly over the years, with each manager creating his or her own little fiefdom, much like the situation at Telstra prior to the flattening of its management structure. The company had more than 30 different job levels and had become so hierarchical that people would do almost nothing without asking their boss. In fact, one of the leaders mentioned, "We don't even email our peers unless we go to our boss first." Clearly, the structure was in the way.

One more aspect of this is near to my heart: what drives great HR organizations. We've researched hundreds of leading HR teams, and among all the practices we studied, rotating HR professionals around the business scores the highest in predicting great performance.

Google, PepsiCo, UnitedHealth Group, Unilever, and other companies with great HR teams have developed HR apprenticeship programs, where new HR professionals spend time doing job rotations to learn how all the areas of HR work. They learn about recruiting, technology, pay, benefits, leadership development, and performance management. Many of them rotate into and out of functional areas as well.

Dave Ulrich's research shows that this kind of job rotation is one of the most predictive principles of strong people practices.[61] Why? Because without such job rotation, the HR department often becomes stigmatized as the place to put people who aren't very good at their jobs. Moving people around gives HR professionals and other businesspeople perspective and respect for the complex nature of what HR people do. Dave should know: ranked as the number one management guru by *Bloomberg Businessweek*,[62] he was the first to say HR needed to become a strategic partner of the CEO with a seat at the table.

Job rotation can also be a wonderful way to make other problems disappear. It reduces bias in people decisions. How many times have you been at work and thought to yourself, "That guy is a sales guy; no wonder he isn't worried about product pricing," or, "She came from operations, so she won't understand marketing"? These kinds of biases are common in old-fashioned companies, but they get in the way of performance and change.

Look at what Unilever was able to accomplish by rotating skills sets during the pandemic. They shifted salespeople from selling food products to a greatly diminished number of restaurants to selling hygiene solutions and transitioned other salespeople who were selling products to beauty shops into a variety of back-office roles. People with next to nothing to do not only learned new skills, they also generated revenue. "We unlocked more than 300,000 hours of work from these varied shifts where people lent a hand where needed," said Jeroen Wels.[63]

Let's suppose you understand this topic now and you want to make your company more dynamic. What do you do? It may be harder to implement than you might think. The reason is that we have built up decades of HR practices that get in the way.

Look at just a few examples: companies hire by reviewing a candidate's job history, promote by moving people up through the ranks with clearly defined titles and levels, and pay people based on salary bands dictated by level and role (see Figure 2.2). These practices have to change.

THE CHANGING NATURE OF SKILLS: WHY THE SHIFT FROM JOBS TO WORK IS URGENT

There's another reason irresistible companies operate this way: this approach centers the company on constantly developing, sharing, and rewarding skills.

Every job, no matter how well you define it, is undergoing radical, transformational change. Why? The rapid maturity of automation, AI, and cognitive technology is breathtaking, making all of us "augmented" by technology in ways we never imagined. And this, in turn, is changing every job description faster than ever.

Emsi Burning Glass scans all job descriptions in the United States, United Kingdom, and Canada to understand job titles, skills, and salary trends around the world. The company's analysis of what's trending in jobs and skills, conducted in partnership with Boston Consulting Group, is drawn from millions of online job postings and indicates that more and more jobs are hybrid—in other words, they combine skills sets that never used to be included in the same job, such as marketing and statistical analysis or design and programming (see Figure 2.3).[64] These skills can only be built internally.

"Fully one-quarter of all occupations in the U.S. economy show[s] strong signs of hybridization, and they are almost universally the fastest-growing and highest paying—and also the most resistant to automation," the study stated.[65]

In fact, a whole new discipline, that of creating "career pathways," is helping companies deal with this change. As jobs become automated, people need to move to adjacent roles if they want to add more value to their careers.

HOW AUTOMATION IS ACTUALLY CREATING WORK

Every job is being automated at breathtaking speed. Marketing managers are now digital-marketing mavens. Salespeople use AI-enabled customer relationship management (CRM) platforms to do sourcing, prospecting, pricing, and negotiation. Engineers are using complex tools to design full-stack systems. Finance professionals are no longer bookkeepers; they're becoming financial managers.

Management itself is becoming more automated. Leaders have systems that show how productive people have been, their progress toward goals, and even their sentiments at work. Zoom, Webex, and Microsoft Teams will soon measure facial expressions to show us who is feeling stressed and which managers are pushing people too hard.

For many years, pundits predicted that machines would automate us out of work. Well, the complete opposite has happened. Every new automation, AI, or robotic tool takes an existing job and makes it more human.

FIGURE 2.2: HOW OLD JOB ARCHITECTURES AND REWARD SYSTEMS GET IN THE WAY

HIRING DECISIONS	Based on prior job titles and job levels, not necessarily on skills or fit
PROMOTION DECISIONS	Based on tenure and time in job, forcing people to "wait their turn"
PAY DECISIONS	Based on job level, title, and functional salary bands, not reflecting true value or individual performance
JOB TITLES	Highly structured, printed on business cards, and expected to go up over time, with people competing for titles and levels
TALENT MOBILITY	Lateral moves considered a negative move, often called a sideways move
NEW SKILLS AND CAPABILITIES	You "manage your own career," implying that individuals have to look out for themselves
REPUTATION AMONG PEERS	Useful for promotion but often based on political behavior and "who you know"
MEASURING OF PERFORMANCE	Typically based on annual rating, delivered often by one manager
MEASURING OF POTENTIAL	Typically based on subjective review by manager or by groups of managers in calibration meetings.

SOURCE: THE JOSH BERSIN COMPANY, 2021

FIGURE 2.3: EVOLUTION OF HYBRID JOBS

OLD FUNCTIONAL JOB	NEW HYBRID JOB	PERCENT CHANGE IN SALARY SINCE 2011
Advertising manager	Digital marketing manager	145% increase
Web designer	Mobile-app developer	135% increase
Data analyst	Data scientist	372% increase
Product designer	Product manager	7% increase

SOURCE: THE JOSH BERSIN COMPANY, 2021

This means people have to upskill, reskill, and rethink their work every year.

My daughter is a 30-year-old marketing manager and also a digital guru: she understands social media, search engine optimization, ad targeting, integrated CRM, and digital-marketing analytics, and she picks this stuff up almost immediately. If she wasn't constantly educating herself on her role, she could fall behind in a year.

This shift also affects the way we must recruit and promote employees. Irresistible companies select employees based on their experiences, not on their experience; on their capabilities, not on their technical skills; and on their ability to learn and adapt, not on their college pedigree or seniority within the organization.

In some recruiting research I did just before the pandemic, I found that the highest-performing companies no longer rely on job experience and college degrees to evaluate a candidate: they look for cognitive ability, ambition, passion, and fit.

Unilever, for example, got rid of labels for talent. "We're sending the message that your purpose and skills make for a successful and satisfying career," Jeroen Wels said.[66] "People make their own choices. A job posts, and everyone has the opportunity to sign up for it. After you sign up, you determine if it is a great match. If you want to jump into a project taking up 20 percent of your time, you ask to be released to venture out in this next step of your career. We're liberating people to take their careers into their own hands by democratizing opportunities."

Zappos doesn't even let you apply for a job. You can browse all the jobs available, but you apply to Zappos itself, and then the company decides where you may fit.[67]

Deloitte's 2021 *Global Human Capital Trends Report* affirms this perspective as the future of work, concluding that the most important way that organizations can unleash the potential of their employees is "to empower them with agency and choice over what they do."[68]

I believe the pandemic proved that people have the initiative and resourcefulness to learn, despite the extraordinary challenges imposed by remote and entirely virtual ways of working. "Workforce potential is not about what workers were recruited to do, or what they are certified to do, or even what organizations or leaders what them to do," the Deloitte study found. "It's about giving workers more freedom to choose how they can best help tackle critical business problems as organizations and ecosystems evolve."

Does this all sound a bit loose? Not at all. Skills development, not hierarchical ascension, is the right organizational framework. A thriving career is T-shaped, with the vertical representing a person's actual job responsibility and skills sets (say, sales) and the horizontal representing experiences absorbed in hybrid assignments outside customary job tasks.

In this new world of amassing skills, continuous development is more important than ever. Executives must let managers and individuals "recraft" their work on a regular basis as machines become smarter each day. At one time, X-ray technicians would simply manage an X-ray machine's movements. Today, the technical part of the job is becoming less important, while the service, communication, empathy, and interpretation parts of the job have grown in value.

Let me give you another example. I worked on a consulting project with a large bank in Asia. The bank gave us access to its thousands of job descriptions; to look for common skills, capabilities, tasks, and roles, we used a series of AI-based tools. Like most banks, it was organized into retail, business, and institutional sections and had a cross-organizational structure by geography. There were a lot of duplicated, inconsistent, and often redundant jobs.

First, of the 60,000-plus job descriptions we found, almost 20 percent were similar to other jobs and merely had different titles, levels, or disparate descriptions. These are people who could easily be developed and coached in groups, could move from project to project easily, and could be grouped into a circle, as I described earlier.

Second, our research found that almost 25 percent of the skills described in these roles were depreciating in value and likely to be automated by technology over the next several years. These people were in jobs that needed to be recrafted: the work needed reengineering, and they likely needed to find new positions.

Now, armed with this information, the bank is going through a massive strategic design process to think about its structure, roles, and jobs going forward. Many companies need this kind of effort.

CAN WE DELETE JOB DESCRIPTIONS? YES

If jobs keep changing and we need people to move from role to role, do we need job descriptions at all? Yes, but it's clearly time to make them broader and more open-minded and to focus on growth.

At Yelp, hundreds of engineers share the same job title—engineer. There are no "junior engineers" or "senior engineers." While there are levels behind the scenes (used for promotion and salary administration), everyone is considered a peer—so people build their reputation and skills through experience and successful work, not through their title.

A large consumer-packaged-goods company revealed to me that listing all its open jobs on its career website was just getting in the way. People were applying for the wrong jobs because candidates could never quite understand which job was best for them. The company now lists types of work; describes daily tasks, travel demands, fellow employees, and required skills; and then asks candidates to apply to a job "family." Through a series of assessments, games, and, later, interviews, the company's recruiters decide which roles are best for a particular candidate. Their quality of hire and retention has since gone up by more than 30 percent—a huge success.

Rather than spend your energy trying to negotiate your way to the top, spend it trying to expand and improve your skills sets. Visualize careers as including many waves that will crest, bring us to the beach—and then will require us to paddle out again to catch the next wave. Each successive crest and re-paddle helps us evolve, build new skills, and enhance our contributions.

Will you sink a few times? Sure, but this speaks to the power of the growth mindset, which Microsoft CEO Satya Nadella instilled in the company's culture. People who adopt a growth mindset put time and effort into understanding why they failed to rebound quickly from setbacks. When this culture of relating one's sense of self to challenges took hold, Microsoft's performance as an irresistible company soared.

GIG WORK HAS GONE MAINSTREAM

The gig economy—where workers take on individual gigs rather than fill long-term positions—continues to grow every year. Companies such as Upwork, Freelancer, Fiverr, 99designs, and others have aggregated talent networks to help organizations close temporary gaps in their workforces with high-quality gig workers. In fact, my research shows that there are more than 70 million workers using these platforms today, and the number is growing at a double-digit pace.

Companies see the shift: more than two-thirds of all companies believe their gig work will grow dramatically over the next three years, according to my latest research.[69] It's already happening. Visit Microsoft, Meta (previously Facebook), and many other companies, and you will see green badges to signify contractors or gig workers brought in for projects or for specialized work. The next evolution is to incorporate gig workers fully into company teams. For example, SellMax holds team retreats twice a year and flies out both internal team members and freelancers, and SimplrFlex invites its contract workers to participate in holiday potlucks.[70]

Inside companies, gig work has also gone mainstream. Our latest research shows that almost 15 percent of all large companies now use what's called a "talent marketplace" to let managers post projects or tasks and employees find and apply for interesting work.[71]

In the "pre-irresistible" era, companies classified workers as employees— full-time or part-time, exempt or non-exempt—and most contract work was managed by the procurement department, essentially appearing on the profit and loss statement as a contract (see Figure 2.4). Today, companies need to be more flexible than that.

Well, it's time to industrialize this new world. Companies like Deloitte and most pharmaceutical companies, for example, formally establish positions for gig workers around projects or assignments, and they manage them as an extended part of their workforce. Outsourcing firms like Genpact and IBM now train their gig workers to learn the culture of their clients. And Uber workers receive training and ongoing communications as if they were full-time employees.

Since all this is relatively new, large companies have historically not had good tools to manage project-based work, making it hard to keep track of where and how this is happening. Those days are over. The gig work–software industry is quite robust, evidenced by a series of acquisitions and initial public offerings (IPOs). For example, Workday acquired Rallyteam, a gig-work platform, and SAP acquired Fieldglass. ADP acquired WorkMarket, another gig-work platform, enabling customers to look for workers right from their HR systems, tapping into the expertise available in the WorkMarket system. ADP then acquired a

FIGURE 2.4: THE IRRESISTIBLE WORKFORCE

TYPE OF WORKER	HOW THEY'RE CLASSIFIED
White collar	Full time, salaried, on the balance sheet
Blue collar	Hourly, full- or part-time, on the balance sheet
Gray collar	Contingent contractor, not on balance sheet
No collar	Gig worker, paid for a piece of work

SOURCE: THE JOSH BERSIN COMPANY, 2021

company called Global Cash Card to provide real-time pay solutions for gig workers.

More interestingly, the pandemic opened up another dimension of gig work. As companies like DoorDash, Uber, and hundreds of other gig-delivery and service companies were born, intermediary tools to help manage schedules have emerged. One of the hottest of these companies, Legion, uses AI to help workers schedule their multiple gigs to optimize their earnings.

Using Legion's AI-driven platform, you could be hired and trained to work for Starbucks, Peet's Coffee, and Philz Coffee, each with different sets of work practices. The system tracks your certification, schedules your time between all three companies, and makes it possible for you to work for Starbucks in the morning, Peet's in the afternoon, and Philz the next day. This is the way work is going.

Gig work is rising in part because people want to make more money. As Z-Work's co-chairman Doug Atkins told *Fortune*, gig work "provides opportunities for people who don't have the right connections but do great work to get jobs they otherwise wouldn't get. And it enables full-time moms to use skills they couldn't otherwise use to earn money."[72]

The idea that we "own a job" is rapidly going away—we may "own" a job and then work in multiple places. The question is whether you, as an employer, will win or lose.

It's time to think of this model inside your company. Unilever and Schneider Electric are now operating like professional services companies. If you need help with a project, you can post a project online, and any employee can apply. People look for work they like, and at the end of the year their performance on these projects contributes to their raise and level in the company. The gig economy teaches us how to redesign our organizations, and it's happening faster than you may think.

Why is this important? As Humera Shahid, Intuit's vice president of talent development, commented in a 2021 interview, "The business landscape changes faster than ever before, and if we're not invested in helping our employees gain the skills and knowledge that they need as we evolve as a company, then we're not going to be successful."[73] It's that important. And, as Shahid said, "[H]ow do we get those skills? You build, buy, or rent."

LONGEVITY WILL FURTHER PUSH THIS SHIFT

There's another important factor driving this shift: longevity. Today, despite the issues in wellbeing I mentioned earlier, one of the greatest gifts of science is longevity. We are living longer every year. The fastest-growing segment of the U.S. population is people aged 80 or older.[74] An estimated 50 percent of Millennials are likely to live to 100. And for those of us in our 60s, if we are healthy today, there's a 50 percent chance we will live well into our 90s.

Although the pandemic fueled more retirements of Baby Boomers in 2020 than in any previous year, many people in their 60s and older have no desire to retire in the traditional sense. Rather, they see retirement as more of a transition: some still want to work full- or part-time. They want to mentor others. They want to share all they've learned.

In today's world of very scarce labor, the question for companies is how to turn the longevity dividend to their advantage. How can we tap the vast institutional knowledge, experience, judgment, and skills of older workers while still creating opportunities for the next generation? How can the elderly remain part of the workforce in useful, productive, and meaningful ways?

I recently had a fascinating conversation with the senior vice president of HR at a large pharmaceutical company. A general manager in his 60s was running a large business unit. The organization wanted to promote a younger, high-potential person into the role while also keeping the senior person engaged in a new role as an advisor, subject-matter expert, and team leader. When the senior individual refused to give up his position, HR faced a dilemma: let him go and lose a wealth of experience by promoting the high-potential employee, or keep the senior employee in place and risk losing a rising star to another company.

This new, gray generation also comes with many creative solutions. CVS developed the Snowbird program, which allows older pharmacists to work in Florida and other sunny climates during peak winter seasons.[75] Michelin allows older workers to reduce their hours without losing their jobs starting at age 55. And BMW and other German companies give older manufacturing workers redesigned workspaces with larger fonts on devices, more comfortable seats, and 70 other small accommodations.[76] In BMW's case, a minimal investment of $50,000 increased productivity at the plant by 7 percent and reduced absenteeism to almost zero.

Irresistible companies eliminate age bias and promote generational diversity not only because it is the right thing to do but also because it significantly benefits the organization as a whole. Research shows that generationally diverse teams innovate better, feel safer, and enjoy a more collaborative climate.[77] As organizations rethink work, the best will take advantage of the longevity dividend to hold on to valuable experience, skills, and expertise, generating better performance across the company.

the challenge: developing new ways to hire

If we want to take advantage of this transition, we must change the way we hire. We can't just fill job slots because jobs keep changing; we have to hire for potential, agility, values, and passion. This means removing bias, getting rid of old hiring models, and changing the way we think about performance.

Consider all the traditional biases we have in our recruitment practices.

EDUCATION AND PEDIGREE BIAS

We put far too much weight on college pedigree. Most big companies rely heavily on college recruiting, and they tend to return to the schools their executives attended. While this is a noble and important practice, research shows that such a practice is not necessarily a good way to find high performers. Consulting firm Ernst & Young (EY) found almost no correlation between GPA or degree and eventual job success.[78] So, they now use pre-employment simulations to evaluate candidates in a real work simulation. Unilever found the same.

Another client, a large insurance company, did an extensive study on job performance and found that college pedigree was less predictive of success in sales roles than factors such as likeability, personality, and hands-on job experience.[79] Their data showed that graduates of community colleges often outperformed college-educated candidates because they often had more grit and entrepreneurial spirit.

I had an interesting conversation with one of the executives at AnitaB.org, one of the leading organizations promoting women in technology. She told me that in the 1970s and 1980s, Apple (where she used to work) hired many engineers, designers, and production people with no college degree at all.[80] The company looked for people with passion, energy, design skills, and experience. Women, minorities, and people without degrees were highly represented.

In the 1990s, however, as Google, Meta, LinkedIn, and other internet companies came to market, companies started to focus on hiring people with straight As from schools such as Stanford, Massachusetts Institute of Technology (MIT), and Berkeley. This created an enormous competition for people with college pedigrees, almost to the point where it was impossible to get a job in companies like Google or Meta unless you had a computer-science degree from a top-rated school.

Google and Meta both later realized this was a mistake and have since greatly expanded their data-driven recruitment program. The companies have reduced the number of interviews, focusing more heavily on passion and drive than simply on technical skills; both also look for culture alignment.[81] This reflects the fact that at these companies, technical skills are simply not enough anymore.

Unilever recently adopted a dramatically new system for recruiting, using gamelike assessments to judge math, writing, and thinking skills. The company uses a neuroscience-based assessment tool that has dramatically improved its quality of hire, almost eliminating the role of education in the recruitment process. Unilever then uses video interviews to assess working style, language, honesty, and personality. (Video interview software can now pick up lies and exaggerations through facial expressions.) The company then brings candidates into the office for multicandidate working sessions to see how well people can solve problems and work in teams. Using this process has enabled Unilever to virtually eliminate all education and degree bias and recruit a workforce that is far more diverse than ever before.[82]

EXPERIENCE BIAS MUST GO

In the world of "work, not jobs," direct experience means a bit less. Most new managers rely on experience bias above all else. When you aren't sure how to get a job done, there is a tendency to find someone who has done the job before. This may have been logical for industrial-age business; a welder who welded pipe in one refinery could do it in the next.

Now, however, it is less valuable than people think. For most jobs, the ability to learn, work successfully within a team, and innovate is more important than direct role experience. When we studied the most impactful recruitment organizations, the most striking differentiator among the irresistible companies is how they recruited for ambition, culture, and potential—not just direct job experience.

Experience bias also works against a company's need to create talent mobility because it encourages managers to hire externally when they have an open slot. Companies such as Yum! Brands, Allianz, IBM, Allstate, and Unilever value internal experience more heavily than external experience in most cases because they know that institutional knowledge is far more important than technical skills.

Consider a rather astounding finding. General Assembly, a large IT and technical training provider, interviewed a series of its financial service customers to understand their challenges in hiring software engineers. What they found was that competing for these "hot skilled" individuals was very expensive: they had to pay very high fees for contract recruiters (up to 40 percent of salary) and steep fees for job advertising and new hire bonuses; what's more, most of these people would only stay one or two years because these employers could not provide stock options.

Instead, these companies tried an internal boot camp to develop software-engineering skills among in-house employees who had math degrees, psychology degrees, or other technical backgrounds. In all three cases, the companies found that they could develop people with skills and productivity that were similar to external hires within 12 to 24 months, at *one-sixth the cost*. The message? Don't always look for people with experience to fill a job; look for people with potential to learn.

the innovation: select to fit

Irresistible companies hire employees based on how well they fit the purpose of the work, rather than on conventional metrics such as education and pedigree, experience, and skills. I call this approach "select to fit"—which requires many companies to throw out their previous theories about what makes a good employee.

Take Bon-Ton Stores, a mid-sized specialty retailer in the northeastern United States that was looking to improve the financial performance of its cosmetics department, traditionally one of retail's highest-margin items. The old rule of thumb was that attractive, well-dressed individuals familiar with makeup made the best salespeople. To test this theory, Bon-Ton Stores hired a consulting firm and conducted a high-performer analysis, segmenting the entire population of salespeople into two groups—the top 10 percent and the rest—and identifying which traits really separate the best performers.[83]

The results were staggering. Nearly everything the retail industry *thought* it knew about what makes a high-performing seller was wrong. Physical characteristics such as height, weight, eye color, and hair color had no relevance at all. Neither did previous experience in sales. Instead, the best predictors of high performance were cognitive ability and rapid analytical-thinking skills.

Executives were shocked. Few had realized that selling cosmetics is such intellectually demanding work. A salesperson must size up the customer rapidly, choose from hundreds of products confidently, analyze the customer's reaction—and often repeat the process several times.

Using these insights, Bon-Ton Stores overhauled its screening, assessment, and hiring process. The company now chooses candidates based on how fit they are for the specific work required, rather than relying on outdated, preconceived notions.

The movie theater chain AMC took a similar select-to-fit approach.[84] Most of AMC's profits come from sales of popcorn, candy, drinks, and other concessions. While movie ticket prices generate revenue, movie licensing generally offsets this, so the business is highly dependent on encouraging customers to buy treats.

To assess what drives concession purchases, the company studied each location and found a distinct pattern: theaters with highest concession sales also had the highest employee engagement and retention rates. In other words, happy employees were creating happy customers—who bought more concessions. This relationship held true regardless of city size, neighborhood wealth, or other metrics normally associated with high sales.

To scale this finding across the entire theater chain, the CHRO embarked on a national program to train employees how to provide customers with an enjoyable experience. However, after several quarters the company saw almost no change in concession sales.

What happened? As the CHRO later told me, "I realized I can't train people to be happy; I have to hire happy people!"[85]

After evaluating the candidate-screening process, he found that AMC was primarily hiring people based on grade point average, degree, extracurricular activities, and experience in service jobs. While these "bias model" traits had some use, they discovered that people who were really the right fit for AMC loved movies, loved the theater, and loved helping people.

Using help from outside consultants, AMC redesigned the screening process and started scanning for movie, theater, and people lovers. After only a few months, replacing the bias model with a select-to-fit model dramatically increased concession sales and generated repeat customers. The following year was one of AMC's most profitable on record.

how to get started

Discuss these questions with your own leaders and teams:

1   When did you last look at your job architecture? Have you assessed all positions for duplications, job circles, and opportunities to make the system simpler?

2   How are people really rewarded in your company? Do you reward capabilities, experiences, and reputation? Or do you reward tenure, job level, political relationships, and job title?

3   How much autonomy do people have to "recraft" their jobs in place? Are service and support people given freedom to solve problems locally, without asking for permission? Do you have ways for people to share innovations in their teams so others can learn from their ideas?

4   Do people have time to think about their work and make it better? Or is everyone in your company overworked and committed to many goals and conflicting priorities? How do you train managers to assign goals and manage teams?

5   Can people in your company move from team to team or group to group without fear? Can they return to their old job if they fail? Do you welcome and encourage regular job rotation without promotion? Do you tell stories of people who moved into new roles and contributed through their relationships and broad knowledge of the business?

6   Do leaders embrace a growth mindset? Do they honestly believe people can move from role to role and team to team and succeed over time? Or do they always look for the proven, experienced candidate and recruit from outside whenever they need help?

7   Does your company believe in continuous development? Can people commit to learning a new skill, craft, or job with support from their manager and the rest of the company? Or is your company one where everyone "manages their own career" and has to figure it out on their own?

how to get it right

Hiring is the most important task for managers or HR leaders. But in my conversations with business leaders, most executives tell me they get it wrong about half the time. Most companies still use the bias model when it comes to choosing employees, when they should be transitioning to a select-to-fit model.

What's the prescription for making this shift to becoming irresistible?

HIRE FOR PASSION, ENERGY, AND MISSION

The best organizations have a strong sense of who they are. They understand what makes them successful and learn to hire people who fit those characteristics. Instead of relying on misleading traits such as previous experience, irresistible companies build unique elements into the hiring process to identify employees who fit.

For example, Southwest Airlines asks job candidates to tell a joke.[86] The company knows that a good sense of humor and friendly nature will go a long way to making it successful.

Similarly, IKEA, true to its mission to help people "improve their home lives through sustainable living," asks candidates to describe their vision of global sustainability. Those who value sustainability, collective thinking, and interdependent decision-making thrive in the culture. This has helped IKEA earn a higher retention rate than Starbucks, in large measure because they understand who fits and hire carefully.

KEEP WORK FLUID

Companies in all industries are rethinking what work really is and focusing on fit in far more expansive, imaginative ways. At Cleveland Clinic, doctors and medical professionals move from project to project without regard to level. Employees at W. L. Gore can work on any project they want, as long as the team needs the help. And at Meta, people can work on multiple projects simultaneously, often even working on weekends to volunteer for projects that interest them. This flexibility is the essence of decoupling jobs from work.

EMBRACE CLEAR, TRANSPARENT GOALS

In organizations that focus on work, not jobs, it's nearly impossible to measure output based on piecework. Moreover, most studies show that financial goals based on production result in poor quality, lack of innovation, and, often, bad behavior.[87]

Consider Wells Fargo, which created strong forced-sales goals, many unattainable.[88] In response, employees developed unethical behaviors to meet these goals, such as opening fake accounts. The impact on Wells Fargo's brand has been enormous, and it all started with reliance on top-down, hierarchical goals.

In lieu of this industrial-era process, the irresistible model uses what some call the objectives-and-key-results (OKR) approach to goal-setting. Top leadership sets direction and priority, as well as budgets and annual plans. But during that process, teams suggest bottom-up goals based on their own aspirations and what they believe they can achieve.

Even a few years ago, this kind of agile goal-setting seemed impossible—largely because companies design software tools such as SuccessFactors and Oracle to do it the old way. I've interviewed dozens of executives who use top-down goals who told me they spent the entire month of January getting their teams to commit to rigid annual plans.

In the real world, this causes real problems.

One client, a hardware manufacturer, told me that nobody in the company wanted to change priorities midyear because bonuses were tied to fixed annual goals. After this company suffered a quality problem in a plant, the inflexible goal-setting process took many months to reset goals and gain agreement.

Research has shown that people who set their own goals are often more ambitious, more committed, and more likely to succeed.[89] In the OKR model, pioneered at Intel, employees set five to seven goals continuously. Some are easily doable, while others are a stretch. Online systems publish the goals so everyone can see them, often linking them to corporate initiatives or other projects.

A new marketplace of software tools has emerged to help manage this process. With these tools, goal-setting is now easier than ever, and teams can use agile systems such as Jira, Basecamp, and others to update, share, and communicate progress on goals. The team should set clear and transparent goals—and individuals should feel ownership of them.

ALLOW TIME FOR SLACK

As companies undertake the shift from jobs to work, they must build in time for workers to rest, think, and organize their work, which has been shown to improve productivity because humans work best in spurts of energy.[90] This has clear implications for staffing.

Research by Zeynep Ton at the Good Jobs Institute found that retailers who overstaff their stores by hiring extra shifts and giving people more free time are far more profitable than those who understaff to save money.[91] The Spanish retailer Mercadona and the U.S. retailer Costco both staff their stores with 20 to 25 percent more workers than competitors, and each has higher profit margins. Empowered employees with slack time can focus on rearranging products, talking with customers, and cross-training peers.

Employees also rate the companies higher on Glassdoor, demonstrating the impact of time for slack on people's feelings about work.

In our research focused on pandemic responses, we learned that a hallmark of a high-performing culture is the health and wellbeing of employees.[92] While this seems obvious in light of the contagious nature of the coronavirus, this realization extended beyond disinfecting workplaces and designing social distancing protocols. Each worker is a person whose life and work intertwine and deeply affect each other. Employers have to seriously listen to employees, as their lives have a significant impact on organizational outcomes.

Anheuser-Busch InBev pivoted from a semiannual employee survey to weekly surveys.[93] Discussion forums like Reliance's My Voice and WhatsApp groups such as those conducted by Deutsche Telekom opened up channels for people to be heard. And Legendary Entertainment provided subscriptions to meditation and coaching sessions to support employees' mental health and wellbeing.

CROSS-TRAIN AND LEARN ON THE JOB

The shift from jobs to work is impossible to achieve without building an environment that enables people to learn. Today, irresistible organizations are reinvesting in learning at staggering levels and are providing a much more employee-focused, on-demand experience. Companies spend $82.5 billion a year on corporate training.[94]

Among the most successful programs are those that focus on "learning for work" and that use a digital format. Let's take a look at Visa University.[95] In its early days in the 1960s, Visa had little competition and did not need to innovate to grow. In the last decade, however, Visa has seen tremendous competition, not only from traditional competitors such as American Express and Mastercard, but also from Apple, Google, PayPal, Square, Venmo, and other electronic payment companies. With the advent of blockchain technology and digital cryptocurrencies, Visa wondered where it played in this new world.

In the old organizational model, the CEO and senior leadership team would devise a plan and tell a group of employees what to do. If they couldn't figure it out, the company suffered. Today, Visa has turned itself upside down—and is encouraging innovation, learning, and creative thinking everywhere.

Visa University has become a world-class hub of innovation, knowledge sharing, online learning, and some of the most advanced digital-learning tools in the market. Employees worldwide can design courses or share what they've learned, and the company gives people time and platforms to learn what they need. New learning opportunities include a "digital currency fluency" curriculum for all employees, which is so well respected that people want to work at Visa just to learn this new business.

FACILITATE AND SUPPORT TALENT MOBILITY

A focus on learning alone, however, is not enough. In a world of constantly changing work, organizations need a process to encourage people to move around to different teams, different projects, and different types of work. Yet this type of fluid talent mobility has often been dis-couraged under traditional business models.

The vice president of HR for a global consumer-products company told me that leadership failure at the organization often occurs when a high-potential person takes on a job in a new division, then fails in that role. Rather than having an opportunity to learn from the experience, these leadership candidates almost always quit—and generally ended up at a competitor.

Today, people with important internal skills, such as engineers, product owners, designers, and customer-service personnel, are so valuable that teams want to borrow them and their expertise to work on many things. Companies can become irresistible by designing reward systems to facil-itate this type of horizontal mobility without requiring employees to seek promotions.

At Cummins, a global engine-manufacturing leader, encouraging inter-nal talent movement stems from a firm belief that learning through experience is extremely powerful. One employee said this emphasis makes Cummins a "playground for learning" and praised "the number of cross-functional moves that take place and how open leaders are to considering high performers for any number of assignments regardless of their technical background."[96] Not surprisingly, enabling these expe-riences not only provides learning opportunities at Cummins but also raises employee engagement.

How can organizations decide when someone should take another job and whether that job would be a good fit? In the old model of work, managers decided whether an employee could leave a group and deter-mined where that employee could go. I would even argue that the old industrial model was based on managers owning their people—meaning an employee needed permission to leave a group, often based on the manager's best interests, not the employee's.

Today, Millennials and most others expect new work and development opportunities on a regular basis. Our research on engagement and

performance shows that employee desire for career growth and exposure is more important than salary. Given this new reality, companies
are experimenting with new tools to help employees facilitate their own
careers, including rules that managers cannot prevent people from leaving their groups. One company I know even measures managers in part
by the rate of promotion out of their group.

UnitedHealth Group and Ingersoll Rand spent several years creating
success profiles for all their major job categories so everyone in the company could look at other jobs, assess themselves for fit, and then apply
for new positions.

AT&T in the United States and Telstra in Australia offer career-coaching
services for employees to help them find new opportunities. Companies
such as Pfizer and GE have internal job networks and task networks that
let people bid and take work internally based on their skills. Scientists
who are isolated in one research and development group, for example,
can now help others solve problems through these networks.

These are not just nice things for an organization to do—they build
the fiber of a resilient and adaptable organization and drive employee
engagement and innovation.

The chief learning officer of a large healthcare company put it this way:
"I tell our managers, 'You do not own the people working for you. You
are just taking care of them. They belong to the organization, and we
must do what is best for the entire organization, not just you.'" Managers
are not bosses anymore—they are coaches, advisors, talent scouts, and
talent producers.

The good news is that managers and leaders can implement these
changes relatively easily. Encourage employees to move around on a regular basis. Eliminate hierarchical and rigid job titles. Reduce the number of levels. Start to pay people based on the demand for their services
and expertise rather than on their tenure or level. Inspire, reward, or
force managers to encourage people to leave their teams, perhaps even

evaluating managers on how many people do so. Provide career coaching inside the company.

Taken together, these steps will help your irresistible company adapt to thinking more about work than about jobs.

coach, not boss

"Management is the opportunity to help people become better people. Practiced that way, it's a magnificent profession."

CLAYTON CHRISTENSEN, HARVARD BUSINESS SCHOOL PROFESSOR
AND AUTHOR OF *THE INNOVATOR'S DILEMMA*, 2013

You know Apple. You know PayPal. But you may not know Erste Group—and you should. Because when Apple and PayPal threatened the longevity of this over-200-year-old central European bank, Erste came up with a brilliant response: coaching.[97]

Yes, coaching. As a market leader in most of central Europe, with 45,000 employees servicing some 70 million customers from nearly 5,000 branches, Erste knew that looking forward to the next 200 years would require a serious look inward. To encourage employees to think of the line manager as a coach, the company adopted the 70-20-10 model: 70 percent challenging assignments, 20 percent developmental relationships, and 10 percent coursework and training.

This active coaching and mentoring scheme encourages learning on the job, respects the power of each individual, rewards appropriately, and builds on the growth mindset that everyone can always do more. The role of manager has radically changed when it comes to agency, and in this chapter, I'll explain it in detail.

the shift: coach, not boss

There are countless books on leadership. Every few years, a company outperforms its peers, so we make its leaders (Steve Jobs, Jack Welch, and Jeff Bezos, to name a few) into role models for decades to come.

While I won't try to discuss all the research on leadership models and psychology, let me give you a few principles I've seen in my many years of work.

First, leaders themselves are flawed people—as are we all. Their role is not to be perfect, to make perfect decisions, or to tell people precisely what to do. Rather, the most effective leaders who stand the test of time know how to get the best out of their people; ultimately, their companies grow because the people in the company grow.

As one of my friends from Sybase used to tell me, "People don't grow into the company; the company grows into the people." The more driven, aligned, and empowered your teams are, the faster your company will grow, the better its products and services will become, and the more service and support you'll provide to customers. It's quite simple.

Second, the right leader for a given time is not necessarily the right leader for the next cycle in a business. The senior vice president of HR at Cisco once told me, "We studied our leadership pipelines in detail and realized we have four types of leaders in the company: a) people who can start new businesses, b) people who can scale and grow businesses, c) people who can fix and turn around businesses, and d) people who can shut down and rationalize businesses. We've tried to build general managers by moving them from role to role, but ultimately what we found was that our best leaders stayed in their lane, and we found them new roles that play to their strengths."[98]

In other words, the idea that we build "general managers" who can do everything is just not true. The best leaders are specialists in something. They have deep domain expertise, and they bring it to their job.

Third, leaders have an enormous, outsized impact on culture, engagement, and productivity. I've witnessed hundreds of situations where a leader was the wrong fit for the team, the project, or the company. And when this happens, the organization underperforms, people get upset and quit, and the culture of the company suffers. So, while we all want leaders to be great businesspeople, decision-makers, and project leaders, above all they need to be great drivers of culture. People watch their behavior, they do what leaders do, and they learn from the way leaders reward or punish activity.

Given these three principles, we have to accept that a massive change is sweeping through leadership. The days of a grumpy older white male CEO telling people what to do and holding everyone accountable to their goals has come to an end, especially in this accelerated period of flexible work arrangements, where physical face-to-face (or over-the-shoulder) leadership is absent or occasional.

Remember that almost 85 percent of all stock market capitalization in companies is based on innovation, intellectual property, services, and brand. Technology is making it possible for small businesses to disrupt big ones in every industry. People want meaning, purpose, and wellbeing at work. And the types of expertise and skills we need are changing faster than ever. What is the leadership model for this new world? It's simple: leader as coach.

LEADING IN A NETWORK

If you buy my argument that companies are networks, that we work on multiple projects at once, and that our functional jobs may be less important than ever before, what should a leader today do?

Leaders are here to drive strategy, lead projects, help people grow, and identify the experts, innovators, and project managers we need. Leaders must understand the network, they must understand how the company makes money, and they must have the influence and followership to persuade people to move in a given direction without just telling them what to do. And on the people side, they must have a deep instinct for talent and people. The simplest way to think of this is that leaders today must shift from being the boss to being the coach.

Yes, we still need leaders and managers. But their tasks, behaviors, and selection must change. The days of a boss sitting behind a desk, telling people what to do, and handing out annual appraisals have gone the way of the dinosaur.

As I like to think about it, the role of a manager at irresistible companies is to get work done, not to manage people. This means we have two types of managers in companies going forward—those who manage projects and work, and those who lead and coach people, or "people leaders." The job description of "manager" has changed, so companies now often use different language for the different roles.

At W. L. Gore, people leaders are called "sponsors." Their job is to get to know people, identify their strengths and weaknesses, coach them for success, and sponsor them for new roles, new positions, and new careers. Sponsors do not "own" promotions and pay but are instead responsible for furthering each individual's career.

People leaders are called "career advisors" at one consulting firm. They help individuals find the next project and prepare for promotion, and they give them candid feedback on their performance, their reputation, and their skills. They don't manage people's time or tell people what to do each day, but they do help people succeed. The people they lead also evaluate them.

At Spotify (which uses the agile model described earlier), the circle leader, or functional lead, often performs people management. Project leaders contribute to determining each person's pay and promotion, but ultimately the coaching takes place at the functional level.

As coaches, leaders must create clear, achievable goals; fit people into the right roles; provide regular feedback about people's progress; and offer continuous opportunities to learn, build new skills, and improve performance. This means reinventing broken performance management processes.

The CHRO of a leading healthcare provider once mentioned to me, "I tell all my leaders that their job is not to 'manage' or 'control' their people; rather it is to 'build, develop, and promote' them. They don't belong to you; they belong to me [the organization itself]. You, as a leader, have simply been given this important responsibility to make sure they all succeed. And we are going to evaluate your leadership capabilities by the number of people who are promoted, leave your group, or move into higher-level roles."

And, yes, leaders have an enormous impact on employee engagement. Glassdoor research shows perceptions of leadership are more important than compensation in predicting a company's employment brand.[99] So it's important to take this topic seriously. Companies of the past promoted people into leadership based on tenure or technical skills; companies of the future look for leaders who really understand how to coach (see Figure 3.1).

A new model is emerging, one of human-centered leadership. This means the leader connects the business to communities, society, and the local economy.

Today's successful leaders lead by example, empowerment, and inspiration instead of by position, level, or title. Irresistible leaders excel at moving people into the roles that are right for both them and the organization. They align teams, develop networks, and reinforce culture and adherence to the organization's values.

As former Secretary of State Colin Powell said, "You know you're a good leader when you have good followers."[100] That vision is about as far away as you can get from the imperious boss sitting in a corner office directing the actions of employees under his command.

FIGURE 3.1: PAST AND PRESENT MANAGEMENT ARCHETYPES

INDUSTRIAL-AGE MANAGEMENT	DIGITAL-AGE MANAGEMENT
Differentiation by scale	Differentiation by speed
Leaders in charge	Individuals and teams in charge
Top-down goals and direction	Bottom-up goals and direction
Focus on output and performance	Focus on alignment and service
Competitive culture	Interdependent and collaborative culture
Success through careful focus on scale, quality, and process	Success through experimentation, iteration, and constant improvement
Decisions made through hierarchy	Decisions made by teams, individuals, and the network
Individual power developed through tenure and level	Power developed through relationships, experience, and knowledge
Emphasis on upward mobility for power	Emphasis on horizontal mobility for breadth
Rewards based on fairness and equality	Rewards based on individual performance
Culture of competition and scarcity	Culture of abundance and growth
Lead through authority	Lead through influence

SOURCE: THE JOSH BERSIN COMPANY, 2021

In sports, great coaches make everyone feel more powerful and engaged. They know how to put people into the right position, where they can succeed. They give team members the subtle guidance they need to improve while the game is being played, rather than just handing down judgment after the season is over. Great coaches help keep people focused on the ultimate goal and ask team members questions they may not have asked themselves. This archetype shatters many of the traditional models of leadership in business.

High-performing business leaders, in fact, share many similar traits with sports coaches:

- *They communicate a clear direction:* They have a crystal-clear understanding of where they are going. Good coaches help a team win through the clarity of their vision.

- *They are good judges of people:* They have a keen and refined sense of how someone will perform. Good coaches know the capabilities of everyone in the organization, and they put the right people into the right positions to play to everyone's individual strengths.

- *They develop winning game plans:* They have an uncanny ability to take complex problems and quickly break them down into step-by-step solutions. From watching the team perform, they identify excellence and incorporate it into the team's playbook.

- *They focus on developing people:* They have an ability to inspire others, improve themselves, and work hard for success. They generally do this by focusing on individuals, their strengths, opportunities, and areas for improvement.

DIFFERING LEVELS OF ENGAGEMENT IN THE AIRLINE INDUSTRY

An airline is a traditional, tightly organized company, right? For many, collective bargaining agreements cover the pilots, flight attendants, baggage handlers, and others. If there is a breakdown in flight operations, the plane will be late or will be grounded, resulting in a customer-service headache with the inevitable harsh tweets and hashtags undermining the airline's reputation. All airlines basically do the same thing: they operate planes, sell seats, and fly passengers. But the industry is sharply differentiated by people and management practices, which in turn drive levels of engagement.

As discussed in the previous chapter, Southwest Airlines, which regularly ranks highly on customer experience net promoter scores, runs itself like a network of teams. Each team includes an airplane, pilots, and a handful of crew members. The team operates independently, with individuals held responsible for on-time departures, safety, food and beverage service, and the overall customer experience. Management empowers them to take whatever actions are needed, within regulatory guidelines, to make that plane work well.

Empowering teams—and holding them responsible—yields amazing results. At Southwest, pilots often roll up their sleeves and help flight attendants arrange bags to ensure on-time departures. Flight attendants help pilots get settled quickly. The entire team feels cohesive and engaged, and passengers notice.

JetBlue, another airline with a high net promoter score, has a similar philosophy. The company invests heavily in corporate learning and hosts one of the most advanced corporate universities in the marketplace. Its people are well educated, and JetBlue carefully manages their careers, holding leaders responsible for the growth of their people.

The contrast between these leaders and those at other airlines is striking.

I recently interviewed an executive at another U.S. legacy carrier—that is, an airline established before 1978.[101] This airline has a legacy of a more traditional, top-down management structure—almost the exact opposite of Southwest's "each plane is a team" approach. A recent set of pension cuts and layoffs damaged morale, and many employees have developed low expectations and distrust of management. A pilot sitting next to me on one flight told me he doesn't really listen to management because, as he said, "I'm the labor, and I consider the union my best representative."

Can we think of a worse model of management?

Recently, a new management team has joined the airline, and the CEO and his team started an impressive feedback program that uses best-in-class technology to deploy pulse surveys to gauge employee attitudes. In my conversations with senior leadership and several employees and pilots, I found that engagement almost immediately rose simply because people could feel that management was listening. While this airline is just now beginning its journey to becoming irresistible, it is in the process of revamping its entire leadership model and changing its leadership development program—all in an effort to create better experiences for both employees and customers.

the problem: performance management is broken

The performance-appraisal process is often like a set of handcuffs for management. This old-fashioned approach was designed for a different era. *Jack Welch & the G.E. Way* describes how Jack Welch created a system of forced ranking (the bottom 10 percent must leave the company each year), implemented a strict system of ratings, and used nine-box grids (see Figure 2.1) to weed out poor managers.[102]

What I've learned from my research is that this process is only useful when your goal is to shrink the company and reduce costs. In every other business situation, it causes problems. Evaluating performance, having criteria for leadership, and discussing teams are all important, but the appraisal itself has gone stale. What's more, creating goal-based performance can create lots of problems.

Let me give you an example. When we sold our research business to Deloitte in 2011, we were generating around $12 million in recurring revenue and growing at around 30 percent per year. Deloitte decided to pile on lots of new management, nearly doubling the size of the team, and created a detailed set of goals for everyone—and the goals were only about 5 percent growth.

Guess what happened? We missed the growth target.

Why did this happen? Before the acquisition, we grew with an abundance mindset. We believed there were infinite opportunities for our services, and every company became a possible customer. Under the Deloitte goal management system, people only looked at their numbers and stopped seeing infinite opportunities in the market. Today, that business continues to shrink.

The appraisal process itself can be a problem. When I worked at IBM, Exxon, and Deloitte, managers delivered a year-end appraisal in December, including a few comments on our success, a few comments on what we could do better, and the infamous performance rating. The managers spent almost an entire month filling out forms for meetings they dreaded. (And rarely could they explain why I got the rating I did.)

In my 45 years as an employee, I probably sat through 40 or more of these uncomfortable meetings, and I can remember *only one* that truly gave me the inspiration or help to do better. In almost every case, I felt the process was a waste of time, a disappointing conversation, or a meeting that left me walking out of the office wondering if I really wanted to continue to work at the company.

In 2006, we conducted a large study of performance management that asked companies to tell us whether their performance management process was designed for competitive assessment or for coaching and development. In other words, was it to weed people out or to help people improve? Some 76 percent of companies said the former, implying that the process was primarily there to improve performance through competition.[103]

In 2015, we did the same survey and obtained opposite results. More than 75 percent of companies now saw the process as one of coaching and development, which is a clear indicator that this area is changing rapidly.[104] Importantly, however, nearly 81 percent told us it was "not worth the time they put into it" to sort, filter, and rate people to allocate salary budgets "fairly."

the innovation: continuous performance management

I once asked Edgar Schein, an eminent researcher of corporate culture, to name the single most important lesson in culture and performance. "It's very simple," he told me. "The most important part of a high-performing culture is people helping each other."[105]

Yes, it really is that simple. The boss becomes the coach.

Remember that managers, like fish in a fishbowl, behave the way they are rewarded. If we want to get managers to be coaches, we have to reward coaching, feedback, development, progression, and continuous learning.

By some accounts, the revolution in performance management began with Adobe in 2012. While reinventing its entire business model around cloud services, it also reinvented management, leadership, and performance practices—with coaching at the center. The company found early on that success comes from continuous performance management rather than once-a-year reviews.

Today, continuous performance management involves seven clearly defined steps:

1 *Goal-Setting.* Create short- or long-term goals, sometimes using the objectives-and-key-results (OKR) method.

2 *Check-Ins.* Hold one-on-one conversations to discuss progress and obstacles, having them as often as individuals need.

3 *Feedback and Goal Reviews.* Conduct regular reviews, quarterly business reviews, or other reviews of goal progress with individual feedback.

4 *Coaching and Development.* Propose suggestions, plans, and assignments to help individuals develop, improve, and grow.

5 *Performance Reviews.* Carry out an annual, semiannual, or more frequent formal review, often with a rating.

6 *Compensation Reviews.* Administer an annual or more frequent review of pay and make payment adjustments.

7 *Development Plans and Next Assignment.* Discuss and plan for job rotation, promotion, growth, or the next assignment.

To drive engagement, goal-setting belongs to the team, whether it is a team of nurses, an airplane crew, a design team, a sales team, or an engineering group. Each team member can then set three to five individual goals that are personal, actionable, and easy for others to understand.

Now, back to OKRs. As mentioned earlier, objectives and key results form a goal-setting framework that helps companies define and track objectives. Google, LinkedIn, Twitter, Dropbox, Atlassian, Spotify, Airbnb, and Uber all rely on OKRs to establish what they're looking to accomplish and how to get it done, using them to create clarity, transparency, and alignment regarding goals.

Typically, a few goals are easy to obtain, others are stretch goals, and one or two may be aspirational goals. New software tools from many software vendors facilitate the process by making each person's goals transparent. An open, transparent process creates a sense of empowerment and accountability, allowing people to feel they control their own destiny at work. At Google, this level of transparency applies all the way to the CEO.[106]

The next steps in continuous performance management relate to providing feedback. People want constructive feedback, even when the news isn't good.

As a young IBM systems engineer, I made a major pricing mistake on a huge multimillion-dollar proposal. We found the error during the presentation to the customer, and I almost fainted. I was humiliated, and my boss was very upset. Once we saw what had happened, we excused ourselves, and I jumped in the car and sped back to the office with tears in my eyes. I thought my career was over.

Luckily, the story ended well, and I learned a big lesson. We had a wonderful relationship with this particular executive, and he felt sorry for me. He understood the mistake, and they let us go back through the procurement process with an update. I had dodged a bullet.

At the end of the year, when my performance review came up, my work generally was praised, although I was criticized for lacking "attention to detail." Ever since that day, I've been known to reread and revalidate every presentation, proposal, or analysis I've done. That's the type of clear, honest feedback and coaching irresistible companies must deliver to help people thrive.

Assessing performance on a once-a-year basis in the way we did when I was at IBM no longer holds value today because the worlds of business and work change so fast. During the brunt of the pandemic, PepsiCo relied on week-by-week pulsing and open feedback to make sure input was current.[107]

Even the word "feedback" often carries a negative connotation. General Electric (GE) has changed its language and now calls feedback "insights" so that people feel more open to conversations. IBM uses a system called "Checkpoint,"[108] and Adobe and Cisco call it a "check-in." Whatever the name, managers must adopt an overall culture of feedback that is productive, even if the news isn't always good.

GE, a company that has been through enormous upheaval over the last few decades, now considers itself a digitally enabled industrial enterprise. In this transition, the company tried to put simplicity and employee development at the core of its performance management efforts. GE has dramatically streamlined its management structure, redesigned goal-setting, and focused on how to drive a high-performance meritocracy.

This is a major shift for an organization that once annually ranked individuals against peers and pushed out the bottom 10 percent of underperformers. GE ended "rank and yank" more than a decade ago and has more recently abandoned traditional performance management and annual reviews for its 174,000 employees in favor of frequent feedback and mobile apps. Crotonville, the legendary leadership training center, is the hub of this management transformation.[109]

Even as GE grapples with this massive shift, most organizations remain hierarchical and bureaucratic, even if they claim they are not. But most know that they and their managers need to move toward a new vision.

how to get started

Discuss these questions with your own leaders and teams:

1   Do you differentiate between the concept of a "project manager" and a "career coach" in your company, or are line managers responsible for everything?

2   How do you select individuals for managerial roles? Is it a process of nine-box grids and talent reviews? How relevant and up-to-date is your management model or framework? Is it a political system based on tenure and friendship?

3   Would you consider removing managerial promotions in your company and letting people go into management without a promotion?

4   How are managers themselves evaluated? Does your model include the ideas of talent production and "manager as coach"? Can managers get away with abuse or overworking their teams to boost their performance metrics? Do you have a form of unbiased survey to evaluate teams against their peers in an open, transparent process?

5   How much money, energy, and time do you put into leadership development? Do you have a dedicated leadership development manager who can assess, build, and monitor your leadership development process? Does your company regularly talk about leadership and analyze the important roles of leaders?

6   Is management considered a privilege or a job in your company? Do managers rotate into and out of their coaching roles, and can you move them easily when they are in the wrong job? Or do they get to "own" their management job for the rest of their career, regardless of how well they help others?

7   What is the leadership philosophy of your senior executives? Do they talk about management practices and coaching? Do they truly believe in a growth mindset? Do they regularly move young, highly regarded people into leadership roles? Do they celebrate and tell stories of development and coaching?

how to get it right

TURN MANAGERS INTO COACHES

Companies spend a lot of time and money selecting and developing managers: the leadership development market is a $14 billion business, and it's growing by the year.[110] Leadership development is complex: as a new manager, you suddenly have to select, hire, train, coach, and assess people—and they come to you with a wide variety of work, professional, and personal issues. You have to learn to listen, advise, and sometimes be tough—all in a way that helps others feel more inspired and empowered to perform.

First, you have to set the rules straight: What behaviors do you reward in management? Will you reward a manager for hitting their numbers while burning out their people? Or will you reward a manager for developing their team while they do their best to perform? At an organizational level, the latter model will far outperform; at a microlevel, the former feels better. High-performing companies today now evaluate leaders through the company's net promoter score or the engagement levels of their people.

Second, do you reward talent consumption or talent production? Do managers get rewarded for hoarding great people and getting them to stay on their teams? Or do you encourage and reward managers for moving people out of their teams and into new development opportunities? At irresistible companies such as General Mills, Nestlé, and Aetna, talent production is the goal of leadership. At many "burnout" tech firms, the opposite is true.

A large defense contractor computes talent production metrics from all its managers and team leaders. It measures how many people are promoted within two years of working for a given person, giving managers the message that coaching and developing people is their job.

Third, our research clearly shows that companies that invest in the development of managers outperform those that don't. Companies that perform at the highest level (in our four-level maturity model[III]) in leadership development generate more revenue per employee, are more likely to anticipate and respond effectively to change, and are more profitable than their peers.

Think about it this way. When contributors move into management, they are essentially changing careers. Suddenly, their entire success is dependent on how well they align, coach, and develop others. Most new managers start their jobs trying to micromanage their teams, essentially teaching them to work the way they did. But over time (often years), they develop the maturity to understand that each individual is different and that each brings value in unique ways.

Leaders must be trained to make this transition in the right way. Patagonia and IKEA give managers the clear direction that collective thinking is part of the company's value system. Helping the environment, designing solutions in a holistic way, and spending time helping others are parts of the reward system. (Both companies also value a focus on the environment, sustainable business practices, and brand purpose—values managers must learn from the company.) These companies both have Glassdoor ratings far above their industry averages (see Appendix 2).

Juniper Networks deliberately created a performance management process that reinforces this culture of leadership and growth. Juniper's latest performance management process evaluates people based on four dimensions: contribution (did you meet your goals?), capabilities (did you improve your skills or capabilities?), connections (did you expand your network, meet new people, and contribute to other projects in the company?), and career (are your career interests consistent with those of the company?).[112] This framework, coupled with a focus on defining "The Juniper Way," gives all managers a common set of tools to make sure they are coaching people in a consistent, strategic, and developmental way.

PUT CONTINUOUS GOAL MANAGEMENT OR OKRS INTO PRACTICE

OKRs have a simple structure: a definable objective (for example, hitting a sales quota) and a set of measurable results that will contribute to that objective. By using this model consistently, individuals and teams develop specific plans that align with goals and then share them. A sales-related objective might be to make the sales quota, and its related key results might be to increase the average sale price by 5 percent and make 20 calls per day on average.

At Uber, an objective might be to increase drivers in the system, and key results might be to increase the driver base by 20 percent in each region and to increase the average driver session to 26 hours. At YouTube, an objective may be to increase average watch time per user, and key results might be to increase total viewership to X minutes per day and to reduce video loading time by X percent.

In a 21st-century company, each team in the network has its own goals and objectives, but teams must still coordinate and know what the others are focused on. What better way than to have a transparent set of goals that anyone can see? New tools are making this easy and possible for any company to do.

Setting goals is not a new idea. The difference is the shift in how goals are set, measured, and updated (see Figure 3.2).

The tech industry is very familiar with OKRs, and the concept is beginning to spread to other fields under various names. All my research shows that, whatever you call it, this approach is critical to collective thinking, teamwork, alignment, and continued high performance.

EVALUATE PERFORMANCE IN A NEW WAY

As I discussed previously, traditional annual performance reviews must go. They're extremely bureaucratic, consume manager attention and time, and impede teamwork and creativity, making many employees feel underappreciated and uninspired. But that doesn't mean we don't evaluate people. All employees want to know where they stand. We have to decide how much to pay people, who gets raises and bonuses, and who gets placed into new positions. These are all parts of management, so we need some framework to do this well.

First, evaluate people in a holistic way, building on their strengths, not their weaknesses. As was affirmed during the pandemic, every individual in the world works in his or her own way, whenever and wherever he or she deems it best to get work done. We all have the potential to thrive in the right job or work conditions.

FIGURE 3.2: TRADITIONAL VERSUS NEW GOAL-SETTING TECHNIQUES

	TRADITIONAL	NEW
How Goals Are Set	Top-down, cascaded from the top, and all aligned	Bottom-up, set by the team, and aligned through financial and budget metrics
Frequency	Set once per year, reviewed at year end, and rarely discussed during the year	Updated regularly and adjusted as needed (Our research shows that companies that update goals quarterly get 30 percent more value out of this process.)
Who Sets Goals	Leaders set goals for people, and managers are in charge and responsible	People set their own goals, and managers coach and support them
How Managers Evaluate Performance	Focus on weaknesses and where goals are behind	Focus on continuous alignment and improvement
How Often Goals Are Updated	Annually	As often as needed
Transparency	Goals are somewhat secret, and nobody really knows how others are paid	Goals are totally transparent, so we know what others aspire to do
Sandbagging	Goals are kept manageable, so it's relatively easy to hit targets	At least a third of goals are stretch goals, so people feel inspired and excited to push themselves to overperform
Focus on "What" versus "How"	Entirely focused on objectives; people are often paid bonuses based on outcomes, with little focus on how they are achieved	Specifically define the "how" using key results, with lots of discussion about how to achieve objectives

SOURCE: THE JOSH BERSIN COMPANY, 2021

The purpose of an evaluation is to compare someone against themselves, *not against others*. What can this person do to be better at their job, or is there a role that might help them perform even better?

Studies show that the most destructive management practice in the old hierarchy was the need to compete for ratings. Most companies have a forced distribution of some kind, so only 10 percent of people can get a top rating, for example. This sets up a whole culture of scarcity, where people compete for a top rating and actually resent those who achieve that rating. In a networked organization where everyone adds value, what possible good can this create? None that I can see.

Compare people against their own goals and aspirations; you, as a manager, are here to help them develop, after all. Consider your own children: do you rate them against each other? Of course not—you want each of them to grow and thrive in their own way. That's the way irresistible organizations work—people find the role, job, manager, and work environment that's best for them.

Of course, with hundreds of managers each doing this, a process of calibration must be in place. Lots of research shows that more than 40 percent of all ratings are manager-specific or based on the bias of the manager.

What seems to work best is what we typically call "calibration meetings" or "talent reviews." These are simply meetings among managers to talk about relative performance. The purpose of these meetings should not be to dole out ratings but rather to make sure people feel comfortable with the coaching and feedback they receive.

In my company, which did away with ratings entirely, we spend time in these meetings discussing the strengths of each person, where they could improve, and what new roles they could possibly do next. Our employee engagement shot up, and we had very little turnover. Such a process works at Yum! Brands, Unilever, and many other companies.

The Indian Hotels Company Limited, a large hotel management enterprise in South Asia, previously hewed to a traditional employee performance management system, scoring employees on a scale of one to five. P.V. Ramana Murthy, the former vice president and global head of HR, told me they changed the process to focus on each hotel as a single entity.

Customers rate their experiences at the hotel, which are scored as points. When the points are compiled, it results in a single score used as a proxy for employee performance. "Everyone in different facets of service, such as the front desk, concierge, and dining facilities, receives the hotel score at their performance evaluation," he said. "In other words, the points given by guests are used to motivate our employees."[113]

PepsiCo redesigned its performance appraisals in 2020 to focus on motivating managers to achieve and maintain high standards of performance via five feedback mechanisms, one of which was coaching and mentoring. You need to decide what you value in your company; the OKR model then becomes a powerful way to reinforce it.

ENCOURAGE FEEDBACK THROUGH FREQUENT CHECK-INS

Companies such as GE, Adobe, IBM, and New York Life all report that in transforming managers from bosses into coaches, one of the most difficult challenges was teaching people how closely they should manage people and teams. People want and need feedback; otherwise, they'll become very anxious.

The answer is a check-in, a semiformal or informal conversation which happens regularly so that employees may speak with their coach (see Figure 3.3). For its part, Adobe has established a set of guidelines and tools for check-ins and tracking managers' progress.

Deloitte and Cisco now use a standard set of questions to facilitate check-ins, which then form an evaluative measurement over time. Deloitte asks the questions "Is this person ready for a promotion?" and "Would you give this person the highest possible increase in bonus?" to encourage coaches to think about an individual's performance objectively. Deloitte

FIGURE 3.3: THE ANNUAL PERFORMANCE REVIEW VERSUS THE CHECK-IN

	BEFORE: THE ANNUAL PERFORMANCE REVIEW	AFTER: THE CHECK-IN
Setting Priorities	Employee priorities set at the start of the year and often not revisited	Priorities discussed and adjusted with manager regularly
Feedback Process	Long process of submitting accomplishments, soliciting feedback, and writing reviews	Ongoing process of feedback and dialogue with no formal written review or documentation
Compensation Decisions	Onerous process of rating and ranking each employee to determine salary increase and equity	No formal rating or ranking; manager determines salary and equity annually based on performance
Cadence of Meetings	Feedback sessions inconsistent and not monitored; spike in employee productivity at the end of the year, timed with performance-review discussions	Feedback conversations expected quarterly, with ongoing feedback becoming the norm; consistent employee productivity based on ongoing discussions and feedback throughout the year
HR Team Role	HR team manages paperwork and processes to ensure all steps are completed	HR team equips employees and managers to have constructive conversations
Training and Resources	Manager coaching and resources come from HR partners who can't always reach everyone	A centralized employee resource center provides help and answers whenever needed

SOURCE: THE JOSH BERSIN COMPANY, 2021

collects these data points at the end of the year to contribute to year-end salary, promotion, and coaching discussions. Companies like Intuit, Google, and others do the same.

Check-ins help both managers and employees improve focus, and understanding and maintaining an organization's focus is a clear step toward higher engagement. An important task for coaches today is to spend time helping people decide what not to do and what to ignore, giving them freedom to focus. A manager who succeeds at this task is a valuable coach; teaching managers how to have regular check-ins is critical in the journey to being irresistible.

To build a coaching culture at Adobe, former CHRO Donna Morris (now chief people officer at Walmart) retired annual performance reviews, adopted agile practices,[114] and developed a series of "pods" designed to bring managers together and help them learn to be good coaches. The pods are social learning groups that meet virtually for 90 minutes each month. Akin to agile sprints, they focus on particular concerns, such as identifying high performers for new roles. One person in the pod serves as the "voice of the customer" to collect feedback on the pod itself.

After a year of working in this agile way, Adobe achieved astounding results: 98 percent of leaders reported that it was well worth their time, 32 percent said the program improved their ability to check in with their people, and the pods received 99 percent positive net promoter scores.[115] These and similar programs, including Atlassian's culture tools and Liberty Mutual's learning management system, give leaders the support they need to understand how to make the transition from manager to coach.

FIX PAY: PAY PEOPLE BASED ON MARKET DEMAND, NOT ON COMPANY LEVELS

In the industrial age, where people were "labor," all pay levels were based on bands, and these bands were tied to one's job level. At IBM, my manager used to tell me where I was in the band, so every year he had a rationale for giving me a modest raise. He once told me, "I can't give you too big a raise because you'll hit the edge of the band." I was too naïve to understand the lunacy of this issue; regardless, I eventually quit.

We've done research on pay practices, and the results are not pretty. Only 33 percent of respondents said their pay practices drove improved performance. Only 7 percent said they were aligned with corporate goals. And 30 percent said practices were misaligned with business objectives.

How did pay practices get so messed up? It's quite simple: we're still using concepts and models built during the industrial age. In today's companies, where one individual can create tremendous amounts of value, we need to reinvent this process and optimize based on the individual, not on the hierarchy.

In 2017 and 2018, we completed an exhaustive study of pay practices to correlate what specific approaches contributed to positive business results.[116] The results were quite surprising.

First, pay equity did not really correlate with much. What people want is transparency, clarity, and explanations about why they make what they make. What they do *not* want is arbitrary "equality" in pay. There is a huge discussion about gender and racial pay equity in business today, and we do need to root out systemic bias. But what the highest performing companies typically do is pay people based on meritocracy and make clear how the rules work.

I know for a fact that at companies such as Google, Meta, Microsoft, and others, there can be two people with the same job who sometimes have a 50 to 100 percent difference in pay. This is not unfair; it's just a reflection of the fact that people perform at different levels.

Second, pay has to be reviewed quite often. Today, most employees can go to LinkedIn, Indeed, Glassdoor, or another website and immediately see if they are underpaid. You as a leader should have this information yourself so you can make adjustments as needed. Cisco's head of compensation told me they do regular benchmark studies and that they share all the information with employees—clearly communicating why they are paying above or below average for different jobs.

Third, think about pay as a market of one. Every individual in your company has a salary history, a level of ambition and drive, and an external demand in the market that sets their salary. This means your process should respect differences. I evaluate pay based on four things: a) how well this person performs as a team member in our organization, b) how well this person achieved their goals and projects during the last period, c) how much value this person delivered to their customers and stakeholders, and d) how much it would cost us to replace this person if they left. If you use a similar model, you'll find that some of your people are immensely valuable but may be underpaid because of level, job title, or manager.

Fourth, remember that in today's working world, financial rewards are only a part of pay. A flexible work environment, benefits, wellbeing program, development opportunities, stock options, career options, retirement programs, and more are other rewards. Many companies in my area offer free meals and snacks at on-site facilities and free laptops and ergonomic desk chairs at remote ones. Believe me, young people are calculating what this is worth when they apply for a job—these are parts of your pay, too. In our research, the highest-performing companies have a very holistic view of benefits; you'll read more about these examples throughout this book.

AN EXAMPLE: PATAGONIA

The billion-dollar sports apparel company Patagonia focuses heavily on empowerment, work-life balance, and high performance, coupled with citizenship in the company, environmental sustainability, and a culture of doing good.[117]

Patagonia even considers employees in functional business units when deciding who will work on teams and projects. CHRO Dean Carter has redesigned the goal-setting and performance process to prioritize engagement, teamwork, and peak performance. It respects the pattern in which people grow in a job, which is often in spurts. He calls the system "regenerative performance."

Every Patagonia employee has both annual and quarterly goals, gets regular feedback, and checks in with managers or team leaders quarterly. But Patagonia's system uniquely links this directly to compensation and rewards. At the end of the year, Patagonia rewards people in two ways: bonuses based on attaining goals and an increase in base pay based on an employee's growth in "market value."

In other words, employees who develop, build new skills, and become well known in the broader context of Patagonia's work have succeeded in expanding their job and therefore receive more money. It's not about promotion per se or about a manager's control of an employee. Instead, Patagonia encourages everyone, in part through its compensation system, to upskill annually.

CONSIDER REDUCING THE POWER AND LEVEL OF MANAGER

In irresistible companies, individuals are in charge. These companies give people the ability and the responsibility to manage themselves while leaders or coaches help align and improve them.

One of the most profound ways to ensure this is to eliminate or reduce the power, status symbols, and the authority of the manager. Let's face it: once we have power over another person or a group of people, we often behave differently. We become judgmental, we bring in our own personal bias, and we can potentially abuse our privilege. As Lord Acton wrote in 1887, "Power tends to corrupt, and absolute power corrupts absolutely."

At Google, committees of peers, rather than one person, decide to make pay raises and promotions to reduce the impact of single-rater bias and managerial power.

Some companies have done away with glitzy managerial titles, and some even push managerial roles down in the hierarchy. Facebook's head of people Lori Goler mentioned to me that one of its practices is to tell aspiring managers, "If you want to manage people, you can apply for the position, but it will not be a promotion. If you truly want to contribute to this company by helping others, we want you to take that job because it's what you really want to do." This kind of thinking can have a huge impact on shifting managerial roles from boss to coach.

LEVERAGE DATA IN MANAGEMENT DECISIONS

Thanks to the new world of cloud-based HR systems and performance management tools, we have enormous amounts of data to characterize an individual or team's performance. We can use this data to provide the coaching and management we need and remove some of the bias and politics from the process.

Here are some examples from my research:

- A large manufacturer studied the personal behavior of the most successful product teams and found that tenure, seniority, and skills had almost no real correlation to success. The most predictable driver of success was the level of collaboration and the connections between the team and the rest of the company. In other words, those teams who had the most internal relationships and empathy for the dealer network, pricing, manufacturing, and other business processes were the most successful. This turned into an entirely new model for team formation and team development.

- A high-technology systems and software company studied the happiness and productivity of its engineers by asking them to voluntarily wear "smart badges" that could assess their location, mobility, and tone of voice over the course of a few months. They discovered that the happiest and most productive engineers were the ones who walked around and moved the most because they experienced more physical activity and social interaction. The company used this information to reorganize work locations, create new cafeteria locations, hold outdoor walking meetings, and create other programs to coach people to move more often.

- An HR technology company studied the prevalence of theft and non-compliant activity and found that bad behavior is contagious. In other words, when one individual did something unethical, other similar behaviors took place on the same floor within a few dozen yards of that person. This led the company to realize that it needed to move and "sanitize" bad behavior once discovered, which gave rise to a new set of practices to deal with compliance training, discipline, and fraud analysis.

- The new tools from Microsoft that are embedded into Office 365 give managers, HR teams, and individuals weekly and monthly reports on how much time is spent on email, how much time is spent on internal meetings, how much time is spent with customers, and myriad other important coaching information. We are now using this information to decide when we are sending too many emails, when a particular meeting should be canceled, and even how to communicate in ways that are more impactful and less unproductive.

- More and more companies evaluate managers themselves through pulse surveys and quarterly feedback surveys. Ascension, for example, pulses all 150,000 of its employees every week. Equinix has achieved steady growth thanks, in part, to sending pulse surveys to its 8,700 employees every six weeks, creating the Equinix Business School, and redesigning performance management. At Ecolab, pulse survey results showed that many younger employees would leave for another company if they thought that company might provide them more feedback—leading to the formation of the Manager's Essential Program. The best coaching a manager can receive is unbiased data about how their team feels compared with other teams in the company. This is becoming a common practice and immediately reveals weaknesses in the managerial chain.

In the future, smarter software will enhance coaching. I don't believe machines will replace managers entirely, but we can certainly imagine a world in which our phones and work devices give us suggestions to improve and in which managers will become the true "human coaches" we all need.

culture, not rules

"I think if you're fortunate enough to be someone's employer, you have a huge moral obligation really to make sure that that person really looks forward to coming to work in the morning."

JOHN MACKEY, CEO AND FOUNDER OF WHOLE FOODS, 2008

Imagine a New England destination where mindfulness, Pilates, Spinning, and yoga classes punctuate a day filled with "smart" salad bars and fit meals that fall under 500 calories; there are racquetball games and a basketball court for group gatherings.

Is this the latest spa to pop up in a bucolic corner of the Northeast? Nope. This is the Hartford, Connecticut, headquarters for Aetna (part of CVS Health), where the health insurance company enacts its ethos of becoming a health*care* company by creating an enriching corporate environment.

Whether employees work on-site or remotely from home (or a combination of both), irresistible companies are pursuing a workforce strategy that elevates employee health, safety, and wellbeing—creating culture, not rules. It's about optionality, and here you'll learn why it's important.

the shift: culture, not rules

Ah, the corporate office. What used to be a buttoned-down, desk-based, in-person experience has radically expanded into a place we go to work, eat, sleep, collaborate, exercise, and even do our laundry, shop, and take care of our personal needs. Office workspaces have become optional now that so many employees work from home. In fact, 7 in 10 executives responding to the *2021 Deloitte Global Human Capital Trends* survey said the shift to remote work has had a positive impact on employees' wellbeing.[118]

How do we define the workplace in businesses where people work in teams and share information electronically while managers are often busy doing their own work, not watching over our shoulders? And how do we build a work environment that overinvests in creativity and agility and focuses less heavily on operational execution?

The answer is a new workplace defined by culture, not rules, with a focus on flexibility, freedom, and fairness—in essence, redefining the office as an end-to-end environment for productivity. Yes, part of this may involve removing cubicle walls or introducing modern digital collaboration platforms, but the big win is culture—creating an open, transparent culture and developing a work environment that supports it.

Many executives believe that redesigning the physical office will suddenly increase productivity, promote collaboration, and increase engagement. This is only partially true. Yes, companies need open work environments, but the irresistible environment is more than just a new office.

Let me give you an example. A well-known Silicon Valley company acquired a fast-growing start-up in San Francisco. The acquired company, which was a very innovative business, had a beautifully open office; gourmet food for breakfast, lunch, and dinner; and world-class office furniture, computers, and technology. The CEO of the acquiring company was so impressed with the facility that he came back to his management team and said, "Let's replicate their environment here."

The team decided to totally redesign one of its older office buildings in the Santa Clara area, moving engineers who worked in old-fashioned cubicles into beautiful open areas, providing free food and snacks, and upgrading the cafeteria to gourmet status.

Guess what happened? Within only a few weeks, engineers started to complain. The space was too noisy, and they couldn't get their work done. There was too much light and distraction. And while they loved the free food, many of them were used to going home for lunch or leaving early in the afternoon to be with their families. The winning culture of this particular group simply did not fit the environment that the company had created.

THE FIVE ELEMENTS OF ENVIRONMENT

What does the word "culture" really mean? For our purposes, I consider it to mean the shared values, attitudes, standards, and beliefs that characterize your organization. As many consultants describe it, it's the water in the fish tank—it's something we all experience every day, but it's not always visible.

Many management and business practices contribute to a company's culture, and leadership plays a tremendous role. In fact, most research shows that leaders create the culture, leaders reinforce the culture, and only leaders can change the culture.

In this chapter, we will discuss five aspects of irresistible culture:

1   The work environment—the physical, environmental, and virtual experience

2   Wellbeing—how the organization supports health, safety, and physical, mental, and financial wellbeing

3   Inclusion—how diverse, open, inclusive, and transparent the work environment is

4 Recognition and reward—how the company treats and rewards people

5 Flexibility—how much agency, optionality, and freedom employees have

Many pressures are forcing companies to focus heavily on these five issues. As we work in teams and take on more fluid roles, the work environment must be more open and flexible to support our work activity. Teams may want shared whiteboards, open places to design and discuss problems, and quiet places to focus. Workers who grew up with technology expect an always-on experience that follows them wherever they are. And as I discussed earlier, workplace stress and overload in both the traditional office and remote-work environments are at an all-time high, forcing leaders to innovate in all areas of employee productivity, wellbeing, and flexibility.

AN OPEN, FLEXIBLE WORK ENVIRONMENT

The word "office" derives from the Latin word for the performance of a task: *officium*. In our 24/7 mobile, tech-fueled world today, tasks are performed anywhere—at a desk, in a hallway, at the airport, in a client facility, waiting for the elevator, or at the dining room table. The work environment is that fluid. Work itself is not.

Let's start with the physical, on-site work environment. Looking back over my own 40 years of work, it's very clear how radically things have changed (see Figure 4.1).

Workplace design really does matter. Steelcase, a company that studies and pioneers new office designs, has found that highly engaged employees are also those who have the greatest control over where and how they work, including having access to privacy when they need it.[119] There is an almost perfect correlation between an employee's level of engagement and his or her satisfaction with the physical workplace.

FIGURE 4.1: THE OLD WORK ENVIRONMENT VERSUS THE IRRESISTIBLE WORK ENVIRONMENT

WORK ENVIRONMENT: THE OLD WAY	WORK ENVIRONMENT: THE IRRESISTIBLE WAY
Fixed office or desk with your name on a nameplate or even on the door	Dedicated or mobile location, depending on employee need
Located in a building near the team, colocated with your department	Often virtual or working from another location but always in close collaboration with the team
Forced to come into work almost every day	Given freedom to work from other locations as needed
Clothing and appearance well defined, corporate in nature, and standardized	Casual and personalized clothing, relaxed guidelines, and no need to dress up every day
Few amenities in the office; go out for lunch or coffee	Coffee, food, exercise, sleep areas, technology services, health services, and many other in-office benefits
Diversity program sponsored by HR and driven by quotas	Focus on an inclusive culture where gender, age, race, and cultural differences are valued
Health insurance and some level of employee-assistance program provided	A wide-ranging program focused on employee wellbeing, including mind, body, financial, and professional fitness, with the goal of making employees more productive

SOURCE: GLOBEST.COM, 2021; THE JOSH BERSIN COMPANY, 2021

FIGURE 4.1 (CONT'D): THE OLD WORK ENVIRONMENT VERSUS THE IRRESISTIBLE WORK ENVIRONMENT

WORK ENVIRONMENT: THE OLD WAY	WORK ENVIRONMENT: THE IRRESISTIBLE WAY
People feel committed to their company and to their boss	People feel socially connected to their team, their organization, and their customers
Buildings organized by function or department	Cross-functional collaboration facilitated by eating areas, conference rooms, and free spaces
Conference rooms reserved for large meetings	Many small conference rooms for joint meetings, discussions, or team meetings
Video conferencing tools only provided for executives	All facilities set up for video conferencing and instant communication
Periodic recognition events, staff meetings, or companywide meetings	Recognition, reward, feedback, and praise taking place on a regular basis in a newsfeed-like, "always on" experience
Productivity tools center around phone lines, email, and copiers	Productivity tools include messaging, video, goal management, and AI-based document and asset management, all with virtual private networks (VPNs) and other security tools to monitor and control intellectual property
Focus on design, art, and work-place beauty	Focus on design, art, external light, open space, flexibility, and direct support of each employee's designed work experience, including team pods and shared whiteboards where needed
Lots of space allocated to employees but often not used (70 percent of office space was unused on a regular basis before the pandemic*)	Space available for many people to use and highly utilized, with the goal of bringing people together and giving people many options of where and how to work

SOURCE: GLOBEST.COM, 2021; THE JOSH BERSIN COMPANY, 2021

What do these highly engaging, productive workplaces look like? Are they open or closed? Do people have private offices or not? Are there exercise facilities and free food? Are people allowed to work from home and not come into the office? If so, should we continue to let people work from home full-time? Or should we force them to come into the office?

According to a December 2020 survey by the Pew Research Center, most employees whose job responsibilities could have been done from home rarely teleworked prior to the pandemic, with only one in five working from home all or most of the time. However, at the time they were surveyed, 71 percent of these employees worked from home all or most of the time. Most said that it was easy for them to meet deadlines and to complete projects on time, without interruption, and that they felt motivated to do their jobs.[120]

Our research suggests that employees are roughly as engaged when working remotely as they are when they work at the office. Frankly, the engagement feedback on work and jobs overall is the highest I have seen in my career as an analyst. People feel very good about working remotely at home, and ratings regarding the effectiveness of managers is equally high.

For more than a decade, it was predicted that work was bound to become more flexible, with employees choosing when and where it was best to get work done. The pandemic just made that shift happen more quickly.

Joe Whittinghill, corporate vice president of talent, learning, and insights at Microsoft, said that "while technology will never be a complete replacement for physical human-to-human connections, there's no question that it allowed productivity, resilience, creativity, and connections to continue to flourish."[121]

In 2021, Microsoft transitioned to offering employees flexible work opportunities as its permanent work standard. Other organizations like Ford, the Teachers Insurance and Annuity Association of America (TIAA), and Citigroup also shifted to a flexible hybrid model of work.[122]

What these decisions highlight is that choice and control are key—giving employees, regardless of their role and job, the freedom to work the way they find is the most productive, supportive, and enjoyable for them.

In doing this, companies need to provide shared workspaces at the office and reconfigured workspaces at home; access to privacy; easy-to-use technology; amenities such as large windows, food, and places to move around; and free time for exercise, quiet breaks, and even naps.

In a sense, the entire workspace should be focused on physical, cognitive, and emotional wellbeing.

HYBRID: A SUCCESSFUL APPROACH TO REMOTE WORK

Since the start of the COVID-19 pandemic, companies have built highly flexible options for work.

Companies were forced to rapidly reinvent their workplaces, products, services, and relationships with customers and employees without a clear guide. Workers needed support, infrastructure, and programs to work well in this new environment, and managers needed training to lead remote teams.

It is amazing that many organizations and people made this transition as well as they did, adapting to remote work at lightning speed. Organizations stepped up their game to provide resources, tools, and infrastructure to continue seamless business operations, increasing productivity in many cases.

For this we can thank the galaxy of new tools and collaborative technologies supporting independent work at home. These include videoconferencing platforms, mobile messaging applications, goal-sharing systems, and document and calendar synchronization, among other tools.

Also deserving of our gratitude is the HR profession, which rose to the occasion to help companies deal with the health risks of the pandemic, endeavored to mitigate workforce stress, and took a leading role in workplace transformation, redefining the role and the nature of leadership.

Through our ongoing conversations with HR leaders around the world, we worked to find ways to benchmark their remote teams' capabilities, to inventory their strengths and weaknesses, and to understand how to build ever-more powerful ways to develop and grow.

Concerned over the diminished human contact wrought by the pandemic, HR strove to build engagement across the remote workforce. Our research indicates that organizations that provide support for workers and their families are 6.8 times more likely to engage and retain their workforce.[123]

Deutsche Telekom acknowledged that people felt lost and confused. To de-stress, the company created a leadership-in-crisis program with workshops, a survival kit, and a reflection kit.[124] Weekly leadership communications were scheduled with employees to help them better deal with ambiguity and uncertainty. Having earned the trust and loyalty of people, employee engagement shot up from 75 percent to 85 percent.

Many organizations provided other forms of support, such as child- and dependent-care opportunities and social interactions for families, including virtual movie nights and free Netflix subscriptions. Connections were established with coworkers to de-stress, disconnect from work, share hobbies, and virtually get together.

Deloitte's *2021 Global Human Capital Trends* report affirms that organizations that integrate wellbeing into the design of work at the individual, team, and organizational levels can build a sustainable future where workers feel and perform at their best.[125]

Such irresistible companies reinforced their message and focus on mission, purpose, and agility, letting people know why their work matters and how it helps create a better world. Hiring was reinvented, jobs were redesigned, people were redeployed, and business and operating models were transformed.

A human-centered approach to people management is now considered the most important strategic goal in defining success in various settings, including during economic growth, unexpected downturns, or flat-out crises. As organizations transform their business models, they also need to reinvent and reimagine their approaches to managing people and talent (see Figure 4.2).

The most successful organizations had already built up these agile people practices through the years and were simply ready to adjust and deploy them when the pandemic struck.

FIGURE 4.2: A HUMAN-CENTERED APPROACH FOR LEADERS AND HR

GOALS OF A HUMAN-CENTERED APPROACH	WHAT LEADERS CAN DO	WHAT HR CAN DO
Provide support for workers' families and lives	Empathize with workers and provide personalized support to help them create a balanced, supportive environment	Redesign family-support programs to go beyond healthcare, and support the mental and physical wellbeing of workers
Use the alternative workforce strategically	Instead of simply placing people, take a strategic view and determine the criticality, timeline, and urgency of needed skills; then, determine what part of the workforce should fill that need	Work with other groups (e.g., procurement) to create strategic and tactical approaches to manage the alternative workforce
Empower teams to experiment and learn quickly	Empower teams and individuals to make decisions, support them in experiments, and model learning from mistakes	Beyond formal learning, help create experiences where people can apply learning, experiment, and learn from mistakes
Adapt performance management	Communicate team goals and priorities frequently, allow people to recalibrate quickly, and focus on real-time feedback	Simplify performance management approaches, focus on what drives performance and learning, and allow people to move at the speed of business

SOURCE: THE JOSH BERSIN COMPANY, 2021

DOUBLING DOWN ON WELLBEING

The most important aspect of the "culture, not rules" mindset is a massive focus on employee wellbeing. This area is one of the fastest-growing marketplaces in business, with companies hiring chief health officers, heads of safety and wellbeing, and directors of wellbeing. As of April 2021, there were 55,000 jobs open for these positions.[126]

For decades, worker wellbeing focused exclusively on evolutionary advances in workplace safety and employer-provided health insurance. In fact, when I joined Exxon in 1978, the company's most important program was refinery safety. We wore hard hats bearing the number of days since the last accident.

The transition from encouraging employee health and fitness to promoting wellbeing and performance began only in the last decade or so. Companies began to realize that white-collar workers needed different programs to improve both health and productivity. The result has been a new era of wellbeing programs sweeping organizations today— programs aimed not simply at reducing insurance costs but also at helping employees perform better on the job.

A pioneer in employee wellbeing is the Johnson & Johnson Human Performance Institute (HPI).[127] This organization offers courses to hundreds of companies under the brand "Corporate Athlete," teaching employees how to deal with stress, become more resilient, and achieve more sustainable performance. While it was initially designed for executives, the HPI now offers training for all types of employees.

More and more companies are starting to realize that wellbeing is also a strategy for engagement. If employees show up for on-site work or to virtual conferences not feeling well—tired, sick, or distracted by home or financial problems—their productivity suffers. What holds people up are their feelings of psychological safety. If they're upset or unhappy, are getting behind on a project, or are not getting along with their manager, is there a place where they can express these feelings?

I recently talked with the CHRO from a large company who encouraged the CEO and senior leaders to schedule all-hands meetings to discuss their own challenges with stress, anxiety, and overwork. Everyone felt relief, she said. The company is now training all its leaders in listening, flexibility, and care.

The CHRO of a large Canadian bank said that in addition to focusing on workplace safety and wellbeing, the organization is teaching managers about mental health and emotional fitness. On top of mandating training on diversity and inclusion, the bank is educating managers on stress, anxiety, and behavioral health.

Managers have a much bigger role than just driving results. We are responsible for taking care of people, monitoring our own behavior, and making sure we are creating a net-positive impact on the entire organization. Irresistible companies are moving wellbeing out of the "benefits department" and making it part of the corporate culture.

THE NEED FOR ADAPTIVE SPACE

What about the physical office? Innovations have been dramatic, and they will continue to evolve. As we saw at Spotify, Atlassian, Adobe, IBM, and ING, the physical space must match the style of work: teams have pods, individuals have private spaces, and buildings have larger common areas.

But innovations must go well beyond physical space. Changes in how workspaces are physically arranged must be accompanied by changes in how people are managed and interact at work. For those workers still in physical offices, those offices are more open, multifaceted, and flexible, with employees often taking the lead in how they are designed.

Steelcase discovered that the biggest driver in workplace satisfaction is not the openness of the office nor the availability of features such as stand-up desks, nap rooms, and quiet spaces. All these were deemed important, but the most important factor was whether people had a great deal of control over where and how they worked, including access to privacy when they needed it.[128] In other words, flexibility, freedom, and inclusion give employees a sense of empowerment.

Some of the statistics were astounding:

- 88 percent of employees feel more engaged and productive when they can select where they do their work.

- 96 percent of employees feel more engaged and productive when they can move around and change posture during the day.

- 94 percent feel more engaged and productive when they can work in teams without interruption.

- 98 percent feel more engaged and productive when they feel a sense of belonging in the company.

In the post–COVID-19 workplace, employees will not return to an office that doesn't feel safe, and most of today's high-density workplaces with extensive reliance on hoteling and shared ancillary spaces will need to be modified, according to a Steelcase report.[129] "Businesses understand that infection transmission within a workplace can not only shut them down again, but also damage their brand and their ability to attract new talent," the report states.

Consequently, future on-site offices must be redesigned to be safe in ways that do not weaken community, creativity, or productivity. In navigating this path, Steelcase is looking at holistic office solutions rooted in the science of infection control. In redesigning and reconfiguring work environments in the future, the company is examining reorienting workstations away from the standard linear setup and reconfiguring freestanding desks to reduce sitting face-to-face.

Open-plan formats, shared spaces, flexible furniture, areas of high mobility, and employee behaviors also are under review in redesigning tomorrow's physical workspaces. "The office must immediately be made safe, but also more resilient and more adaptive," the report states.

When a large consulting firm in Canada planned the office design for its new facility, it looked at the highest-performing teams and found several important characteristics.[130] First, these teams spent more time together than others did. Second, they worked better across service lines; for instance, tax experts worked with management consultants. And third, they moved around often.

Using this information, the firm thoughtfully designed its new office space. Its facility features 18 different types of workspaces—from lounges and collaborative environments to individual stations—all designed to match the work environment with the type of work being done. An open staircase connecting all six floors serves as a visual sign of the importance of collaboration in the culture, as the physical environment encourages formerly siloed functions and service lines to interact more closely with each other; colleagues in different functions are visible rather than isolated in closed areas.

This is a wonderful example of how a change in the workplace revolutionized an approach to work itself. The goal was not simply to bring disparate groups of employees together but also to foster innovation, disruption, and collaboration. While traditional offices are comprised of 80 percent personal workspaces and 5 percent collaborative workspaces,[131] this consulting firm allocated 65 percent to collaboration. Thanks to research showing that companies that provide employees with access to natural light gain 18 percent in productivity, 90 percent of seat space has access to daylight, with the building featuring floor-to-ceiling windows. Our research shows that office designs such as these reduce absenteeism and promote greater loyalty among employees.

ADP's Chelsea Design Center deliberately feels intimate and informal to encourage people to work together and think outside the box. An enormous video screen in the center of the room permits any design team to virtually collaborate with other teams to design programs and software together.

Much of the workplace redesign during the last decade has focused on bringing people closer together physically. Companies such as Apple and Google have found that accidentally bumping into others creates a new social experience at work, strengthens culture, and promotes innovation and creative thinking.

Michael Arena, vice president of talent at Amazon Web Services, writes about this in his book *Adaptive Space*, explaining the need for physical proximity and discussing the idea of the "third place" we have in our personal lives beyond our on-site offices and homes.[132] The coffee shop, the café, or the bar gives us another place to talk, chat, and be with others. It frees us from the burdens of work and the responsibilities of home.

For most of us, our office or desk represents "getting work done," not "thinking outside the box." When it's time to break down the business model we live in and think of something new, we often go off-site or take a walk. Companies need such adaptive space at work as well.

TAKING OWNERSHIP FOR INCLUSION, DIVERSITY, AND FAIRNESS

No single topic is more important than the topic of diversity and inclusion. In today's era of team-centered organizations, nothing is more valuable to employees than a sense of feeling included and respected at work. In irresistible companies, diversity and inclusion are not just HR programs; they're also critical to creating the right work environment. Diversity and inclusion must permeate all aspects of work and affect employee performance and engagement at all levels.

Many companies struggle to even identify exclusionary behavior and practices. Research by scientists at Massachusetts Institute of Technology (MIT) and Columbia shows that there are rampant microaggressions (subtle ways of putting people down) throughout companies.[133] Kieran Snyder, CEO of Textio, a company that ferrets out bias in assessments, once worked at Microsoft. She tells the story of walking into a room set aside for a math lecture. Two male attendees told her that the design lecture was across the hall, assuming she didn't belong in a discussion about math.[134] This type of behavior is unfortunately all too common in teams. It must be stopped, and the CEO is responsible for making sure it does not happen.

Bias in recruitment, promotion, and pay is also far more common than people realize. Salesforce conducted a study of gender bias and found that women in equivalent positions were making 11 percent less than men. CEO Marc Benioff fixed the problem immediately by increasing payroll by $3 million to fix the gap. He has also vowed to eliminate this problem at every company Salesforce acquires in the future.[135]

Deloitte has studied diversity and inclusion for years. In one such study, *Waiter, is that inclusion in my soup?*, the firm found that teams that feel included and diverse outperform their peers by a staggering 80 percent on financial and operational measures.[136] Similarly, research by my former colleague Juliet Bourke demonstrates that gender-diverse teams feel safer, that racially diverse teams are more innovative, and that generationally diverse teams have more successful outcomes. Diversity is not just the right thing to do—it drives performance.

Diversity, equity, and inclusion (DE&I) are also critical components of an organization's customer brand. Companies that lead in DE&I surveys, such as Sodexo, General Mills, Unilever, Nestlé, Cummins, Timken, and Chevron, are well known for their positive records among customers and job candidates. These companies generally score above industry averages on Glassdoor ratings.

Our latest research, *Elevating Equity and Diversity*, goes even further.[137] This research, which we concluded in 2021, shows that highly diverse companies far outperformed their peers during the coronavirus pandemic. A focus on psychological safety and belonging not only helped minorities feel engaged, but it also allowed everyone to bring their "whole selves" to work.

Several studies have shown that socially conscious companies outperform those that are driven solely by financial considerations. The authors behind *Firms of Endearment* studied these companies and found that those that define their values through a multitude of stakeholders, including employees, customers, investors, and the overall community, outperformed the S&P 500 eightfold over a 30-year period.[138]

Today, we have many new forms of diversity to consider: gender, age, race, nationality, physical ability, mental ability, and even emotional state. SAP, for example, has been a pioneer in this market, creating an entire Business Beyond Bias program and product line.[139] SAP creates special programs for autistic people (who often test software); the company also heavily promotes women into leadership and carefully measures inclusion and diversity in promotion, rewards, tenure, attrition, and talent measures.[140]

Diversity training, while interesting and useful, rarely changes behavior. Plenty of studies have shown that investment in such training does not reduce lawsuits or change the level of diversity in the company.[141] A longitudinal study of 829 companies over 31 years showed that diversity training had no positive effects in the average workplace.[142] Research shows that the more you train people (which, if done poorly, can mean simply scolding employees for their implicit bias), the less likely you will see a diverse management culture.

What should you do? Chevron, one of the most advanced companies in this area, treats diversity and inclusion like safety, tolerating no bias and addressing it as a business-process problem, not just as an education problem. Chevron uses diversity committees that look over every major talent decision, inspecting and auditing whether minority candidates were given a fair chance.[143] Any time an individual is promoted, given a raise, or moved into a new role, a committee of external peers looks at the decision, evaluates the criteria, and decides if the decision was fair.

This type of process does three things no training can do. First, it institutionalizes fairness into the system using a clearly defined business process. Second, it holds everyone accountable for understanding and promoting inclusion. Third, it takes power away from individual managers so that no executive or supervisor has the power or influence to behave in an exclusionary way.

Finally, let me add that great companies see diversity as a business strategy, not as an HR program. The chief diversity officer at Target, Kiera Fernandez, is a senior business leader. She looks at Target's diversity and inclusion strategy in its products, pricing, store locations, supply chain, and internal practices—in other words, in all aspects of the company.

For example, Target's mission is to "help all families discover the joy of everyday life."[144] Implicit in this mission is the goal to help low-, medium-, and high-income families in any community find and afford great products for everyday living. This means Target locates stores in low-income neighborhoods, hires and pays people in a fair and inclusive way, and proactively promotes minorities into management. The company wins diversity awards year after year.

As many clients have explained to me, diversity is not a problem to be solved; rather, it should be the natural state of the environment at work. In other words, inclusion creates diversity, not the other way around. Instead of teaching people about differences, we need to teach them how to listen, work together, and respect each other. As IBM used to say in the 1980s, respect for the individual is the most important value.[145] These are the cultural values irresistible companies understand.

EMBRACING A CULTURE OF RECOGNITION AND LISTENING

As I described in Chapter 3 ("Coach, Not Boss"), much of our corporate culture revolves around the way people are rewarded. And rewards go far beyond money and benefits.

Maslow's hierarchy of needs is a good guide for great management (see Figure 4.3). The lower levels of the hierarchy (pay, benefits, and workplace safety) must be satisfied first, and once they are, employees aspire to more. This is what great companies do. In my analysis of the Glassdoor database, for example, I found that employees' perception of opportunity and culture are 3.5 times more important than salary in predicting the overall Glassdoor rating (see Appendix 2).

Recognition has a tremendous impact on performance. My research suggests that companies with high-recognition cultures have as much as 30 percent lower voluntary turnover ratios on average.

FIGURE 4.3: BUSINESS APPLICATIONS OF MASLOW'S HIERARCHY OF NEEDS

MASLOW'S HIERARCHY (TOP TO BOTTOM)	APPLICATIONS IN BUSINESS
Self-actualization	Mission, purpose, growth, and career progression
Esteem and accomplishment	Meaningful work, recognition, and positive feedback
Love and belonging	Teamwork, management empathy, consideration, patience, and flexibility
Safety	Workplace safety, health, wellbeing, and inclusion
Physical needs	Adequate pay, benefits, and work tools

SOURCE: THE JOSH BERSIN COMPANY, 2021

During monthly branch meetings in my early days at IBM, the branch manager would stand up and hand out $1,000 checks to one or two employees who had done outstanding things during the last year. These traditional recognition events were inspiring to some degree, but I remember telling myself, "I will never get one of those," and often thinking the checks were a political prize, not true recognition.

Today, I'm happy to report that a new world of meaningful recognition has arrived—one in which we can give people positive feedback and praise with "likes," "points," or "kudos" using social tools. I've now interviewed dozens of executives that use these tools, and they are all from organizations on the right-hand side of the Glassdoor bell curve. This is not because people are just "nice" in these organizations: it's because giving thanks creates actual physical benefits. Research shows that saying "thank you" produces oxytocin in our bodies, which in turn makes us happier, more trustful, and more collaborative.[146]

Listening to employees has an impact similar to recognizing their achievements. Unlike customers or investors, employees vote with their lives to work for you. They tie their family earnings, time, and personal energy to your company. So, when they have problems or good ideas, you really have to listen.

Too often, CEOs and other leaders look at listening to employees as a periodic engagement survey to improve retention. While this is clearly a good idea, it doesn't go far enough. The new world of engagement is one of listening on many channels and letting employees speak up, give suggestions, and contribute to every decision you make.

Irresistible companies do this and outperform their peers. Make listening to employees a cultural value. Every leader, from the CEO to the first-line supervisor, should be encouraged to slow down and listen, create a place of psychological safety where people feel liberated and safe to speak up, and take notes on what they say.

Conduct town hall meetings, team feedback sessions, and post-mortem reviews, and create suggestion boxes where people can recommend changes, point out problems, and suggest solutions. For example, IBM has global online "jams" to help leaders redesign everything from pay practices to work-at-home policies.[147]

Microsoft surveys more than 2,500 employees every day and makes sure people only get one survey per quarter.[148] The data helps Dawn Klinghoffer, the head of people analytics, immediately detect issues like burnout and stress, guiding the redesign of work practices to alleviate harmful conditions.[149]

When you listen to employees, you will discover amazing things. As the CEO of a large pharmaceuticals company told me, employees are essentially a surrogate for your customers. When employees are upset or unhappy, you can bet your customers are, too. So don't think about "employee voice" as an HR thing. This is a critical business process. Employee sentiment, feedback, and voice are not only important for hiring, retention, and engagement—they're a direct representation of the customer experience.

PAYING PEOPLE A FAIR AND COMPETITIVE WAGE IN A WORLD OF TRANSPARENCY

What about the bottom layers of Maslow's hierarchy? Thanks to radical transparency in salary and benefits, pay practices are slowly starting to change. Irresistible organizations have to understand a few important issues.

First, unlike in the past, when pay was a big secret and managers held information as power, pay levels today are transparent. Vendors such as ADP, LinkedIn, Glassdoor, Payscale, Salary.com, and others have crowd-sourced salaries and are quite accurate in showing employees what others make at similar jobs in other companies. Employees can look up their job title, level, tenure, and location and almost immediately see what others are making. HR managers used to buy this data from survey firms; today, it's freely available on the internet.

This is a fairly radical shift. In the industrial model, people were paid in bands by level, and, as I mentioned earlier, managers had to justify moving people out of their respective bands. We treated people as workers and didn't really respect the idea that each individual has a market of their own.

I never questioned my pay at Exxon or IBM because I knew it was institutionalized in the job architecture and was almost entirely tied to my annual appraisal. My manager had the ultimate power over my pay, so while there was a review process, I was somewhat dependent on him for my financial future.

Today, this is all undergoing radical change. Companies such as Google specifically remove managerial power in the pay process. A committee of peer managers discusses an individual's pay, and the first-line manager is only a contributor to the decision.[150] Pay often varies widely between peers—it's not unusual for a very highly regarded engineer, for example, to make 30 to 50 percent more than someone sitting right next to them.

Second, we need to pay people based on clear work criteria, not just on their job. Consider the shift from "jobs" to "work." How do you make sure someone is fairly paid when their job changes from year to year based on the projects they join? In companies such as Cisco, Juniper, and Patagonia, pay is based on multiple factors: job performance, skills and capabilities, reputation, network, the ability to lead, and the potential to grow. Peer groups can assess these criteria regardless of level, giving each individual his or her own "pay band" based on experience.

Dean Carter, the CHRO of Patagonia, developed a simple structural model that gives employees a good sense of the future. At Patagonia, your base pay is increased based on your teamwork, core job performance, and skills development. Your bonus is based on your personal goal achievements. The two are separately measured, so if you achieved your goals but did not contribute to the team, you may get a bonus but not a raise.

Third, paying people well is a strategic competitive advantage, not a burdensome expense. Traditionally, CEOs have "bargained" with their employees by keeping hourly wages as low as possible, often waiting for employees to complain. Their belief system is based on the idea that the less they pay people, the better for the business.

Today, I would argue that the opposite is true. Paying a fair wage attracts stronger candidates, increases the level of commitment to the company, and creates a more productive workforce. Many hourly workers today are living in financial insecurity; research shows that fewer than 4 in 10

Americans could pay a surprise $1,000 bill from their savings.[151] Many American households have no savings at all, and the average credit card debt is $6,270.[152] Nearly 70 percent of older Millennials are still paying off their student debt a decade or more after graduating.[153]

Our research on pay shows that the highest-performing companies communicate their pay practices openly; they clearly market their strategy; they offer a holistic set of benefits; and they vary pay by location, tenure, and job based entirely on merit.[154] In our study, which examined more than 60 different pay practices, we found that these companies are 7 percent more profitable and generate 28 percent more revenue per employee, proving that a sound and competitive pay strategy really does pay off.

We need to personalize pay for each individual. This means companies must use design thinking (surveying and interviewing regularly) to understand what employees want and need. A powerful tool to use here is conjoint analysis, a process of asking people to compare the value of disparate things to understand their relative worth. Conjoint analysis is often used in product marketing.

Companies that use conjoint analysis can build what is called an "efficient frontier" of pay and benefits to see precisely what each individual employee group values. Just as we apply these kinds of tools to customers, we should apply them to employees. People with young families highly value vacation time and leave; people nearing retirement highly value healthcare. If you study the drivers, you can build an irresistible pay practice in your company.

DRIVING TRANSPARENCY AT ALL LEVELS

Now, transparency: I've have been flooded with articles, blogs, tweets, and social media posts of employees citing harassment, gender pay inequity, discrimination, and other forms of bad behavior in public. Websites such as Glassdoor, kununu, Fairygodboss, and anonymous networks such as Blind and Hyphen now make it easier than ever for employees to share, post, or comment on behaviors at work.

This new level of transparency has opened a Pandora's box in corporate life. Building a culture of trust means managers, leaders, and executives must become comfortable with sharing information—financial news, customer and product issues, internal operational problems, and the impact of work on individuals. In my Glassdoor analysis, I looked at the impact of leadership and CEO ratings on other metrics and found that company ratings and culture ratings are almost entirely correlated with an employee's perception of the CEO and senior leadership. Undoubtedly, transparency is a key principle of irresistible companies (see Appendix 2).

how to get started

Discuss these questions with your own leaders and teams:

1   How well do you think your leaders understand their roles in driving and creating a corporate culture? Do you talk about it? Are they aware of their roles?

2   Do you understand your corporate culture today? How often do you survey your employees?

3   How modern and up-to-date is your work environment? Do people find your workspace supportive? Is it time to reconsider the physical experience of the workspace?

4   Do you have an adequate wellbeing program or a wellbeing strategy? Have you considered how important it could be for performance and productivity?

5   Who owns inclusion and diversity in your company? Has it been delegated to an HR leader, or do the top business executives hold themselves accountable? Would you be proud to have your diversity

metrics cited on the front page of the newspaper? If not, what are you doing about it?

6   How would you evaluate your culture of recognition? Do people recognize and thank each other for little things, or is recognition reserved for high performers and top earners? Do you have systems or programs to help people thank and recognize each other?

7   How expansive, flexible, and modern is your rewards program? Have you evaluated the utility of the benefits you provide and looked at updating them regularly? Are they relevant for all segments of your workforce?

8   Does the concept of transparency and flexibility scare your top leaders? Or are they comfortable sharing information, personal stories, and challenges the company faces?

how to get it right

BUILD AN INCLUSIVE CULTURE

Inclusion must be part of your organization's culture, not simply an HR program. Companies that are truly inclusive take ownership at the top. They rigorously measure diversity and bias. They implement dashboards that hold managers accountable for fairness and diversity in all decisions.

At Chevron, a diversity committee oversees every major talent decision.[155] Members can ask a manager why someone was promoted and can ask to revisit a diverse candidate to determine whether that candidate was qualified. This focus on diversity is key to Chevron's business strategy.

Anka Wittenberg, former senior vice president of diversity and inclusion at SAP and current chair of the board of directors at the World Childhood Foundation in Germany, champions a strategy that focuses on gender diversity, cross-generational diversity, diversity in culture, diversity in ability (inclusion of neurodivergent individuals and people with disabilities), and, of course, diversity in race and origin.[156] At SAP, she set—and achieved—a goal of filling 25 percent of leadership positions with women.[157] SAP also hires people across the autism spectrum. The tech giant's Autism at Work program is considered a model for other companies seeking similar value from hiring neurodivergent individuals.[158]

Software can identify gender bias in job descriptions and analyze talent decisions to see if managers interview more white males or promote more people of a certain class. Technology can also visually recognize race during interviews and watches the eyes of interviewers to see if they are giving candidates a fair chance.

The problem of innate bias may never completely disappear, but those who run companies with high levels of engagement must make extra efforts to root it out and to embed inclusion in the organization's culture.

USE DESIGN THINKING TO CREATE ENGAGING, INCLUSIVE WORKSPACES

Companies can design workspaces to reflect this inclusive culture—and, of course, the unique needs and types of work that the company must do. But the stampede toward open office plans alone can reflect a one-size-fits-all mentality that often fails to account for the unique needs of each individual organization.

Two of the most compelling offices I've visited belong to consulting firms: the first is the workplace in Canada I described earlier, and the second is an office in the Netherlands.[159] These buildings are essentially mobile office complexes filled with high atriums, beautiful open windows, and technological amenities everywhere. Windows adjust automatically to optimize light and reduce glare. Stairwells are open so people can meet and talk. The buildings reflect the fact that the firms deliberately design teams to work in cross-functional ways. These workspaces reflect the companies' commitment to creating cultures where people feel happy, engaged, and included.

PAY A FAIR WAGE

My analysis of more than 4,500 companies in the Glassdoor database shows that the greatest predictor of important financial metrics such as high cash flow and profitability per employee is employees' perception that compensation and benefits are fair (see Appendix 2). In other words, the most profitable and cash-rich companies have employees who feel satisfied about their compensation.

I've seen this repeatedly. Retailers that pay more, such as Wegmans, Costco, and Starbucks, far outperform their peers. Engineers at companies like Google and LinkedIn and production experts at Halliburton are typically paid more than their counterparts at competing firms.[160] These companies have realized that fair wages and above-average pay for high performers signal that an organization cares about its people. In turn, people who feel valued are more engaged and energized to give their best to the organization.

FIND PERKS WITH A PURPOSE

In today's flexible work environment, employees always seem to be working. To make offices more enjoyable, many employers offer features such as standing desks, nap rooms, table tennis, foosball, and even bowling alleys. One well-known San Francisco office has an open bar filled with the world's finest whiskey.

Despite this proliferation of perks, my research shows that entertainment alone does not really engage employees. A better approach is to target perks toward a specific purpose, such as attracting new employees, easing financial burdens, or encouraging employees to put more time into the job.

For example, Dropbox provides three healthy meals a day so its employees, who are often young San Francisco engineers who can barely afford an apartment, can save money by eating at work.[161] The company recently changed dinner service to 7:00 p.m., which encourages people to stay later at work.

Prior to the pandemic, another technology company, Pivotal Labs, which has since been purchased by VMware, served a gourmet hot breakfast at 8:00 a.m. every morning and shut it down at 9:00 a.m., encouraging employees to come in on time.[162] Employees arrived early, ate together, and then joined in a 15-minute company-wide standup meeting at 9:00 a.m. As an observer, I found the experience energizing and powerful: people stood together, chatted, and then ran off to their projects at 9:15 a.m.

TAKE A HOLISTIC APPROACH TO WELLBEING

Wellbeing encompasses much more than fitness centers, nap rooms, or even good compensation. Companies must take a holistic approach by understanding what factors drive employee stress, anxiety, and fatigue— all of which hamper performance.

People need to take more time off from work. Between 1978 and 2000, Americans took an average of 20.3 days off every year. As of 2020, the average number of paid time off (PTO) days for U.S. workers plunged to 10, according to the U.S. Bureau of Labor Statistics.[163] A group called Project: Time Off, in collaboration with American Automobile Association (AAA), calculates that Americans fail to use 662 million vacation days a year.[164]

Company leaders can set an example by taking their allotted vacation. This helps to break the work-martyr syndrome that consumes so many workers. Emailing while on vacation sends the wrong message. At Illumina, a pioneer in genetic science, the company takes a "Jaycation"—a vacation named for former CEO Jay Flatley, which shuts down the company twice a year.[165] FullContact, a Denver software company, gives employees a $7,500 bonus if they follow three rules: 1) take a vacation;

2) disconnect while on vacation; and 3) avoid working on vacation.[166] Sounds like easy money, but just try it sometime.

Shorter meetings—and fewer of them—also relieve the feeling of being overworked. Several companies with which I work schedule 20-minute meetings or hold quick standup meetings so employees don't waste time and can get some exercise. Other companies take a different approach to meeting overload. Patagonia regularly has staff meetings at the beach, lets people wear casual clothes, and encourages people to surf during the day when the weather is good,[167] and Aetna promotes walking meetings.[168]

There are dozens of other ideas worthy of consideration and experimentation:

- *Healthy food and nutritional snacks:* Laszlo Bock, former CHRO of Google, tells the story of how employees resisted the idea of healthy snacks. He simply put the sugary food at the back of the cabinet, making it harder for employees to find it.[169] The result: people lost weight, and employee engagement rose.

- *Nap time:* People need to rest, so many companies offer nap and quiet rooms at the office.

- *Bring a furry friend to work:* Glassdoor, Amazon, Zynga, and Tumblr, along with 17 percent of American businesses, allow people to bring their pets to the office.[170]

- *Offer VTO along with PTO:* Salesforce gives each employee five days a year of "VTO"—volunteer time off. This benefit attracts Millennials, who flock to the company. And a large consulting firm has an annual impact day when the entire U.S. business takes a day to work in local communities.

- *Tap technology:* Microsoft, Oracle, SAP SuccessFactors, and dozens of smaller companies have started to build wellbeing platforms into their HR software. These vendors let employees take training online, join competitions, and track their activity and exercise.

RECOGNIZE THAT LEADERSHIP MATTERS

Perhaps a leader's most important task in the new world of work is simply setting a good example. Open offices tend to inspire a culture of communication and openness. I have found that CEOs at companies with above-average engagement ratings generally make a point of sitting in an open office. In contrast, sending emails all night or calling meetings on weekends essentially tells a team that you don't respect their personal or family time.

Some Japanese companies have a tradition that no one leaves the office until the boss leaves. At its extreme, this has resulted in the sad phenomenon of *karoshi*, or "overwork death." In 2015, the Japanese government identified 2,159 preventable deaths caused by suicide or other forms of work-related stress, leading Prime Minister Shinzo Abe's cabinet to consider new laws to prevent high-overtime work.[171] The goal is to empower a new generation of leaders who won't stay late or force others to do the same.

You as a business leader, team leader, or manager have an immense responsibility to set a good example. When you take time off, cancel early meetings, avoid emails on weekends, and promote fairness, inclusion, and wellbeing, you empower and energize your people to perform well together in a simply irresistible company.

5

growth, not promotion

"You will either step forward into growth,
or you will step backward into safety."

ABRAHAM MASLOW, PSYCHOLOGIST AND CREATOR
OF MASLOW'S HIERARCHY OF NEEDS

You might not know Telstra, but as Australia's leading provider of mobile services, it's the country's version of AT&T. In 2020, the telecommunications company made the decision to no longer tie an employee's job to a specific location, permitting a level of work flexibility that seemed radical just a few years earlier. Equally revolutionary is Telstra's decision to accept that every person is different when it comes to working.

We know this to be true: some of us are raring to go first thing in the morning, others kick into gear midafternoon, and more than a few people find evening hours to be extremely conducive to getting things done. Despite this knowledge, many organizations want everyone to work at the same time and often in the same place, supervised by a manager to make sure productivity is humming.

Not at Telstra. "We've changed the managerial model to focus on the social contract with employees," said Alex Badenoch, Telstra group executive of transformation, communications, and people.[172] "Instead of watching people to make sure tasks are performed, managers provide clarity around their objectives. Their sole purpose is to talk with employees about their purpose and development, which instills pride in the values of the organization."

Think about it this way: if you want your company to be irresistible, you need the organization to learn as fast as it can. This means that learning should be essential to your entire people strategy so that people can grow, earn more money, and advance—regardless of level or job title.

RETHINKING DEVELOPMENT IN A NETWORK

As discussed in previous chapters, irresistible companies focus on people and work, not on hierarchy and jobs. They define their success by the output they produce, the customers they serve, the brand they create, and the work they provide, and they add value in every possible way.

When I was running Bersin & Associates, I was always reluctant to give people management roles. We hired people who had great skills, we gave them challenging things to do, and everyone worked together in a highly productive way. We managed to stay profitable almost every month we were in business, largely because I tried to eliminate middlemen whenever I could.

But eventually the time comes for something new, and you realize you don't have the right people, skills, or capabilities to pull it off. The sales team starts to underperform, so you wonder if you should train them better. The finance department struggles to find the profit model, so you hire a consultant. The marketing team doesn't understand search engine optimization (or any of a dozen new ideas), and you feel like you're falling behind. What do you do? Do you go out and hire these experts? Or do you try to build them yourself?

In times of low economic growth, plenty of experts are looking for jobs. I built Bersin during a recession when there were many talented people looking for work. But in tight economic times, like the period we're in today, there just aren't enough skilled people to hire—so you have to develop them yourself.

As I've studied this topic over the years, I've continuously found that the highest performing companies always have one thing in common: they embrace a culture of learning. People are able to take time to learn, they have a culture of sharing and development, and managers are coaches, mentors, and educators at heart.

Organizational learning takes many forms. In some cases it's teams taking time to step back and talk about what's failed. In other cases it's giving someone a new assignment to help them develop new skills. And in others it means taking a course, completing an assessment, or finding a mentor.

In any company there is a natural stress between execution and learning. Should I answer my emails or read the article I want to read? This dichotomy is going on in all our heads every day while working, and when our company gives us the time and ability to learn, we take the time to do it. Thomas Watson, the founder of IBM, gave us all desktop signs that said "THINK" because he famously said, "Being busy doesn't make a company grow; thinking about how to do things better does."

When you have a skills gap, you *could* try to hire someone to fit it, but that's often a terrible idea. The people you hire from outside may be expensive, hard to find, and often don't fit your culture. When we worked with General Assembly, we interviewed a series of banks about their challenges hiring web-development experts. After looking at all the expenses of recruiting, hiring, bonuses, and high salaries, we found that sending an existing employee to a boot camp and giving the person nine months to learn how to code was a whopping six times cheaper than hiring a developer from outside.

So, how do we do this in a network? Irresistible companies focus on growth, not promotion, as their learning strategy.

WHAT DOES GROWTH VERSUS PROMOTION MEAN?

In a nutshell, the "growth, not promotion" management principle simply means that we optimize around growth in everything we do. Yes, people are promoted, but that is not the goal; rather, it is the outcome.

In my early days at IBM, Exxon, and Sybase, I spent a significant amount of my time worried about how to get promoted. While I wasn't overly focused on it (I was a very late bloomer), it kept bothering me because it seemed to be the primary way people were rewarded.

Since I wasn't a very good politician, I didn't get promoted that often—so I managed to make myself happy by doing my job well. And now, looking back on a 45-year career, it was the smartest thing I did along the way.

A few months ago, I was talking with some colleagues, and they were astounded by the number of positions I've had. I was a maintenance engineer; I was a systems engineer; I was a sales representative; I was a marketing manager; I was a product expert; I spent time as a staffer to a senior executive; I was a business development leader; I was a product management leader; and, later in my career, I was the vice president of marketing, vice president of sales, vice president of product management, and, even later, a CEO and industry analyst.

While a few of these jobs were promotions, the majority of them were lateral moves. I took these new jobs because they were fun, because I had an opportunity to learn something new, and because the company needed me in those positions. Looking back, I was growing every year.

Unfortunately for my employers, a lot of these new opportunities required that I leave the company at which I was working because I was unable to traverse the hierarchy. The companies I worked at were very hierarchical at the time, so I had to create this growth pattern by going from place to place.

Today, as companies become more and more networked, we have to create this environment inside companies and let people grow regardless of whether they are promoted or not. I'm not saying promotion is bad, but when people know they're learning and improving their skills, they know their market value is going up even if their job title doesn't change.

How do we do this?

THE URGENT NEED TO REINVENT CAREERS

First, let's talk a bit about careers themselves. They're no longer the upward-sloping curve we all learned about as kids.

This is because of the digital transformation of businesses in almost every industry sector. As companies transformed to become more agile, customer-responsive, and employee-focused, every role in business, from finance and IT to engineering and sales, came to rely on automated processes and technology tools, solutions, and platforms to get work done.

Since technology development is dynamic, everyone in every function must constantly learn new ways of performing their essential functional tasks. Not surprisingly, technical skills are in high demand—but so are skills in sales, customer service, healthcare, and general project management. A good career is one that builds all these skills together.

For you as an employee or a manager, continuous learning has become one of your most valued skills. As I like to say, "The learning curve is the earning curve." And this curve keeps moving.

A study by Burning Glass Technologies, now Emsi Burning Glass, which analyzes jobs, skills, and salaries around the world, found that in only a few years, salaries for data scientists skyrocketed by more than 300 percent and later declined, in part because a new job family called "machine learning" and another called "cybersecurity" took data science's place as the hot new jobs.[173] Every one of us has to stay continuously current, regardless of our role.

In marketing, for example, the job of the marketing manager used to be designing and implementing advertising, lead generation, public relations, or other outreach programs. Today, it is all that, plus search engine optimization; social-influencer marketing; TikTok marketing; managing the Salesforce, Hubspot, Marketo, or Google AdWords system; putting together estimates and budgets for marketing campaigns; analyzing the performance of ads and webpages; and writing creative content. If you aren't familiar with the latest digital marketing technology, you've fallen behind.

Most professionals understand this: the number one reason people give when they leave a company is "I wasn't learning anything."[174] So if you're not helping your people learn, they're probably looking around. As I studied the data from the Glassdoor database and looked at many other studies of employee engagement, I was surprised to find that among Millennials, the opportunity to learn and advance is a stunning three times more important than salary in an employee's willingness to recommend their company as a place to work. This translates into retention, engagement, and commitment.

At an organizational level, these are issues of life and death: if we cannot attract and retain the most highly skilled people, we are doomed to fall behind.

At a personal level, career development is essential to our lives. A 2018 study by LinkedIn found that the number one thing people want to learn is skills that will make them better at their jobs, followed immediately by skills that will help them become better leaders and skills that will help them achieve work-life balance. These are existential issues.[175] To acquire these skills, LinkedIn's updated 2021 skills report cites learning and development through upskilling and reskilling at the top.[176]

We all have to get better at what I call "personal reinvention." Stop thinking about yourself as a salesperson or as a senior consultant. You can be whatever you want to be—this is the new way to manage a career. Rather than go to school, get a job, and retire, we now live in a world where we learn, work, and hopefully enjoy our lives in a series of continuous cycles well into our 70s and beyond.

HOW CAREERS HAVE RADICALLY CHANGED

In the early 1900s and throughout the 1950s and 1960s, we had a career model that went roughly as follows: we went to school (primary and secondary education); we went to a college or a craft school or took an apprenticeship; and then we went to work. And we worked for 30 years until we could retire.

The entire economy was built around this model. We sent our children to school for 18 years; they learned math, reading, and other basic skills; and in high school they learned science, social science, and other disciplines that made them ready to enter society. College was a time to pick a major and then pick a career.

In high school, I took the Strong Vocational Interest Blank, which was a standard job assessment given to every student. It picked up my interest in science and travel and told me I should become an astronaut. I actually used that test later to decide to study engineering, and I even considered joining the Air Force. These and other tools were signals I received that helped me decide what kind of career I would want some day.

There are a lot of problems with this model—the biggest being that we all live much longer and whatever job, career, or company we chose is likely to change, disappear, or radically transform during our lives. Today, only about two-thirds of Americans retire at 65, and despite a slight jump during the pandemic, this percentage is dropping every year.[177]

Most of us are very alive and vital in our 60s and 70s, and we have a lot to give back to the world. These are the years when we can bring all our experience, skills, and perspectives to work, which many of us want to do. Plus, many studies have shown that retirement is a frightening and negative experience for most people,[178] and others show that retirement creates loneliness, isolation, and a loss of self-esteem.[179] When I was forced to retire from Deloitte, I started hearing stories of partners who had heart attacks soon after retirement—so, of course, I decided I would never retire!

These flaws have been obvious for years. A more recent drawback with this model is that it assumes that education is over once you start to work. Of course, this is ridiculous—we all know this isn't true. But does your company have reskilling programs, boot camps, new job training programs, and other types of apprenticeships for people in their 50s and 60s in your company? I doubt it. All these wonderful things are designed for youth, so "tenured" employees are on their own. It's a huge opportunity to change, and companies such as IBM, CVS, and others are slowly fixing this.

The new world is one where learning, working, and recreation occur all the time. And this is where irresistible companies have to go.

IRRESISTIBLE COMPANY CAREER MODELS

Irresistible companies are figuring this new model out. They focus on an individual's growth, not promotion—moving forward in responsibility, expertise, and salary without necessarily being forced up the pyramid. We now know that a fulfilling career involves formal learning, stretch assignments, new projects, and opportunities to contribute across the company on many different teams. People feel a sense of continuous personal progress, they learn new skills, and they steadily become more valued without a choreographed ascent through management ranks. As I like to think of it, careers are experiences, not ladders.

This change has significant implications for the organization. For starters, it means modifying hierarchical career ladders to embrace continuous learning, which allows employees to build skills on demand, explore new disciplines, and learn from their peers. For example, suppose a salesperson wants to rotate into marketing? And then into customer service? And then into a new geography, perhaps overseas? This is a good thing for everyone: the employee, the business, and the customer. Can we reward this as a career move? In companies such as Nestlé and IBM, this is a common occurrence.

Second, the corporate university or the learning and development (L&D) department is no longer just a center of learning but is also a curator of external and internal learning in many forms. In many ways, corporate learning today is more like Netflix than it is like a college catalog: we find the channel or program we want, we follow the experts we admire, and we learn when and where we want. We have to build a set of strategies that facilitates learning all the time, not just while attending a course.

Certainly, formal training continues to be important: it still makes up more than 30 percent of the $140 billion spent around the world on corporate learning and is projected to reach a market size of $417 billion by 2027.[180] But, as all our research has shown, learning is now done in a blended way, using experiences, experts, simulations, and even virtual reality. (Farmers Insurance trains automobile-damage claims specialists[181] and Walmart its customer-service associates[182] using 3D virtual reality.)

Consider HP's Brain Candy program.[183] Mike Jordan, HP's global head of talent and learning, realized the company needed a learning solution to enable technical specialists all over the company to share their knowledge with each other. HP develops about 65 percent of the program's content and shares it internally with customer support, engineering, sales, and other business functions. More than 1,000 learning paths have been created. It's a hub where employees can find content, courses, and people and looks more like Netflix or Hulu than traditional corporate learning. In its first year alone, the program led to 100,000 completed learning activities. It's popular among all types of employees at HP— from Baby Boomers to Generation Zs.

Then there's Denver-based Guild Education, which connects companies to educational opportunities for their employees, helping many of the 64 million working Americans without a degree obtain one.

Other companies are developing similar, self-directed strategies. Capital One has an entire internal university dedicated to technical and digital reskilling and has now proven that it is far less expensive to build digital skills than it is to hire software engineers away from software companies. Shell Oil Company, which has always been a strong investor in employee learning, has built an entire virtual university (with real-world mentoring) to help engineers, financial analysts, and other professionals learn about geology and the business of finding and producing different forms of energy. And Bank of Montreal, Visa, and Bank of America have built entire online learning platforms that let employees share content across all their functional areas.

This demand for continuous development is important for other reasons as well. Not only does it help employees improve their own skills and individual careers, but it also enables companies to protect themselves from job obsolescence. Research by Emsi Burning Glass has found that single-function jobs (for example, coder, graphic designer, or financial analyst) are slowly declining in value as automation improves.[184] What is increasing in value (as measured by salaries going up) are what we call "hybrid jobs"—jobs that require a multitude of skills.

An example of a hybrid job might be a mobile-app designer, an Internet of Things engineer, a large-account sales manager, a marketing manager, or even a production specialist. These jobs require technical skills, project management skills, leadership skills, and communication skills. Everyone, regardless of background, will have new things to learn.

During my career, I vividly remember realizing that my technical skills at IBM were no longer enough and that I needed to learn about sales, communications, team collaboration, and even marketing to advance. It took me 40 years to develop all these skills: today, companies can offer these hybrid-job-development opportunities internally, helping people reskill and upskill all the time.

As I talk with executives from companies such as Visa, Capital One, and others, I always hear the same story: "We started with digital reskilling, but then we realized people wanted project management, communications, goal-setting, and other skills—so we expanded the program to teach soft skills." This is yet another aspect of the future of work—expanding our human skills to add human value to every job in the company.

Sure, people have to be willing to reinvent themselves, but the reality is that spending an entire career in the same job role is outdated. Today's career models are permitting people to advocate for moving from role to role, from job to job, and even from function to function. So, advocate. The only thing holding you back is a fear of trying something new and failing at it. That's where HR can help and lead this modern career progression—by creating a scaffolding of psychological safety so people know that trying and failing is okay as long as learning is continuous.

How do we actually implement this? After years studying this topic, we developed a framework for learning that explains what companies need.[185] It reflects the fact that all employee growth is based on four Es: education (training), experience (projects and jobs), exposure (mentors, coaches, and peers), and environment (an organization that gives people time, rewards, and opportunities to learn). We will explore the four Es more later in the chapter.

Every manager and individual has to think about growth, not promotion, in their career. Are you asking for a developmental assignment? Are you willing to take a project outside your functional area? Does your manager propose and support your desire to learn something new? Are you willing to do these things without any guarantee of a promotion or raise as a result? These are the keys to success today.

Think of a career as a series of experiences in new roles following what the individual and company need and desire. You as leader have a set of projects, roles, or jobs to staff and fill. Each individual has his or her individual career goals, desires, and strengths. We need to match these in a dynamic way. As I write this book, a new breed of career management tools is hitting the market, making it easier than ever to fill this gap.

UnitedHealth Group, for example, built an entire self-assessment portal to help employees in any role assess their skills, map them against hundreds of jobs, and find new opportunities within the company. IBM has a cognitive career advisor powered by Watson. And companies such as Ingersoll Rand, Schneider Electric, and Unilever have invested in entire career assessment, coaching, and development portals designed to help employees and managers identify new roles. (This is a big growth area for artificial intelligence [AI], by the way, where new HR tools can now find the best next role for an individual in the company.)

Far removed from its days as a staid old phone company, AT&T now operates in one of the most dynamic, competitive industries in the world. To ensure that the company has the skills to compete, the HR department has identified ascending jobs (as compared to descending jobs) and now pushes people to develop the necessary skills for high-demand roles of the future.[186] In AT&T's case, that means developing skills in ascending areas such as data science, cybersecurity, and mobile systems—not in outmoded, descending areas such as COBOL and digital subscriber line (DSL).

AT&T has built a world-class learning environment, including online programs, microcourses, content-sharing, and a wide variety of formal and on-the-job programs. The company maintains a culture of development—or risks the consequences. The mandate is simple: every employee has every opportunity to develop and stay relevant. For those who don't, it's best for both sides to move on.

Not all companies are so strong-willed about development, but they should be.

In the industrial age, it was enough for companies to tell employees what to learn. Today's employee has the responsibility to stay vigilant, continuously learn new skills, and explore new capabilities as soon as the need appears. That applies to everyone, up through the C-suite.

Not long ago, I met with the CEO of the largest telecommunications company in India. He told me he had recently taken an online course in Python. When I asked why, he said quite simply, "If I have to manage people who do this stuff, I need to know what it is." This is the mentality that leaders should model and inspire at work.

Irresistible companies have some formal training for new hires but focus more on a smorgasbord of learning opportunities, such as micro- and macrolearning available on demand; online content, from short videos to longer courses; and a heavy dose of coaching along with support from the team.

Teams that give people time to learn and value development (and those that constantly coach others) are consistently cited as the best to join, another benefit of fostering a learning culture at all company levels. A good but perhaps surprising example of this culture is the U.S. Armed Forces. Earlier in my career, I worked with a senior leader who trained many of the Navy's admirals. I learned from him the philosophy of the U.S. military: "We do two things around here: we train and we fight. When we aren't fighting, we're training. And when we are fighting, we're learning."[187]

For companies, the challenges are different, but the principle of continuous learning is the same. Yum! Brands, Allianz, General Mills, and many others reward job rotation and encourage employees to move from sales to marketing to IT to HR. This creates organizational agility and helps companies adapt to change. Employees sense that even if a promotion eludes them, they can reinvent themselves within the organization, which translates into higher engagement through a strong sense of empowerment and growth.

THE NEED FOR A LEARNING CULTURE

At Exxon and IBM, I would spend three to four weeks at a time in a highly scripted training regimen, which took me away from my job and imposed a huge expense on my employers. Today, this type of formal training still occurs, but for the most part, online learning platforms that offer webinars, videos, and reading materials across an immense range of topics have supplanted the trip to the corporate training facility.

Leadership must stay closely involved. Former SAP chief learning officer Jenny Dearborn led a sweeping initiative to reinvigorate the entire company's leadership model, the sales training academy, and the company's focus on diversity, culture, and engagement.[188] Her team eliminated hundreds of duplicative programs, consolidated multiple learning management systems, and unified the global L&D function under a common strategy.

My son recently had one of the most integrated, multifaceted learning experiences of his life at the SAP Academy for Sales and Presales. People from all over the world come together for almost nine months in a series of projects, formal learning activities, networking events, and executive interactions. The program is rigorous, detailed, and demanding. But it works, and it reflects SAP's willingness to heavily invest in learning, even at the beginning of an employee's career.

Ultimately, building and maintaining a learning environment is a matter of culture. If a company or a team is too focused on output and not focused enough on learning and growth, it will not achieve the desired results. When Satya Nadella joined Microsoft, he immediately realized the company needed to reward listening, experimentation, and growth, not just revenue and execution.[189] He sent a companywide email to employees, which explicitly stated that Microsoft's future would be built on a collective, inclusive, growth mindset:

> We fundamentally believe that we need a culture founded in a growth mindset. It starts with a belief that everyone can grow and develop; that potential is nurtured, not predetermined; and that anyone can change their mindset. Leadership is about bringing out the best in people, where everyone is bringing their A game and finding deep meaning in their work. We need to be always learning and insatiably curious. We need to be willing to lean into uncertainty, take risks, and move quickly when we make mistakes, recognizing failure happens along the way to mastery. And we need to be open to the ideas of others, where the success of others does not diminish our own.[190]

Learning lies at the heart of this philosophy of business. Since Nadella took over as CEO, Microsoft's stock price has more than quadrupled, and the new product pipeline is competitive and exciting. Visiting the company, I feel a new energy around innovation and a new style of listening. As one executive told me, "Microsoft used to be a company of the smartest people in the room. Today, we are the best listeners in the room. And this is paying off."[191] That's the power of a learning culture.

What have we learned about a learning culture? It is not really an HR or an L&D problem—it's a management philosophy, a set of rewards, and a series of stories. In our high-impact learning culture research, we found that some of the most important practices include rewarding people for taking risks, taking time to reflect and discuss mistakes, giving employees the autonomy to learn from their errors, and pushing people to take stretch assignments with the support to succeed.[192] These are management principles we can all embrace if we really want to become irresistible.

As Jeff Bezos states on Amazon's website, "I believe [Amazon is] the best place in the world to fail [...] To invent you have to experiment."[193]

the innovation: always learning, always growing

We know how to build a culture of learning. It requires a strong respect for curiosity, something that is often missing in business. A recent study found that curiosity and agility were the top characteristics of employees at companies successfully navigating the pandemic,[194] but our high-impact learning culture research shows that only top executives are rewarded for this trait.[195] As you move down the pyramid, people are less likely to ask questions. This is a problem.

In our research, which mapped more than 40 management practices against long-term business results, we found that the most important practice in learning is being willing to discuss mistakes. If a young employee asks why something happened, how would you react? I hope you'd take a few minutes and discuss the possible answers.

At one point in our research journey, we decided the new theme for corporate training was continuous learning, a thread now widely used in HR. If you think about your company as a continuous-learning organization, you'll end up in the right place. Young professionals understand the need for this; it's the way they were raised.

Right out of college, my daughter took a job in email marketing and quickly learned to use tools for website management, email content management, search engine optimization, and marketing analytics. She sees the writing on the wall and recently told me, "Dad, I want to become a data scientist. Marketing doesn't really use my skills anymore." She has recently changed jobs and is now really getting her hands into the data.

THE IMPORTANCE OF NEW HYBRID JOBS

Research by Emsi Burning Glass shows that almost every job goes through a similar cycle.[196] In the early days of a new type of job, it is unique, highly paid, and hard to recruit for. People flock to that job, education and training programs become available, and the industry develops more tools. Then, a few years later, that job becomes more hybrid, requiring both technical skills and skills in judgment, application of the technology, and social skills.

Consider, for example, that the number one skill required for all LinkedIn and Indeed job postings (more than 30 million job postings per year) is *communications.* This complex skill—that of writing, speaking, persuading, and leading people—remains the top need in business.[197]

Doctors and nurses, for example, continue to be in high demand (in fact, healthcare is now the largest employment segment in the U.S. economy[198]) because their skills sets and population are limited by years of study, followed by accreditation. Yet, in reality, a nurse's job is hybrid, requiring technical, communication, and listening skills, along with empathy and integrated thinking. Because of the need for this upskilling, salaries in nursing have increased dramatically during the last 15 years.[199]

Both HP and IBM have gone through wrenching workforce transformations as their businesses have shifted from traditional computing to digital technologies, analytics, and AI. In both cases, the companies offered employees many incentives to re-educate themselves. Over time, those learning opportunities translated into new careers for those who seized the opportunities to acquire new skills.

And let me add one more point. In the current Fourth Industrial Revolution, otherwise known as Industry 4.0, a lot is said about how coding skills and software engineering skills are the future of the economy.[200] While in high demand, history tells us that such jobs only make up around 10 percent of the economy. Leadership and communication competencies are in the highest-demand categories of all skills sets sought by employers, with the demand for so-called soft skills (also known as durable skills) making up nearly two-thirds of the more than 80 million job ad postings in 2021.[201]

how to get started

Discuss these questions with your own leaders and teams:

1   Do you have existing career models, and, if so, how recently have you revisited them? Can you convene a working group to widen the aperture and to consider more horizontal and growth-oriented models with your HR team?

2   Have you studied the actual career history of your highest performers and most highly regarded people? Can you use these as role models to redefine what high performance means?

3   What tools do you provide to help people find internal positions, roles, and projects? Do you post all open jobs internally, and do managers have an incentive to hire internal staff? When people take on a new role, is there an implicit time and a managerial incentive to help them learn their job, even when they come from an internal source?

4   How do you share, promote, and measure expertise? Does your company have regular brown-bag sessions, knowledge-sharing, or leader-led training programs? Do your technical and managerial professionals take part in onboarding and training programs? Is it easy to find experts, and are they rewarded?

5   Have you seriously looked at revamping your corporate-learning infrastructure? Do you have a formal place to learn or a corporate university? Learning today needs to be in the flow of work, with employees nudged by AI-based technologies with tips, support, and advice as needed. If you haven't invested in this area over the years, now is the time—technology and solutions are more mature than I have seen in a decade.

6   Do senior leaders fully understand the role of careers in your company, and do they sponsor people, incentivize and recognize parallel moves, and encourage people to learn every day? The growth mindset starts at the top. When senior leaders reward growth, not promotion, this sends everyone the right message.

how to get it right

CREATE A CAREER FRAMEWORK AND GIVE CLEAR GUIDANCE TO EMPLOYEES AND MANAGERS

The first and most important thing is to build a real career framework for your people. While only 19 percent of companies have traditional vertical career models today, employees still want guidance. What is my next step? What skills are in high demand in the company? Should I move into management or project leadership, or should I become a technical specialist? What are the potential promotion schedules and paths I can expect?

All these questions are up to you to answer. Many companies (such as Ingersoll Rand and UnitedHealth Group) have detailed "success profiles" for every major role, enabling employees to actually browse and shop for new jobs just like an external candidate. These companies use tools, including Fuel50 or internally developed portals, to help employees search for new positions and see new opportunities. Fuel50's platform even lets managers post developmental assignments and part-time projects.

Make time to sit down with your top leadership team and discuss the most urgent skills needed over the coming few years. This conversation will bring up many discussions about what is strategic and what is tactical.

When Marsh McLennan shifted its insurance business from commodity brokerage to full-service sales, the chief learning officer worked with the CEO to develop a set of new account management and relationship skills.[202] They used this framework to train and assess the entire global organization; it also helped people decide if they belonged in the transformed company or not.

Today, companies such as IBM, General Motors, and Unilever are all doing the same. As they look at these skills of the future, they also find that personal capabilities such as collaboration, inclusion, global awareness, and innovation are more important than ever. Write them down, give them to managers to use in their performance discussion, and revisit them each year.

Companies are updating their leadership models every 24 to 36 months as their businesses and the environment change. It gives employees a clear view of the capabilities they should aspire to and whether or not they fit into their company's leadership track.

ALIGN YOUR REWARDS TO THE COMPANY'S FUTURE NEEDS

When someone changes jobs, does your company reward or penalize them? What if a tenured employee moves into a new department but is initially untrained? Will the company penalize or reward the individual for creating this career opportunity? Does the manager have an incentive to hire this internal candidate instead of looking for an expert outside the company?

How are promotions decided? Does your culture value technical expertise? Business results? Collaboration and teamwork? Customer service and customer retention? These reward philosophies should be crystal clear so people can push their careers in the direction in which they are most likely to succeed.

One of the most difficult issues facing companies today is a lack of clarity about the future. One major consulting firm knows, for example, that automation and AI will disrupt the audit business. What are the skills sets and role of the auditor in the future? Are there other services beyond auditing these professionals can provide, perhaps of a consultative nature? The firm is actively exploring this issue to give the audit professionals a career path to follow.

NASSCOM, one of the largest IT professional networks in the world, is in the early stages of building a career framework for the future of IT.[203] It is researching new roles in security, cloud computing, operations, mobile, and other technologies. From that work, it plans to publish a series of career paths for the future and then align thousands of training programs toward this path.

Salesforce launched a new app in 2020 that makes it even easier for people to use its innovative development portal called Trailhead.[204] Trailhead is a fun, gamified learning environment that lets anyone interested in learning more about Salesforce and its many related tools access a vast library of courses and resources on every Salesforce-related topic—all for free.

Remember one important thing: continuous career development helps your company and your people in myriad ways. It helps individuals stay relevant; it improves engagement and retention; it strengthens your brand so you can attract high-performing people; and, of course, it makes sure your employees are skilled and relevant to your business.

Spending on career programs ranges from $200 to $4000 a year in different companies, but our research shows it always pays off.[205]

BUILD A CORPORATE UNIVERSITY, WHATEVER THAT MAY MEAN

The corporate university is back—and this time with a vengeance. However, today, it looks quite different from what it was before. (We now call it a capability academy.[206])

In the early 2000s, as e-learning became immensely popular, companies spent billions of dollars on learning management systems, and many set up physical or virtual corporate universities as well.

As digital learning grew and we all became addicted to our phones, video platforms, and other forms of social networking, these corporate-learning platforms grew stale. We found that non-HR professionals often rated their corporate-learning experience with a negative net promoter score.[207] It simply has not kept up with the consumer-learning experience.

It's time to go back to this concept. Companies such as Apple, Boeing, McDonald's, General Electric, and IBM have reinvented their corporate-learning platforms and are finding them more important than ever.[208] Why? Because a physical location can be a truly adaptive space—a place where people can meet others, think outside the box, and free their minds to learn. With so many jobs occurring at home, this is just another great way for people to socialize.

Consider Deloitte University. A decade ago, when business was tough, the Deloitte partners had to decide how to save money on meeting spaces, training locations, and other forms of high-cost collaborative programs. The firm put together a proposal to build a first-class physical university focused solely on training, collaboration, and leadership development. The alternative to this investment (which was more than $200 million) was to build a virtual university, one that would try to emulate this experience online.

After a very contentious debate, more than 50 percent of the partners voted to move forward on a physical space, and the company built a state-of-the-art facility that companies around the world now envy. Deloitte built the university around design thinking: every minute of the experience is positive, collaborative, and productive. It has a wide variety of modern meeting rooms, a world-class gym, and a never-ending supply of coffee, healthy food, and places to hang out.

Deloitte, which today employs more than 312,000 professionals around the world, thrives on continuous learning, career growth, and collaboration. Deloitte University has turned into a valued place to learn, a place to meet, and a place for consultants to rest and revitalize themselves. The corporate-learning facility is considered one of the top 10 in America.[209] Now, Europe and Asia are replicating the model as well.

CAPABILITY ACADEMY MODEL

Today, as companies arm up with skills technology and lots of online learning, an even more exciting model has emerged: the capability academy. The capability academy is a team of people dedicated to building and strengthening long-term capabilities in a given functional area.

Sales and leadership academies are common examples, but now companies build academies in data science, cybersecurity, actuarial economics, and even digital marketing. These academies are led by business leaders and are supported by HR and L&D teams.

Capital One, for example, built an entire cloud technology academy as it moved its processing and systems to the cloud. Cemex, the largest provider of cement, built a supply chain academy to help its employees understand the complex supply chain for aggregates and binding materials. ServiceNow is building an internal academy for experts in IT service delivery and employee experience. Intel is building an academy for all the technologies and mathematics of AI. And companies like Allstate and Liberty Mutual have built academies for actuarial economics, claims management, and other strategic skills.

While corporate universities remain important, they should be focused on the strategic capabilities to make the company succeed. Your role as a business leader is to sponsor, participate, and support this approach. It keeps your company current and relevant as technology and business evolve.

CULTURE: VALUE DEVELOPMENT AND LEARN FROM YOUR COMPANY'S MISTAKES

While "culture" is a vague term, we've found 10 critical best practices you can follow[210] to create a strong learning culture (see Figure 5.1).

This research, which took almost two years to complete, identified a set of high-impact companies that embrace these practices well.[211] The companies in the top 10 percent of this analysis were 32 percent more likely to be first to market (in other words, they were leaders in innovation), rated 37 percent higher in employee productivity, rated 35 percent higher in responsiveness to customer needs, and were 17 percent more likely to be market-share leaders. Clearly, a learning culture matters.

TAKE A HOLISTIC APPROACH

Online courses are just as critical as in-person courses in a learning culture. Indeed, it's better to take a broader approach. We call this approach the four Es—education, experience, environment, and exposure—as described in Figure 5.2.

This broad approach to learning is now easier to establish than ever. Companies can offer Coursera, Udacity, LinkedIn, Skillsoft, General Assembly, Pluralsight, and hundreds of others through curated platforms that teach employees technical and professional skills online. Massive open online courses (MOOCs) are free to anyone who wants to develop their skills or learn more about a topic. Some are even offered by educational institutions such as Stanford and Massachusetts Institute of Technology (MIT). Coaching platforms like BetterUp guide managers and other employees to be superior coaches, inside or outside the

FIGURE 5.1: 10 BEST PRACTICES IN A LEARNING CULTURE

1	Leaders are open to bad news.
2	Asking questions is encouraged.
3	Decision-making processes are clearly defined.
4	Employees are given projects beyond their current knowledge to stretch them developmentally.
5	Employees have influence over the work they do.
6	The company rewards and values employees who learn new skills.
7	The company values mistakes and failures as learning opportunities and provides structured opportunities for reflection.
8	The company believes that learning new skills is a valuable use of time.
9	Employees perceive that learning and skills development is a valuable use of time.
10	Employees take active responsibility for their personal development.

SOURCE: THE JOSH BERSIN COMPANY, 2021

FIGURE 5.2: THE FOUR ES OF CORPORATE LEARNING

EDUCATION	Formal and informal training delivered in person, on the job, or online—typically through a course or formal training process
EXPERIENCE	Developmental assignments, projects, and work tasks that give people skills and confidence in new areas
ENVIRONMENT	A set of cultural and management practices that facilitate learning, including coaching by managers, demonstration that learning is valued, time allocated for reflection, and discussion about mistakes
EXPOSURE	Opportunities for people to meet leaders, internal experts, peers, and outside thought leaders to learn, develop, and expand their perspectives

SOURCE: THE JOSH BERSIN COMPANY, 2021

company. And internal sharing platforms let employees quickly share, recommend, or author content for others.

This new world of microlearning has exploded as new platforms deliver what is often called "personalized learning" or "adaptive learning." These platforms deliver and recommend training based on an employee's role, his or her required training, and his or her learning history.

Several years ago, the chief learning officer of BT Group (formerly British Telecom) attended a Bersin research conference. As an HR leader with an operations background, he believed that one of BT's biggest challenges was continuously training service staff to repair, maintain, and replace legacy telephone systems around the world. Quite frequently, a service technician arrives at a site, looks at the antiquated systems, and simply walks away, unable to figure out what to do.

Not only does this waste money, but it also irritates customers and hurts BT's brand. And given the vast amount of equipment installed around the world, no amount of formal training could give every employee the knowledge to understand every machine.

The chief learning officer told me he decided to try something new. He gave every service representative a small video camera. Whenever they fixed a piece of old equipment, they videotaped what they did and then posted the video on the company's learning portal. Other technicians could view the videos and then rate them, with the more useful ones rising to the top. Within just two years, this experiment in shared knowledge saved the company millions of dollars in maintenance and repairs. In a sense, the chief learning officer built the YouTube of BT.

EDUCATION: LEVERAGE DATA AND AI

One of Starbucks' biggest problems is teaching baristas how to understand all the different types of coffee it serves. Using AI tools from a start-up called Volley, Starbucks can automatically scan the company's latest manual on coffee, produce easy-to-read tips, and test baristas on new coffee blends—all without formal training.

A new technology standard, the Experience API (xAPI), now allows corporate platforms to track any form of digital learning in the company, from reading a blog to completing a course.[212] This has enabled companies to build advertising-like recommendation engines based on the learning behavior of others. Companies such as Mastercard, Visa, and Bank of America are now using these learning-experience platforms to give all employees a platform that recommends, curates, and delivers training relevant to their jobs.

EXPERIENCE: REWARD EXPERTISE

Most tech companies have a career path for engineers that often leads to a title such as "fellow" or "senior technical staff," which represents the pinnacle of achievement in technology companies. One of my best friends from college has been a design engineer for more than 40 years and is now a highly esteemed expert in his field of high-frequency chip design. He has earned the job title of fellow—and while he manages people and directly manages projects, this gives him an immense sense of pride and respect in the organization, incentivizing others to follow in his footsteps. It's a common practice in engineering and technology companies and one I believe must grow in organizations in the future.

You could build similar "fellow" roles for project leadership, financial leadership, or other technical disciplines throughout your company.

ENVIRONMENT: FOCUS ON MANAGEMENT AND LEADERSHIP

Creating a successful learning culture requires incorporating a philosophy of learning into all aspects of an organization. Leaders must think about all the ways the culture manifests itself. For example, is the company rewarding team members for taking time to stop, debrief, and reflect on what went wrong if a project fails? Or is the company simply punishing the team? Irresistible companies don't shy away from mistakes; they talk about them openly.

Similarly, is the company rewarding managers for producing talent with skills that can be spread across an organization? Or are they more likely incentivizing managers to hoard talent? One company with which I've worked actually pays managers for the number of people promoted *out* of their groups—a strong reward system for leaders who focus deliberately on developing others.

The list continues: Does the company give managers the budget and freedom to access learning tools both inside and outside the organization? Does the company reward teams for sharing their learning with others? Is learning available continuously or just during regularly scheduled training sessions? And does the company give people the opportunity to try new skills in new roles, or does it confine them in rigid jobs?

Developing a learning culture takes hard work and sustained effort, but it is an indispensable part of the transformation to irresistible.

EXPOSURE: RESPECTING AND REWARDING THE VALUE OF RELATIONSHIPS

In the traditional vertical model of careers, people advanced through tenure, power, and responsibility. Today, more and more research shows that the most influential people in an organization are those who have built strong, respectful internal and external networks.

In irresistible companies, a highly successful tenured professional might best be identified by his or her followership. Do people respect and follow this person? Does this person listen and understand what others are doing? Does this person bring new ideas and know where to go to make things happen?

These capabilities—taking time and energy to build relationships and to understand how the company works—have become one of the most important building blocks of a prosperous career. As you throw away the traditional model, make sure you give people the incentive, time, and rewards for meeting others, understanding the business, and building followership in the company.

6

purpose, not profits

"Unless you focus on purpose,
you cannot deliver performance."

INDRA NOOYI, FORMER CEO OF PEPSICO, 2010

It was a slippery start, so to speak, when the Dutch company Margarine Unie and the British soapmaker Lever Brothers merged to form Unilever in 1930.[213] Today, the company is one of the best examples of an irresistible organization dedicated to the greater good.

To backtrack: since its founding, Unilever has grown to include dozens of the world's most well-known brands, including Lipton, Ben & Jerry's, and Dove. For years, the company has been concerned about customer health, environmental impact, and social good. Unilever was the first to develop a sustainable process for manufacturing tea, becoming certified by the Rainforest Alliance to make sure Lipton is grown in a sustainable way around the world.

Leena Nair, the CHRO of Unilever, has purposely weaved this focus into the fabric of the company, creating a global program called People with Purpose.[214] Unilever has trained more than 30,000 employees in the value of purpose and asks them to write a personal purpose statement describing their life purpose, career purpose, and how they want to be remembered over time.

These purpose statements show the inclusive nature of Unilever because they encourage people to bring their authentic selves to work. But they go much further: managers and leaders use them to help decide what is the next best role, who is suited for a new business or a new project, and how the company can reorganize itself to optimize the purpose of its people. Nair calls it a program to "ignite the human spark in everyone."[215]

Because Unilever uses this program worldwide, its HR department has enormous opportunities to understand the employee experience and make it better all the time. People talk about their purpose statements, they share them, and they use them to make recommendations for change. This dynamic process lets Nair's team identify who the highly active learners are, who is fulfilling their purpose, and what jobs are available that suit their needs. Talent mobility and the ability to find the right job within Unilever are sacrosanct values, bringing purpose and citizenship to this irresistible company.

the shift: purpose, not profits

Profits are important to a company because they affect the company's ability to secure financing and attract investors who can increase working capital and fund business growth. But purpose is the real fuel of a company. It gives people the energy, enthusiasm, and creativity to add value in many ways. And today, amid worries about income inequality, immigration issues, bias, and discrimination, purpose has shifted into a new era, one I call "citizenship." This means helping the society around us. In a business, we want our people to always think about what they can do to make the company better, what they can do to make their teammates successful, and, of course, what they can do to please customers, shareholders, and the community.

Purpose at Unilever extends beyond employee personal purpose statements to encompass society at large. In early 2021, the company announced a wide-ranging set of commitments and actions to build a more equitable and inclusive society by raising living standards across its value chain, creating opportunities through inclusivity, and preparing people for the future of work.[216] One of the initiatives was for everyone who directly provides goods and services to Unilever to earn at least a living wage or income by 2030. The company already pays a living wage or income and wants to secure the same standards for more people beyond its workforce.

Jeroen Wels, Unilever's executive vice president of HR, told me about another ESG-focused companywide program. ESG, of course, refers to the environmental, social, and governance factors used by investors, customers, rating agencies, and the public at large in evaluating a company's sustainability. The Unilever program is called Raise a Hand, Lend a Hand. "We encourage people here to raise their hand if they need support to address our growth opportunities, risks, and other priorities and for those whose time is underutilized to lend a hand to their colleagues," he said. "It's a catalyzer to create some fantastic impact."[217]

I also met with the head of consumer insights at Unilever, who told me that customers now want products and services developed and designed for their local communities—grown locally, manufactured locally, designed for local needs, and positioned as relevant to their local community.[218] This is why Unilever, General Mills, Nestlé, and others make so many local brands, flavors, and products. People want to contribute to their local economy.

She also shared that customers today no longer want products; they want experiences. When you get on a plane, shop on Amazon, walk into a store, or go to a restaurant, you don't just want a good seat, good electronics, and good food; you want a good experience. This means that companies must give their people a sense of empathy, understanding, and true concern for their customers. It means shifting the focus from revenue and sales to customer satisfaction and retention—and showing their people why and how their mission matters.

As I studied the Glassdoor data for industry trends in employee engagement, I was surprised to see that three of the industries that are rated highest by employees are education, government, and healthcare (see Appendix 2). These are not the highest paying industries, and these are certainly not the most dynamic or technologically savvy areas of the economy. But what they are filled with is purpose. People who work in these industries feel like they are truly helping others, so they like their work and their respective organizations.

Glassdoor's *Workplace Trends 2021* data builds upon these trends.[219] The study emphasizes that more and more employees expect progress, not just pledges, regarding corporate diversity, equity, and inclusion (DE&I). This is now one of the five top workplace trends, along with expectations for flexible remote/on-site job experiences in the future. Interestingly, the study also suggests that employers seem to want the same thing due to the ability to hire workers anywhere across the world and to reduce office-related expenses under flexible frameworks.[220]

How do we define and implement purpose in a company? It starts at the top, and it has to involve a series of stakeholders throughout the company. Many banks, for example, have now decided that they are not in the financial-services business but rather in the business of helping people improve their lives through the effective use of money, such as purchasing a home or funding college tuition.[221] Pharmaceutical companies such as Pfizer and Sanofi are now wellness companies, and Starbucks not only sells coffee but brings people together in a "third place," as described in Chapter 4.

At Target, a very well-run company whose mission is "to help all families discover the joy of everyday life," the emphasis is on the words "all families." I recently talked about DE&I with Kiera Fernandez, Target's chief diversity and inclusion officer.[222] She said the company treats it like a business function, meaning that, just like other functions, it establishes strategic priorities, goals, and metrics. "This way, it's embedded into our day-to-day operations: an inclusive culture that personifies our purpose to bring joy to all families," she said.

Stories abound of companies redefining themselves through mission and purpose. Whole Foods, for example, started the sustainable food market. DaVita focuses on its heart patients' health and lives. In the United Kingdom, Sainsbury's stated purpose is to "feed the nation." And Santander Bank and the Royal Bank of Canada talk about their purpose of helping customers and communities better manage and improve their financial lives.

Here's another story of finding purpose.

During the last decade, Philips realized that its lighting business had become a commodity and was no longer generating profits comparable to its faster-growing businesses in medical and other products. Philips planned to spin off its lighting business into a separate company, hoping to boost the valuation of its faster-growing operations.

Rather than spin it off to die and commoditize, however, the executive team decided it would try to reinvent Philips Lighting. The company hired a consulting firm that went through a three- to six-month process of interviewing employees at all levels through a series of small stakeholder meetings. The consultants asked the following questions:

·   "What is our legacy? What is our history?"

·   "What is our culture? How do we want to treat our people?"

·   "What do we want to be? How can we become something new?"

In each session, the consultants asked the employees to think about things they wanted to keep and things they wanted to "throw away."

Employees wanted to keep the company's engineering culture, its focus on quality, and its focus on developing its people. And they wanted to maintain its legacy as a pioneer in the lighting industry.

What they wanted to throw away was the focus on margins and products, the lack of creativity and innovation, the old-fashioned way Philips managed its people, and the company's relentless focus on costs. And they wanted to find a way to serve people and get closer to their customers.

After six months of this process, the leadership team studied the results and then launched a new strategy. Philips would no longer sell light bulbs but would now sell integrated lighting systems—digital end-to-end systems that companies could use to heat and light buildings, control external light and heat, and make people's workdays better, more energizing, and more productive. This leveraged all of Philips engineering and technical strengths but required a major change in product strategy, engineering, and how the company worked with customers. Now, Philips Lighting was more of a consulting and services company, so employees could get closer to their end customer.

Philips was able to reinvent itself. The company now defines its mission through the lives it improves and defines its strategy as "light beyond illumination." This is Philips Lighting's mission statement:

> *Philips has been revolutionizing lighting for over 125 years. We pioneered the world changing development of electric light and LED, and are now leading the way in intelligent lighting systems. Our deep understanding of how lighting positively affects people enables us to deliver innovations that unlock new business value to our customers. We offer rich lighting experiences that make people feel safe, comfortable, focused, energized and entertained.*

> *As Philips Lighting, we are leading the ongoing development of connected lighting systems and services. By leveraging the Internet of Things, we are transforming buildings, urban places and homes. To increase energy efficiency, and manage working environments in a more environmentally friendly way. To make cities safer and more responsive. To help our healing and improve our well-being. And to create experiences at home like never before.*[223]

Who wouldn't want to be a part of this company?

A HISTORIC PERSPECTIVE

Should companies focus on profit or society? Economists have debated this for years, starting with Adam Smith in the mid-1700s discussing the "invisible hand" of the economy. The original perspective is that when companies make money, the economy grows, which in turn creates jobs, wealth, and overall economic wellbeing:

> *As every individual, therefore, endeavours as much as he can both to employ his capital in the support of domestic industry, and so to direct that industry that its produce may be of the greatest value; every individual necessarily labours to render the annual revenue of the society as great as he can. He generally, indeed, neither intends to promote the public interest, nor knows how much he is promoting it. By preferring the support of domestic to that of foreign industry, he intends only his own security; and by directing that industry in such a manner as its produce may be of the greatest value, he intends only his own gain, and he is in this, as in many other cases, led by an invisible hand to promote an end which was no part of his intention.*[224]

Adam Smith and other early economists theorized that by building an economy of rugged individualism, incomes and wealth would grow, people would deliver goods and services to meet the needs of buyers, and the world would become a better place. But as history has clearly shown, these theories have fallen short many times.

Since 1776, we have suffered through many deep recessions, stock-market crashes, weather and other natural disasters, and the unforeseen disruptions of technology. Every 7 to 10 years we have a stock-market correction, and people lose their jobs, see their retirement accounts decline, and suffer from health problems due to stress.

Then, of course, there's the economic impact of climate change, income inequality, the lack of pay equity by gender or race, workplace harassment, and other social issues. According to the Pew Research Center, by 2050, most Americans expect income gaps to widen, living standards to decline, environmental conditions to worsen, and political divisions to intensify.[225]

Today, as I write this book, Edelman's most recent Trust Barometer tells us that the country will not make it through our varied crises without companies playing a critical role in addressing the challenges we face.[226] The majority of the 33,000-plus global respondents say brands owe it to their employees to speak out against systemic racism and racial injustice and that they must take necessary steps to ensure their organizations are racially representative of the country as a whole. More than two-thirds (64 percent) of consumers will choose, switch, avoid, or boycott a brand based on its stand on societal issues, up from 51 percent in 2017.[227]

What I found particularly insightful and instructive in the respected annual consumer survey is that the public trusts businesses more than any other institution, including government and the media. More than three-quarters of respondents worldwide and 72 percent in the United States said they trusted their employer to do what is right.

The onus, of course, is on businesses to do just that. This is not a new idea, either. In the 1940s, Johnson & Johnson established its credo,[228] which remains relevant today in the company's synergistic and holistic responsibility to doctors, patients, employees, and shareholders.

> *We are responsible to our employees who work with us throughout the world. We must provide an inclusive work environment where each person must be considered as an individual. We must respect their diversity and dignity and recognize their merit. They must have a sense of security, fulfillment and purpose in their jobs. Compensation must be fair and adequate and working conditions clean, orderly and safe. We must support the health and well-being of our employees and help them fulfill their family and other personal responsibilities. Employees must feel free to make suggestions and complaints. There must be equal opportunity for employment, development and advancement*

for those qualified. We must provide highly capable leaders and their actions must be just and ethical.

We are responsible to the communities in which we live and work and to the world community as well. We must be good citizens— support good works and charities, better health and education, and bear our fair share of taxes. We must maintain in good order the property we are privileged to use, protecting the environment and natural resources.[229]

In the 1960s, George Goyder's *The Responsible Company* outlined ways shareholders could influence companies to act on behalf of society and the environment.[230] And John F. Kennedy established the Consumer Bill of Rights in 1962, creating guidelines for protection, transparency, and the importance of considering the environment in products and services.[231]

In 1970, the United States had its first Earth Day, bringing more than 20 million people out into the streets for a peaceful demonstration for environmental care. Greenpeace was founded in 1971 and brought a sense of activism to the movement. The 1980s saw the rise of more environmental movements, and two college dropouts in Vermont founded Ben & Jerry's, proudly announcing that they would donate 7.5 percent of their profits to the local community.[232] The company (now owned by Unilever) has continued to pioneer its focus on the community, fairness to employees, and environmental awareness over the following three decades.

In the 1990s, as the world became concerned about climate change, the World Trade Organization, the World Business Council for Sustainable Development, and the Kyoto Protocol were created to coalesce all business to act to repair damage to the environment. And in the 2000s, the first Certified B Corporations, or B Corps, were approved, companies like Patagonia and Ben & Jerry's that pledged to make only safe, ethically sourced products. Every Black Friday, including 2020's virtual Black

Friday, Patagonia gives 100 percent of the day's profits to nonprofit organizations that protect air, water, and soil quality.[233]

Looking forward, we will see a steady increase in focus on business's broader role in society, often pioneered by forward-thinking leaders.

VALUING COMPANIES BY CITIZENSHIP

Business books of the 1950s and '60s extensively discuss driving shareholder value and the need to make a profit. A large portion of global equity markets continues to focus on financial results, embracing the idea that business exists for that purpose alone: to make a profit.

I would argue differently. While profits fuel a company's growth, irresistible companies are essentially institutions that garner loyalty, commitment, and energy from their employees. And in today's service-driven world, they attract the same level of energy and loyalty from customers. Profit, rather than being a goal, is an outcome.

There's even a term for this now (there's a term for everything!): "conscious capitalism," the conviction that businesses must operate ethically and with a higher purpose as they pursue profits, serving the needs of humanity and the environment.

In Target's 2020 year-in-review report, the company listed among its greatest achievements the fact that it helped farmers save 12 billion gallons of water, increased the starting wage to $15 per hour six months earlier than planned, and added solar installations to more than 500 store rooftops, exceeding its goal.[234] Target also donated the equivalent of more than 87 million meals in pounds of food to families across the country. Who wouldn't want to work for this company?

During the course of many business cycles, including the current one, companies with excellent employee experiences outperform those with poor employee experiences. In higher-performing companies, employees are willing to sacrifice during downturns and then outperform during growth times.

The word "citizenship"—defined as "the character of an individual viewed as a member of society"[235]—best explains this strategy. In the context of a company, it means taking care of your employees, your customers, your shareholders, and the communities in which you live.

I consider myself a capitalist at heart. I do believe that well-run companies are good for everyone: employees, customers, and investors. But even if you only take the investor view, you come to the same conclusion.

Look at Warren Buffett, whose strategy has been based on investing in companies with strong moats (barriers to entry) and who famously discussed his addiction to Coca-Cola (a sugary drink with no real nutritional value) and See's Candy (a wonderful company), as well as his enthusiasm for Geico and other financially successful companies. Buffett is what many call a "value" investor: he buys companies and stocks based on their cash flow in an attempt to unlock value that others have not seen. This strategy, discussed by Benjamin Graham in the 1930s, values companies based on expected future cash flow (dividends and stock appreciation).[236]

What research now shows is that citizenship is a surrogate for financial value. Intangibles like citizenship, which make up almost 90 percent of U.S. stock-market value, include such aspects as innovation, brand, service, and intellectual property. When a company is inspired and its people are happy, these measures of value go up—and when citizenship is poor, bad behavior is the result.

Consider the case of Volkswagen, which disclosed in 2016 that it had been regularly cheating on its diesel-emissions standards and misleading U.S. regulators. As the story leaked, the company's stock plummeted, and governments around the world investigated, resulting in a series of fines and a humiliating experience for the company, its leaders, and many German citizens. Its stock price has been nearly flat for almost 20 years, underperforming General Motors by almost 30 percent over that period of time.

Did the company truly pay for its behavior? Yes, but while its stock has suffered and the company has lost lots of money, investors are again bullish on the company, due in large part to the automaker's plans to more than double electric-vehicle sales in 2021 in a goal to become the global market leader for electric mobility by 2025 at the latest, the company's CEO pledged. In other words, no matter how bad a company behaves, our memories are short, and we can revert back to Benjamin Graham's principles in valuing a company.

THE DELOITTE MILLENNIAL SURVEY: EVIDENCE OF MAJOR CHANGE

To get a deeper sense of why citizenship has become so important, let's look at the economic and social lives of our youngest generations: Millennials and Generation Zs. The *Deloitte Global Millennial Survey 2020* reveals the pandemic has reinforced both generations' desire to drive positive change in their communities and around the world.[237] They will continue to push businesses and governments to put people ahead of profits and to prioritize environmental sustainability, the survey found.

Other findings are equally striking. When asked to choose their top concerns, Millennials chose climate change and protecting the environment first, followed by healthcare and disease prevention, unemployment, and income inequality. Generation Z respondents also chose the environment first, followed by unemployment and sexual harassment. In a follow-up pulse survey, the issue of greatest concern remained climate change and protecting the environment, emphasizing the importance of the issue to both generations.

By far, the majority of respondents in both cohorts agreed that climate change is occurring and is caused primarily by humans. Roughly four in five respondents across the generations also said that businesses and governments need to make even greater efforts to protect the environment. The COVID-19 pandemic has catalyzed the vast majority of respondents to be more sympathetic to the needs of different people around the world, has inspired them to take positive actions to improve their own lives and communities, and has given them a strong sense that everyone around the world is in this together.

The *World Happiness Report 2020* arrived at similar conclusions. For one thing, not being able to work during the pandemic had a negative impact on overall wellbeing, particularly among young people and low-income and low-skilled workers.[238] Overall workplace happiness decreased year-over-year in the United States, with a higher number of people reporting feelings of anxiety and depression. Moderating these feelings were supportive management and job flexibility, two important drivers of workplace wellbeing. The study states, "Past research suggests that the more employees work from home, the more likely they are to depend on their supervisors' frequent contact. Since the onset of the crisis, many workers have reported feeling unprepared to fulfill their responsibilities, again underscoring the need for good communication between managers and employees."[239]

One other finding of the study struck me: the fact that social connections continue to be an essential driver of subjective wellbeing and buffer the negative impacts of hard times. As I mentioned earlier, my daughter works for a small but fast-growing software company in San Francisco, which, like many other tech companies, is located in an area with a large degree of unhoused people, substance abuse, and poverty right on the street. So, every day, my daughter leaves her apartment in Nob Hill, walks to work, and passes by people who are unhoused, hungry, and suffering from substance abuse disorders.

Recently, she started a small program for employees to take a day off to serve food and help out in the local community kitchen. The executives at her company were not initially on board, but as more employees became involved, they realized the value of coming together to give back to their community. The program is now a companywide effort. Despite limited resources, its leaders understood this is part of their role in society.

This ethos is real, it's powerful, and it's growing.

SALESFORCE: AN EXAMPLE OF AN IRRESISTIBLE COMPANY

One of the fastest-growing companies in the world is Salesforce, which produces a software platform that automates and improves customer relationship management and sales. Thanks to the leadership of its amazing CEO Marc Benioff, it has become one of the most iconic and well-run companies in the technology sector. Salesforce was the first cloud company to reach $1 billion in sales (2009)[240] and then the first to reach $10 billion (2017),[241] and it has done this while maintaining a Glassdoor rating of 4.5 (in the top 10 percent of its industry) in 2021.[242] Nearly every employee (97 percent) approves of Benioff, and the company is constantly rated in best-places-to-work lists.

Salesforce has been able to manage growth—one of the most stressful times in a business—in an exemplary way. (While all CEOs dream of stunning growth, it often means that most people are in jobs over their heads; processes and systems are always behind; employees can't find office space; and the company is constantly reinventing new products, customer programs, and services.)

Just recently, I spent a half day with Salesforce's head of employee experience, and she shared their Ohana Book project, which exemplifies the company's focus on its people.[243] Salesforce not only offers VTO (volunteer time off); it also promotes gender pay equity. (As mentioned earlier, CEO Marc Benioff famously gave all the women in the company a series of raises over the last few years and has pledged to revisit this issue annually.[244]) Salesforce actively publishes its diversity and inclusion metrics and invests heavily in education and in community activities. Benioff has personally donated hundreds of millions of dollars to local hospitals.[245]

Benioff and his senior leadership team clearly understand that being irresistible is based on the principles outlined in this book and that only by being a good citizen can the company attract the talented people it needs to grow.

DEFINING CITIZENSHIP HOLISTICALLY

It's easier than you think to find companies that are great citizens. Companies such as Unilever, IKEA, Wegmans, Toms Shoes, Patagonia, Whole Foods, Philips, and Maersk Line all define themselves as broad members of society. Most of these companies start their journey through the founder's original passion, and over time their level of thinking tends to expand.

Being a good citizen means thinking about all the stakeholders you have as a business: obviously your investors and customers, but also your employees, their families, and the communities in which you recruit, operate, and serve. Citizenship today means delivering products that don't hurt people or have an adverse environmental impact. The public expects companies in diverse industry sectors to take transparent actions to achieve net-zero, the term describing the balance between the amount of greenhouse gases they produce or emit and the amount they remove from the atmosphere.

Citizenship also means creating a climate of inclusion and income equality internally and honoring the world's need for better healthcare externally. Business leaders have immense power in their roles, and despite the need for companies to grow, profit, and beat the competition, if they want to survive over time, they must consider all their stakeholders.

how to get started

Discuss these questions with your own leaders and teams:

1   Does your company have an up-to-date mission statement, and is it real and specific enough for people to get excited about? If you do have one, can you point to programs, artifacts, and investments that support it directly?

2   When your company makes a decision about what business to grow, what product to build, or what acquisition to make, do your executives view these decisions through the lens of the mission? Or do they focus on revenue, market share, and competitive position?

3   Have you conducted a culture survey of the company, and do you understand where people feel committed to the mission and where they don't? We did such a project at a healthcare company and found a profound mission-driven culture in patient care but a dysfunctional, negative culture in finance and operations. You can fix problems like this one.

4   As the famous statement goes, "I asked one of the janitors at NASA what their job was, and his answer was, 'I'm here to put a man on the moon.'" Would your employees be able to answer this question in a similar way that reflects the purpose of your company?

5   Do you hire for passion, purpose, and fit? Or do you look for the highest-trained professionals, regardless of whether they want to be part of the culture? How do you measure employee purpose? Do you ask people to write down and share their values with others?

6   Have you made employee listening a cultural value? Every leader, from the CEO to the first-line supervisor, should be encouraged to slow down and listen, create a place of psychological safety where people can speak up, and take notes on what employees want. When you listen, hear, and react to what employees say, you not only make better decisions, but your employees also feel more engaged.

how to get it right

Think about where you spend your time as an employee, manager, or executive. Do you spend time volunteering in the community? Are you on the board of any local educational or nonprofit organizations? Do you give time or money to local causes?

As I analyzed the Glassdoor database for irresistible companies and looked at the brands that outperform, I was amazed that the companies that rated high were those that consistently do good things in the community (see Appendix 2).

Bain & Company, for example, has been voted one of the best places to work for 13 consecutive years by Glassdoor.[246] In 2021, despite the life- and work-changing tumult brought about by the pandemic, the management consultancy was cited the number one best place to work. That should not come as a surprise, Glassdoor says, as Bain creates solutions and delivers results that shape the world for the better. In the previous 10 years, the firm invested more than $1 billion in *pro bono* services to bring their talent, expertise, and insight to organizations tackling today's urgent challenges in education, racial equity, social justice, and the environment.[247]

Among a company's stakeholders, employees are considered number one by a growing number of organizations, in large part because of their heroic efforts to keep business flowing during a once-in-a-century pandemic. But even five years ago, some enlightened CEOs were headed in this direction. I remember attending a user conference hosted by a fast-growing HR tech company whose CEO and founder got up in front of 7,000 customers and said, "I want you to know that you are not my most important stakeholders. You are my second-most important. I think first about taking care of my employees because I know that they will take care of you."

Many companies felt the same way during the economic crisis the pandemic unleashed. In a way, they had to—without employees managing the stress of work and life, the engine of business would have seized up like my grandfather's Buick. Despite the pressures on profits, companies like Bank of America, Morgan Stanley, Starbucks, and PayPal committed to a no-layoff policy in 2020 and 2021.[248]

Research supports this move away from layoffs, as has been noted by *Newsweek* and other publications:

In Responsible Restructuring, *University of Colorado professor Wayne Cascio lists the direct and indirect costs of layoffs: severance pay; paying out accrued vacation and sick pay; outplacement costs; higher unemployment-insurance taxes; the cost of rehiring employees when business improves; low morale and risk-averse survivors; potential lawsuits, sabotage, or even workplace violence from aggrieved employees or former employees; loss of institutional memory and knowledge; diminished trust in management; and reduced productivity.*[249]

The better answer? Reduce executive compensation when times are bad; this is good citizenship. In 2020, that was the approach taken by Signet Jewelers, Southwest Airlines, WestRock, Cracker Barrel, UnitedHealth Group, and other companies, according to data compiled by Equilar.[250]

Whereas ESG factors were a nice-to-have a few years ago, today a company's adherence to positive environmental, social, and governance policies can have a material impact on its business profits and profile. ESG to me is just another way of saying "responsible citizenship." For several years running, in his annual letter to the world's CEOs, Larry Fink, the CEO of BlackRock, one of the largest investment firms in the world (with $9 trillion in assets under its management[251]), has told investors that he will not invest in companies that don't practice good citizenship. "Without a sense of purpose, no company, either public or private, can achieve its full potential," Fink has said.[252] In his 2021 letter, he warned shareholders and stakeholders of all companies that no issue today for businesses ranks higher than that of climate change:

In the past year, people have seen the mounting physical toll of climate change in fires, droughts, flooding and hurricanes. They have begun to see the direct financial impact as energy companies take billions in climate-related write-downs on stranded assets and regulators focus on climate risk in the global financial system. They are also increasingly focused on the significant economic opportunity that the transition will create, as well as how to execute it in a just and fair manner.[253]

His message to companies is clear and compelling. You are an institution of people's dreams, hopes, and lives. Yes, you have to make a profit, but what you do to deliver that profit, how you operate, and how you take care of the environment, employees, and communities are what really matter.

7

....

employee experience, not output

"If we win the hearts and minds of employees, we're going to have better business success."

MARY BARRA, CEO OF GENERAL MOTORS, 2013

Deutsche Telekom is one of the most dynamic telecommunications companies today. As one of the largest providers in the world, the organization is constantly adopting new technologies, developing new services, and moving into new businesses. It now owns a large stake in T-Mobile and Sprint and is now among the top 100 companies globally.[254]

To maintain its agile and fast-moving strategy, in 2017 the company embarked on a companywide focus on design thinking.[255] Design thinking, a process of studying customers (or employees) and then building iterative solutions to their problems, has become a valued innovation in software, product design, and marketing.

In addition to training all its leaders on the process, the company adopted design thinking in HR and IT. Reza Moussavian, the senior leader of the company's digital transformation, worked with the team to create 14 detailed personas for the entire employee population.[256] These personas are now used to design every HR, IT, and employee program in the company.

"Design thinking has been transformational for the company," said Moussavian. "We use the process for recruiting, management, leadership development, pay, and every program we build. We design, test, and iteratively improve all our employee investments using this methodology."[257]

Today, Deutsche Telekom continues to grow at above-industry growth rates, and its Glassdoor ratings are higher than Telstra, AT&T, or Verizon.[258] In fact, the company is considered one of the top 10 employers in Germany.[259]

A NEWFOUND FOCUS ON EMPLOYEE EXPERIENCE (EX)

Among the many changes driven by COVID-19, the biggest of all was the new focus on what's called employee experience. The idea, put simply, is that we can't just design jobs and work practices; we have to look at employees' total experience at work.

In the past, companies focused on annual (and later pulse) engagement surveys to understand employee satisfaction. Today, this is a discipline of design: studying what employees do, understanding their work and job needs, and then designing the systems, workplaces, and rewards that help them thrive.

In 2021, we completed a massive study of employee experience where we looked at more than eighty different management practices.[260] The findings were profound: among all the things we can do to make work better for employees, a focus on trust, productivity, inclusion, and belonging win out. Throwing perks and benefits has little real impact.

Irresistible companies understand this, and they build employee-centric systems, frontline worker platforms, and many forms of listening, communication, and feedback to make sure employees are supported. These are the practices that create results—not pushing for output.

EMPLOYEE-FOCUSED TOOLS SAVE THE DAY

No book about work would be complete without a robust discussion of the role of technology. The pervasive impact of technology in the workplace was evident before the pandemic-influenced remote-work experience. But it was this crisis that truly cemented the value of technology as a disruptive force, altering how people will work in the future.

As I said in a podcast in August 2020, Zoom and Microsoft Team meetings, Slack channels, and virtual reality and online training programs all work exceedingly well.[261] For years, companies discussed their digital transformations as works in progress. The pandemic digitally transformed almost every company overnight.

The combination of wireless mobile technologies and automated accounting-software solutions in the cloud helped companies close their books and forecast earnings at a time when chief financial officers and entire accounting teams were working from home. Workforce management tools helped people collaborate remotely and were reengineered by some providers to check in on employee wellbeing.

Prior to the pandemic, leaders were perplexed by many questions: What will work look like in the future? How will technology shape it? How will people adjust to it? How will organizations cope with it? And how can we use technology to our advantage? Those questions for the most part have been answered. Both organizations and individuals adapted to the new work demands thanks to technology.

As one of my partners at Deloitte liked to say, "As goes life, goes work." In fact, the barriers between work and life have almost disappeared. If your company isn't thinking about technology across work *and* life, you will fall behind.

Consider Autodesk, one of the world's most successful developers of 3D-engineering design and manufacturing software. The company employs thousands of engineers and software developers and is well known as one of the premier employers in the San Francisco Bay Area.

During the last seven years, Autodesk created dozens of Slack channels for different engineering teams, projects, interest groups, and recreational activities. Great—and not so great. The teams were happy but unable to share common practices or cultural cohesion. A simple tool had become overly complex.

The HR department decided to integrate all these Slack channels into one. The result was a total change in the way the company works. "We have tied the teams together," Guy Martin, Autodesk's former director of open source and facilitation, told me.[262] Today, more than 5,000 members of the company's Slack community can collaborate with anyone, anytime, anywhere. People have been liberated to be productive on their terms. And if they need assistance, they can find it at the company's remote-work resource center. Autodesk now sees its mission as reimagining the workplace through design and technology to promote cohesion and trust.

Like any tipping point, the transition to hybrid workspaces and flexible work arrangements is in its nascent, imperfect stage. We know some of the downsides of remote work, such as Zoom fatigue, overwork, and rising stress and anxiety. We also are aware of the positive effects, such as equal or enhanced productivity. Meanwhile, advances in artificial intelligence (AI), voice and facial recognition, virtual and augmented reality, chat and conversational systems, and technologies that read and analyze data and text are all moving at light speed.

Will these technologies make our jobs obsolete? Yes and no. Machines will perform a rising number of mundane, repetitive tasks, but people will migrate to more human work. Not every job can be automated or be replaced by robots, in any case. Millions of years of evolution have gifted humans with brains that guide eye and hand movements that scientists and engineers are a long way from duplicating. Already, we can find job boards with a wide variety of new roles (robot trainers, operators, and curators, as well as developers and designers), many of which require even more human skills. Routine work is what is going away; the jobs of the future will be more human, creating demand for skills in empathy, design, fine motor skills, interpretation, communication, persuasion, and management.

Look at how Mayo Clinic, one of the world's leading healthcare organizations, has improved teamwork, information-sharing, and patient care with technology. Through a mobile app called AskMayoExpert, physicians can find information on diagnosis, treatment, cause, and prevention from other specialists and sources in the network. Users can ask and answer questions, and all information is tagged by topic, location, care process, and key facts. This highly interactive system is now widely used, with doctors obtaining access to experts more than 10 times a day.

The issue for us is how fast we can design, invent, or discover new jobs as machines come in and automate more work. Let me offer three things to consider.

First, the future will be better than the pessimists believe. One consulting firm studied the impact of AI and robotics at hundreds of companies. The research suggests that while technology worries people in routine jobs, in reality, it is making jobs better.[263] Think about the old role of the bank teller stuffing checks into envelopes. The job is different now but also better: today, a branch employee does sales, service, and customer relations, human interactions that make life and work more fun and interesting.

A study of the 200-year-old history of automation reveals a clear pattern. For the first few years, we worry and fret about these tools as we wonder how radically they will change our lives. Then, as they prove themselves and deliver scale, we build new human capital practices around them. Just as the founders of Meta and Twitter could not predict the huge number of human curators they would need to run their social networks, we cannot always predict how many drone operators or AI operators[264] we will need to manage our new machines.

Second, it's important to apply design thinking and look at automation as a way to improve and scale the customer experience, not as a way to reduce labor cost. Retailers have experimented with kiosks for years, but many of the labor-saving ideas failed. Only as the technology has become smart enough to customize an order and really listen to a customer have these platforms started to sell. (Wendy's ordered smart kiosks for 1,000 of its stores.) And behind the scenes, employees are still cooking food and serving customers; they just aren't standing still writing down what you want.[265]

Design thinking and automated technologies were ready to go at S&P Global during the pandemic.[266] The company designed a suite of apps for its 22,500 employees, such as apps for data analysts to conduct their analyses, write up reports, and collaborate with colleagues at home. If they needed to come into the office, the company sent cars that were previously cleaned to reduce infection risks. They also prepared for every possible safety, health, and productivity problem, even schedul-ing floor monitors at all 59 offices worldwide to ensure adherence to social-distancing mandates.

Your job as a business and HR leader is to take an active role in curat-ing and designing the jobs of the future. In our research, we found that most companies are buying or implementing new AI technologies, but far fewer are partnering with HR departments to redesign work. That is why every chapter of this book is about redesigning work in a way that makes it easier for people to be productive.

My third observation is less positive: don't be fooled into thinking all these snazzy new technology tools are going to be good for your people, your organization, or your business. Advertising revenue drives many technology products, so be careful that these products focus on the employee experience. If you don't, you could be putting your company and people at risk.

the problem: technology friend...or foe?

Let's be honest: as technology gets better, faster, and smarter, it's also becoming more intrusive. Many organizations are following the lead of Fitbit, Apple, and other producers of wearable technologies to gather information about employees with a view toward improving the work experience and environment. Companies are not only tapping into the data that commercial wearables provide but are also incorporating this technology into their own workplace practices.

A few years ago, a large consulting firm outfitted its employees in Canada with smart badges that provided many insights into how people worked. The study found a variety of important things: people perform best when they are near sunlight; projects are more successful when cross-service line teams know each other (this is due to the power of relationships, as we've discussed earlier); open offices facilitate more innovative projects; and people burn out if they start work on Sunday evening and don't leave the client until Friday.

While technological innovations can improve our lives and our work, we must also understand that technology and technology providers are not always benevolent. Their mission is to make our lives better—and to sell products.

Social networking, for instance, is part of a wave of products that focus on engaging us with our mobile devices. But engagement can easily turn into addiction. Who hasn't sat in a meeting where people pay more attention to their phones than to their colleagues? These tools can easily lead to the unfortunate side effect of making people less focused on those around them and more self-absorbed as social-networking platforms consume their lives. Such characteristics are polar opposites of those that make for effective team members.

Tristan Harris, a former user-interface designer from Google, writes about how technology companies use psychological tricks to keep users completely focused on their tools.[267] According to Harris, everything, from the layout and tempo of these systems to how the menus are designed and how the social feedback works, is designed to keep users tethered to their devices. He calls this "hijacking our psychological weaknesses." Rather than engaging workers in their jobs, these technologies compete for our attention and make us less focused and productive.

While technological change is a constant, the pace of change is accelerating. The replacement wave over the next three to five years seems particularly significant and important for the workplace.

Take the ongoing challenge of email. Email was originally modeled after snail mail, and it served business well until the volume of emails became overwhelming. Today, email has become a real-time communication device that demands endless attention. Employees receive far too many emails and spend far too much time dealing with them. A September 2019 study from Adobe indicates workers spend about 5 hours and 52 minutes each day checking their work and personal email.[268] The risks extend beyond wasting time. Studies show that every time a new email comes in, our heart rate goes up, our blood pressure rises,[269] and we are distracted from other tasks.

Nowadays, employees spend as much time messaging as they do emailing, sometimes more. During the pandemic, the *State of Texting 2021* report by Zipwhip found that messaging gained popularity due to the crowding of email channels.[270] The task for irresistible companies is to harness the technology beast to make people more engaged and productive in their work, carving out time for rest and focus.

the innovation: a new breed of tools is coming

Business leaders today face a dizzying array of choices when it comes to choosing technology—their job is to make it all work. Today, HR managers must partner with the many chief officers in information, data, digital, and security within IT in new ways, acting as the conscience of the organization to make sure tools address the integration of life and work and are designed to enhance the employee experience—the experiential value of work.

I talk with executives about this all the time (and I meet with dozens of vendors each week). While these new tools all look great, it's important to ask some questions: Can people use these tools easily? Do they help make work-life balance better? Do they integrate well with other tools and security systems? And can they be extended and customized as needs change?

Remember that the goal of today's technology is to disappear—to be so useful you don't even know you're using it. According to Sierra-Cedar's 2020 global study of technology, it is absolutely necessary for companies to shift HR systems "from administrative support tools to strategic instruments finely tuned to engage and optimize the workforce."[271] The study added that HR applications are now "at the center of an organization's ability to manage workforce productivity and enterprise culture."

Technology solutions such as Microsoft Teams, Slack, and Google Workspace are trying to help resolve the issues of productivity, ease of use, and enhanced people experiences. Will they actually make the integration of life and work easier? I'm really not sure yet. But I can guarantee you these vendors will listen—the competition is intense.

In the area of HR and work management tools, the marketplace is totally disrupted. Many of the established human capital management (HCM) systems are built around the hierarchical model of work, but changes are afoot. Providers like Ultimate Kronos Group (UKG) recently unveiled a new workforce management suite of solutions called Life-work Technology, recognizing that life and work are intertwined. The technology is said to factor into people's emotions and preferences to empower employees to thrive both at work and in life.[272]

Another innovative toolset called Team Space is being used by Cisco to help teams set goals, recruit and manage new team members, coach each other, administer feedback and check-ins, and help people understand their strengths. The new market for team-based tools for performance management, feedback, learning, and engagement is encouraging, and I believe many HR technology providers will continue to push boundaries.

Another recent offering that is likely to transform the market for enterprise software is Microsoft Viva, a digital platform built on Microsoft 365 and specifically designed as an employee experience platform (full disclaimer: I advised Microsoft on the development of the product).[273] Out of the box, Viva connects with a wide array of applications, such as Glint, LinkedIn Learning, and content from Headspace, Skillsoft, and dozens of others. In addition to these applications, Viva is a vastly functional integration platform that lets the IT and HR departments standardize the employee experience.

Nearly every company I talk with is now actively redesigning its workplace to make work-life balance better. For example, Deutsche Telekom's head of digital experience has developed 24 job personas that detail the work needs, information needs, mobility, and activities of different work segments.[274] The company now uses these personas to select new tools, design new systems, and even develop training and performance-support programs for its employees.

Ultimately, the role of HR in an irresistible company is to actively study, curate, and help design the right technology solutions to fit the organization's mission and stakeholder strategies. If you do your homework, work with IT, and focus on the employee experience as a proxy for productivity, you can do some amazing things.

When you pick up your phone and use your favorite app (be it Waze, Uber, DoorDash, or Twitter), you can rest assured that behind the scenes a team of designers is working feverishly on your behalf to make the experience better every day. Our jobs as leaders and HR managers in our companies is to get away from thinking about technology as a labor-saving tool and focus on it as a performance-enhancing solution—all in the interest of making our employees' lives better.

DON'T FORGET THE ROLE OF DATA

As an engineer, I'm always thinking about data—and let me close this chapter with a few thoughts on this important topic. At the time of writing this book, newspaper headlines are filled with stories about gender pay inequities, workplace harassment, bad work behaviors, systemic racism, and leadership failures, much of it exposed through social media. Irresistible companies must use the power of data to identify, root out, and solve these problems wherever they can.

Managing employee data is more important and difficult than ever. As I've blogged about for years, the entire area of people analytics has grown up from a backwater data warehouse in the HR department to a highly strategic program that impacts every management decision we make. Companies now monitor productivity, location, bias, and discrimination by looking at patterns of hiring, promotion, and pay. We can use organizational network analysis (ONA) to see who is talking with whom and thereby understand drivers of productivity, as well as fraud and abuse. Smart systems can read job descriptions and internal documents to ferret out your sentiment, bias, or even stress—giving us highly actionable information about what's going on in every team in a company.

If you are an HR or business leader, I urge you to take the people-analytics part of your job seriously. If you don't have a team dedicated to managing, governing, and analyzing this data, you should. The sophisticated tools to integrate and manage data are easier to use than ever, and I believe irresistible companies will soon be smart enough to know when a team is too big, when a manager is in the wrong role, when an employee's spirit is flagging, or when a career path or skills set is out of date. We have the intelligence to do this today—you just need to get your data act together to take advantage of it.

how to get started

Discuss these questions with your own leaders and teams:

1 How well does your technology infrastructure function today? Is it making work easier, or is it getting in the way? If you don't see it as a positive, go to your chief financial officer and start a project to explore improved HR and work management tools—it will drive employee engagement, productivity, and better data over time.

2 What is the age of your existing core HR systems? If they're more than five years old, they're probably hard to use, expensive, and highly customized. Are they still up-to-date? Much of the Fortune 1000 has replaced these arcane systems with new cloud-based platforms; it may be time for you to do the same.

3 What is your relationship with IT? Is the department committed to spending time on employee-facing systems? While most have a help desk and PC-related tool support, I would suggest that much of their new role should shift into redesign of the workplace, with your help. Meet with them at a senior level, and make sure it's on their list of digital transformation projects to fund.

4 What is the state of your people-related data? Our research shows that most companies are actively cleaning up and integrating all the information they have about their employees. Are you in this group, and is this project well funded so that it can do the work well and build an infrastructure that scales over time? This is an investment you must make; the payoffs are huge, but it often takes at least a couple of years to do well.

5 Have you taken a product management approach to your data? Every piece of data you get from employees should go into an employee experience road map. Companies like AstraZeneca and Schneider Electric have employee experience product teams that look at all employee journeys and then use survey data to improve the trek ahead. The concept of HR professionals as product managers is another aspect of the future of HR.

how to get it right

Assign a team to study and test new workplace technology; this team should work with IT to make sure security, standards, and integration issues are addressed.

Research the tools on the market, and consider the fact that many of the best solutions you deploy will be things you integrate or build, not just products you buy.

Look at your employee experience in a holistic way. Follow the example of Deutsche Telekom and others—segment your workforce, invest in research to look at how people work, and develop solutions attuned to the most important segments of your company.

Remember, as our research points out, that the most important factor in employee experience is not technology; it's trust.[275] Do your people feel a sense of purpose and mission? Are you and your peers good at listening and responding to people? Are you able to react and respond when employees point out problems? A core part of empowering employees is what I think of as shortening the distance between signal and action and making sure people know that you care.

Irresistible companies are not afraid to test and experiment. IBM, for example, developed its new performance management tools, its new career explorer, and its online managerial coach through internal development, hackathons, and experiments. Many of the remote-work, hybrid-work, and work-at-home policies developed during the pandemic started as experiments.

Employees will help you with this work. A final example I'll mention is the famous PepsiCo Process Shredder that rolled out in early 2019.[276] During the early days of the pandemic, PepsiCo went out to its employees and asked them what, if anything, they would change or delete to make their work experiences better. Tens of thousands of employees suggested ideas, and they all voted to see which was number one.

Guess what was the most despised process at the time? It was the employee performance management system. It was complex, bureaucratic, time-burning, and often considered unfair. The management team quickly took this information as a mandate and within only a few months simplified the process for the next cycle. Other programs that promoted wellbeing and management support quickly followed, all driven by a focus on employee experience first, output second.

conclusion

"Labor is prior to and independent of capital. Capital is only the fruit of labor, and could never have existed if labor had not first existed. Labor is the superior of capital, and deserves much the higher consideration."

ABRAHAM LINCOLN, U.S. PRESIDENT, 1861

This book has been a labor of love: love for business, organizations, and people. I wrote it over the last five years, and almost every idea was accelerated and made urgent by the COVID-19 pandemic. But the bottom line is simple.

Irresistible companies understand that by unleashing the power of the human spirit, their company can go faster and farther than ever expected. Business should not be an effort to force labor to do what managers want; rather, it should be an enterprise to empower people to build organizational success. I can promise you that an irresistible company attracts top people, customers, and partners. It is one that people admire and respect, and it is one that adapts, grows, and endures.

The seven innovations I've detailed in this book are easy to understand yet profound in their implications—and harder to implement than you may think. They represent a set of new management philosophies in

HR, all of them underpinned by an essential truth: people (or labor, as Lincoln elucidated in 1861) are still the most important element of a business.

In today's economy, where innovation, service, and brand matter more than ever, you should always be thinking about how you can energize, empower, and support your people.

A shift from hierarchy to teams will unleash energy, belonging, and commitment. A shift from jobs to work will empower people to reinvent themselves and to always bring their best. A shift from boss to coach will give people and management a sense of growth and development. A shift from rules to culture will bring people together and attract great candidates. A shift from promotion to growth will create collaboration, development, and skills. A shift from profits to purpose will create more energy, passion, and commitment. And a shift from output to employee experience will propel employees forward on a journey of mutual value.

While not new ideas, I call them "innovations" because, today, you must embrace them at scale. They are no longer just programs or practices to consider but are now fundamental to your success. Together, they will help you build an organization that performs, endures, and grows.

I continue my own journey studying and learning how to adapt management and business to the world around us—and I welcome your thoughts, feedback, and stories as our organizations all strive to become irresistible.

This is not the end but the beginning of a perpetual discussion.

a final note on the pandemic

At the time of this writing, the world is beginning to fight back the COVID-19 pandemic. Now that vaccinations are on the rise, companies are struggling to hire like never before. Almost 35 percent of the U.S. workforce left their jobs in 2021, and nearly every employer is challenged to engage its employees.

When the pandemic began, most companies expected to shut down. Retailers, airlines, hospitality companies, and many manufacturers let people go. Companies like American Airlines, Sainsbury's, MGM Resorts, and Verizon imposed massive furloughs. Yet, somehow, the economy managed to bounce back.

The lesson we learned is what I call the "unquenchable power of the human spirit." Individuals, when they're given the right support, will always adapt to change. And this is the irresistible message.

When you trust in the energy of your team, empower people to invent, and support people with safety, fair pay, trust, and growth, your company will always thrive. The essential lesson of the pandemic is woven throughout this book. If you let your people drive your business forward, you as a manager, leader, or HR professional will experience success.

That's what being irresistible is all about.

appendix 1: about organizational endurance

First, let me define what "irresistible" means and how I came up with the term.

As I studied HR and talent management over the decades, I realized that measuring employee engagement was not sufficient. Most companies have happy employees while they're growing, but then, when they slow, engagement drops quickly.

What we really want to evaluate is what I call "organizational endurance"—the ability of companies to be irresistible today and long into the future. This means building an organization that has the management muscle to grow, change, flex, and adapt, all with a focus on purpose, mission, and values.

As I've met with many CEOs and CHROs over the years and discussed these issues with many employee engagement companies, I've come to the conclusion that there are really four things to consider.

MISSION

Does the company have an enduring mission or purpose, one that survives generational change? Johnson & Johnson, for example, is built on a credo to take care of the doctors, nurses, patients, and mothers that use their products.[277] It was developed and chiseled into the wall of its New Jersey headquarters in 1943. It goes beyond responsibility to customers; it also describes the company's responsibility to employees, communities, and shareholders.

IKEA is built on a mission to "create a better everyday life" with well-designed home furnishings at low prices so as many people as possible can afford them.[278] IKEA also cares about its responsibility to the environment, to a sustainable planet, and to its communities.

Patagonia often calls itself "a cause, disguised as a company."[279] The CEO and founder Yvon Chouinard actually believes he is in business to save the planet.[280] Starting as a company that made tools for climbers, the organization still focuses on building products that cause the least harm to nature, with products that endure for decades.

I've worked for many companies that lost their mission, and in the process, they often lose their irresistible status. Some organizations falter and regain their balance. Microsoft, for example, spent many years driven by the mission to democratize computing through its software. But then it chased the internet, mobile, and other trends and lost its way. Now, the company has come back home, with a mission of empowering people and organizations through its products.

I could go on and on about mission, but suffice to say that it's the guiding light illuminating the clear path forward.

PRODUCTIVITY

As I've studied employee engagement over the years, I always noticed something interesting: the companies with the most engaged employees also seem to be growing the fastest. They are clear on their goals, they understand their market, and they get things done.

As I dug into the issue, I figured out why.

These companies don't just think about making their employees happy; they think about helping employees stay productive. They design their organizations, their rewards, and their managerial strategies around how to get work done.

Irresistible companies, those often in the top 10 percent of the Glassdoor database, have terrific financial results. In fact, as I analyzed the data, I found that these excellent companies are more than twice as likely to be rated fast-growing, with the vast majority citing strong business growth, compared to less than half for the entire sample.

While the word "productivity" has a somewhat cold, economic feeling, it's really an important topic. Research by Teresa Amabile in *The Progress Principle* found after studying the work logs of thousands of employees that the most rewarding thing at work is "getting something done."[281] People really enjoy helping others, pushing their projects forward, and completing activities. The key is to make these experiences efficient and meaningful.

Research I conducted a few years ago with LinkedIn found that the single thing that inspires people to work the hardest is "the nature of the work itself."[282] When people like their jobs and they feel they can progress in their career, they are happy.

On the whole, however, productivity has been a big issue over the last decade. And, in many ways, this problem is one of the reasons I wrote this book.

Here's the issue: productivity is generally defined as output per hour of work (or dollar of labor). As we transition to the digital economy, global productivity has been slowing, and not just because of the pandemic.[283] This is a serious economic problem. Productivity is the engine that fuels wage growth, employment, and business sustainability. Despite the enormous amount of automation we see at work, we have not yet found a way to effectively adapt to this change.

Some economists blame the aging population. Others cite the younger population. Many point to the lack of infrastructure investment. (Commute times have gone up by almost an hour a day in the last 10 years.) Some even think the measurement system is wrong.

My experience shows it's something different: the digital world of work requires that we rethink how organizations operate. This lowered productivity is a symptom of companies struggling to adapt. While new technology and tools proliferate and are incessant, we are still doing work the traditional way. We need to adopt the seven practices in this book to make productivity skyrocket.

Lagging productivity and employee engagement are not problems; they are symptoms of a fundamental change in business. The way we add value has changed. Companies no longer add value through scale and efficiency; they add value through innovation, invention, and service. This means we have to run companies differently.

As I've discovered in my travels around the world, high-performing companies organize, manage, and structure themselves differently. In embracing these changes, we will see productivity (and engagement and happiness) go up in ways we've never seen before—provided we undertake the seven innovations detailed in this book.

ENGAGEMENT

Human resources managers use the term "engagement" to define how well our companies operate. According to many sources, typically around one-third of employees are fully engaged at work. Gallup, the polling organization that developed the first employee-engagement survey, just released its 2021 findings and found that engagement increased to 39 percent, up from 36 percent in late 2020.[284]

We're going in the right direction overall, but while many companies are well above average, many are well below. Irresistible companies, I've learned over the years, generally rank at the top of engagement surveys. The only pattern I've seen among these companies is the quality and focus of their management. They are focused on their people, they understand that people are their product, and they continuously invest, re-engineer, and focus on management practices that empower people.

The engagement industry is a billion-dollar marketplace of consultants, tools, books, workshops, and events focused on this topic. In fact, the terms "organizational culture" and "employee engagement" have become such catchphrases that companies can compete in dozens of nationwide companies for a best-place-to-work title.

Engagement is a good topic. But ultimately, as I've discovered, the solution is more than just conducting surveys. It requires a fundamental focus on management and people, a true understanding that each individual matters, and a plan for how to build a company around engagement goals.

Not long ago, I met with the senior executives at Genentech, which rates as one of the most engaged and irresistible places to work. The CEO of Genentech believes so strongly in people, he tells his scientists and staff that "mission trumps profits" and that if you're not helping make society healthier, you're not working on the right thing.[285] Genentech is doing everything in its power to remove complexity, increase productivity, and elevate the employee experience. This is what irresistible companies do.

Irresistible companies, which are growing far faster than their peers, have a unique ability to focus on their people first. They endure during good times and bad. This employee-first focus will become clear and actionable as you read the seven innovations in this book.

HAPPINESS

Happiness is the essential human mood that brings us to work ready to help, contribute, and innovate. This measure is plummeting at an alarming rate.

Funded by the Organisation for Economic Co-operation and Development, the *World Happiness Report* looks at data from more than 100 countries. In 2020, a slightly smaller number of countries were surveyed because of the pandemic, but the findings were similar: the world's happiest countries are Finland, Denmark, Switzerland, Iceland, the Netherlands, Norway, Sweden, Luxembourg, New Zealand, and Austria. The United States, which has previously ranked as the 13th happiest place in the world, slipped from 18th to 19th place in 2020.[286]

Why is this going on, and what can we as business leaders do about it? The three issues at stake here are trust, fairness, and social cohesion.

Trust is definitely down. In the 2020 Edelman Trust Index, the majority of respondents made it clear that they expect businesses to speak out against issues like systemic racism, to make products that don't harm the environment, and to help the world reduce greenhouse gases.[287] Seven in ten respondents said that trusting a brand to take such actions is more important now than in the past. We as businesspeople must ensure that our business leaders and managers heed these societal demands.

The second happiness issue is fairness. Today, income inequality is becoming a crisis. The Gini index, which describes the level of wealth disparity in a given country (a Gini of 1.0 means one person has all the wealth in society, and a Gini of 0 means everyone has exactly the same level of wealth), is skyrocketing. According to the 2021 Gini index, the gap between the richest and poorest has never been wider.[288]

Even though the employment rate continues to rise and the stock market is high, our cities are filled with unhoused people. The end of 2020 brought the sharpest rise in the U.S. poverty rate since the 1960s; one in seven Americans now has annual family resources below the poverty threshold, with 4.4 percent described by the Urban Institute as being mired in deep poverty.[289]

Many surveys of Millennials in developed economies suggest that they believe they will be "less well off" and "less happy" than their parents. They see property prices going up as wages stay flat, and they take gig jobs to make more money. They believe the world has become unfair. We can certainly address this in our management practices, but this is why diversity, inclusion, pay equity, and transparency have become paramount.

The third issue is social cohesion. As Robert D. Putnam discusses in his iconic book *Bowling Alone*, we live in larger homes, are more separated from our neighbors, and are spending more time on our cell phones. We have fewer friends, and we don't have as many close relationships.[290]

I'm not going to turn this book into a political manifesto, but I will tell you this: we, as business leaders, can and must fix this. We can create a sense of trust in our companies and a sense of social cohesion if we just manage our companies better.

appendix 2: finding irresistible companies using data

The research for this book came from hundreds of research studies, interviews, and case studies we performed at The Josh Bersin Company and Bersin by Deloitte (previously Bersin & Associates). In each of these studies, we look at a wide variety of management and HR practices and correlate them to business outcomes, essentially uncovering the secrets that drive success.

In addition to this kind of research, I have also done extensive analysis of the Glassdoor database. Glassdoor collects millions of employee ratings for tens of thousands of companies, asking employees to rate their companies overall and in the areas of culture, leadership, pay, work-life balance, career opportunities, and equity. I analyzed this database in detail and looked at the nature of high-performing companies and the relationship between these factors.

The findings are very important. First, highly rated companies (what I call irresistible companies) can be found in any industry, at any size, and at any age. In every segment (industry, company size, age), there are a handful of companies that far outperform their peers. Many of these companies are not well known, but they are long-lasting, sustainable, enduring organizations.

Second, highly rated companies (Glassdoor ratings above 4.3) are also very highly rated in culture, leadership, and career growth. In fact, these factors are three times more important than pay or benefits in predicting the company's overall ratings. So, using the data, we can see that growth, empowerment, and trust are predictors of performance.

Third, in almost every industry and company-size group there is a bell curve, or normal distribution, of ratings. In other words, there is no "best industry" or "best size" for a company; success does not depend on these factors. One may expect, for example, that technology companies or small companies are always rated the highest. This is not true. The statistics show a normal distribution in almost every dimension you analyze.

The Glassdoor research also finds that business outlook (growth) is directly related to most of the measures of employee engagement. This is both a cause and effect: these highly engaged companies attract high performers, they retain their people, they can more easily adapt and move people from role to role, and the energy and enthusiasm of their employees translates directly to an improved customer experience.

Overall, this research points out something profound: the most important factor in irresistible companies is their *management*. Great leaders and managers can create great organizations in any industry, of any size, and in any location.

In this book, I tried to meet with, talk with, or get to know all the irresistible companies I could find, and you will see many of them in examples throughout the book. You will also see how these companies consistently manage their businesses in a people-centric way year after year. They understand the seven secrets, and they practice them in a variety of ways.

endnotes

1   *Morality: Restoring the Common Good in Divided Times*, Jonathan Sacks /
     Basic Books, September 2020.

2   "Why you will probably live longer than most big companies," IMD /
     Stéphane Garelli, December 2016, www.imd.org/research-knowledge/
     articles/why-you-will-probably-live-longer-than-most-big-companies/.

3   Authors like Isabel Wilkerson in *Caste: The Origins of Our Discontents*
     (Random House, August 2020) argue that all forms of discrimination are
     driven by our need to put people down and create hierarchy. So, one could
     almost argue that hierarchy is a human weakness.

4   "Institutional innovation," Deloitte LLP / John Hagel III and John Seely
     Brown, March 13, 2013, https://www2.deloitte.com/us/en/insights/topics/
     innovation/institutional-innovation.html.

5   Interview with Janice Semper, Boston Consulting Group, 2019.

6   "The power of number 4.6," *Fortune* / Jia Lynn Yang, June 8,
     2006, http://archive.fortune.com/magazines/fortune/fortune_
     archive/2006/06/12/8379238/index.htm.

7   "Introduction: The social enterprise in a world disrupted," in *2021 Global
     Human Capital Trends*, Deloitte LLP / Erica Volini et al., 2021, https://www2.
     deloitte.com/global/en/insights/focus/human-capital-trends/2021/social-
     enterprise-survive-to-thrive.html.

8   "PepsiCo improves onboarding with Appical app," *Employee Benefit News (EBN)* / Phil Albinus, February 14, 2018, www.benefitnews.com/news/pepsico-improves-onboarding-with-appical-app.

9   "Neocortex size as a constraint on group size in primates," *Journal of Human Evolution* / R.I.M. Dunbar, December 2, 1991, www.sciencedirect.com/science/article/abs/pii/004724849290008J?via%3Dihub.

10   Proprietary interviews, 2016, 2018.

11   "Atlassian Team Playbook: Building strong teams with Plays," Atlassian / www.atlassian.com/team-playbook.

12   *Simply Irresistible*, The Josh Bersin Company, 2019.

13   "How the Ritz-Carlton Creates a 5 Star Customer Experience," CRM.org / Catherine Morin, December 13, 2019, https://crm.org/articles/ritz-carlton-gold-standards.

14   Interview with Jeroen Wels, Unilever, October 7, 2020.

15   Interview with Lori Goler, Meta, April 2018.

16   Interview with Barry Murphy, Airbnb, 2017.

17   Interview with Dom Price, Atlassian, 2018.

18   *The Mythical Man-Month: Essays on Software Engineering*, Fred Brooks / Addison-Wesley, 1975.

19   "To agility and beyond: The history—and legacy—of agile development," TechBeacon / Peter Varhol, https://techbeacon.com/app-dev-testing/agility-beyond-history-legacy-agile-development.

20   "Manifesto for Agile Software Development," Manifesto for Agile Software Development / Ward Cunningham, 2001, https://agilemanifesto.org.

21   Interviews with Joe Militello, Pivotal, 2017, 2018.

22   *The Lean Startup: How Today's Entrepreneurs Use Continuous Innovation to Create Radically Successful Businesses*, Eric Ries / Currency, September 13, 2011.

23   Interviews with GE digital HR team, 2016, 2017.

24   *Drive: The Surprising Truth about What Motivates Us*, Daniel H. Pink / Riverhead Books, April 5, 2011.

25   "The Progress Principle: Using Small Wins to Ignite Joy, Engagement, and Creativity at Work," Teresa Amabile / Harvard Business Review Press, http://progressprinciple.com/books/single/the_progress_principle.

26   "Great managers still matter: The evolution of Google's Project Oxygen," re:Work with Google / Melissa Harrell and Lauren Barbato, February 27, 2018, https://rework.withgoogle.com/blog/the-evolution-of-project-oxygen/.

27   "Google's Project Oxygen Pumps Fresh Air into Management," TheStreet / Brad Hall, February 11, 2014, www.thestreet.com/story/12328981/1/googles-project-oxygen-pumps-fresh-air-into-management.html.

28   "Google's Optimal Teaming Mapped to Safety, Belonging, Mattering," SmartTribes Institute / 2017, https://smarttribesinstitute.com/wp-content/uploads/Googles-Optimal-Teaming-Mapped-to-Safety-1.pdf.

29   "Developmental sequence in small groups," *Psychological Bulletin* / Bruce Tuckman, 1965, https://content.apa.org/record/1965-12187-001.

30   Interviews with Michael Arena, General Motors (GM), 2016, 2017, 2018.

31   "The Risky Business of Hiring Stars," *Harvard Business Review* / Boris Groysberg, Ashish Nanda, and Nitin Nohria, May 2004, https://hbr.org/2004/05/the-risky-business-of-hiring-stars.

32   "Amazon's Innovation Secret — The Future Press Release," The Amazon Way / John Rossman, March 15, 2015, http://the-amazon-way.com/blog/amazon-future-press-release/.

33   *The new shape of work is flexibility for all*, Mercer LLC / Lauren Mason, Kelly O'Rourke, Mary Ann Sardone, and Kate Bravery, 2020, www.mercer.us/content/dam/mercer/attachments/private/us-2020-flexing-for-the-future.pdf.

34   "What 12,000 Employees Have to Say about the Future of Remote Work," Boston Consulting Group / Adriana Dahik et al., August 11, 2020, www.bcg.com/publications/2020/valuable-productivity-gains-covid-19.

35   "How the Coronavirus Outbreak Has and Hasn't Changed the Way Americans Work," Pew Research Center / Kim Parker, Juliana Menasce Horowitz, and Rachel Minkin, December 9, 2020, www.pewresearch.org/social-trends/2020/12/09/how-the-coronavirus-outbreak-has-and-hasnt-changed-the-way-americans-work/.

36   "New Research Shows That Flexible Working Is Now a Top Consideration
      in the War for Talent," International Workplace Group (IWG) / IWG,
      May 12, 2019, www.prnewswire.com/news-releases/new-research-shows-
      that-flexible-working-is-now-a-top-consideration-in-the-war-for-
      talent-300818790.html.

37   Interview with Sachin Jain, PepsiCo, May 2020.

38   "More than half of employees globally would quit their jobs if not provided
      post-pandemic flexibility," EY / May 12, 2021, www.ey.com/en_us/
      news/2021/05/more-than-half-of-employees-globally-would-quit-their-jobs-
      if-not-provided-post-pandemic-flexibility-ey-survey-finds.

39   Interview with Alex Badenoch, Telstra, August 11, 2020.

40   "Embracing a Flexible Workplace," Official Microsoft Blog / Kathleen
      Hogan, October 9, 2020, https://blogs.microsoft.com/blog/2020/10/09/
      embracing-a-flexible-workplace/.

41   "Jeff Bezos's Productivity Tip? The '2 Pizza Rule'," Inc. / Áine Cain, June 7,
      2017, www.inc.com/business-insider/jeff-bezos-productivity-tip-two-pizza-
      rule.html.

42   "Neocortex size as a constraint on group size in primates," *Journal of Human
      Evolution* / R.I.M. Dunbar, December 2, 1991, https://www.sciencedirect.
      com/science/article/abs/pii/004724849290081J?via%3Dihub.

43   *The Silo Effect: The Peril of Expertise and the Promise of Breaking Down Barriers*,
      Gillian Tett / Simon & Schuster, September 1, 2015.

44   *Adaptive Space: How GM and Other Companies Are Positively Disrupting
      Themselves and Transforming into Agile Organizations*, Michael Arena /
      McGraw Hill Education, 2018.

45   Interview with Michael Arena, GM, September 22, 2020.

46   Interviews with Dell HR leaders, 2010, 2017, 2018, 2020.

47   "Redesign Not Downsize," *Online Journal of Issues in Nursing* / Sharon
      Coulter, January 6, 1997, www.nursingworld.org/MainMenuCategories/
      ANAMarketplace/ANAPeriodicals/OJIN/TableofContents/Vol21997/
      No1Jan97/Redesign.html.

48   "Discover the Spotify model," Atlassian / Mark Cruth, www.atlassian.com/
      agile/agile-at-scale/spotify.

49   "Spotify Engineering Model with Squads, Tribes, Chapters and Guilds,"
      Growly.io / Emilia Barska, March 8, 2017, www.growly.io/spotify-
      engineering-model-with-squads-tribes-chapters-and-guilds/.

50   "ANZ blows up bureaucracy as Shayne Elliott takes the bank agile," The
      Australian Financial Review / Joanne Gray, May 1, 2017, www.afr.com/
      companies/financial-services/anz-blows-up-bureaucracy-as-shayne-elliott-
      takes-the-bank-agile-20170428-gvumc2.

51   "Embracing Agile," *Harvard Business Review* / Darrell Rigby, Jeff Sutherland,
      and Hirotaka Takeuchi, May 2016, https://hbr.org/2016/05/embracing-agile.

52   Interview with Alex Badenoch, Telstra, March 2020.

53   Interview with Lori Goler, Meta, 2017, 2018.

54   Interview with Amelia Gandara, General Electric, 2018.

55   "Number of freelance workers in the United States from 2014 to
      2020," Statista / May 11, 2021, www.statista.com/statistics/685468/
      amount-of-people-freelancing-us/.

56   *2018 Deloitte Millennial Survey*, Deloitte LLP / 2018, https://www2.deloitte.
      com/content/dam/Deloitte/global/Documents/About-Deloitte/gx-2018-
      millennial-survey-report.pdf.

57   "The gig economy in 2021: Strategies for recruiting temporary workers,"
      Monster / December 2020, https://hiring.monster.ca/employer-resources/
      recruiting-strategies/the-gig-economy-in-2021-new-strategies-for-
      recruiting-temporary-workers/.

58   "P&G, Google swap workers for research," *Silicon Valley Business Journal*
      / November 20, 2008, www.bizjournals.com/sanjose/stories/2008/11/17/
      daily51.html.

59   *2017 Global Human Capital Trends*, Deloitte LLP / 2017, https://www2.
      deloitte.com/us/en/insights/focus/human-capital-trends/2017.html; *2018
      Global Human Capital Trends*, Deloitte LLP / 2019, https://www2.deloitte.
      com/us/en/insights/focus/human-capital-trends/2018.html.

60   Interview with Tracy Keogh, Hewlett Packard Enterprise, 2019.

61   "Dave Ulrich," Stephen M. Ross School of Business, University of Michigan /
      https://michiganross.umich.edu/faculty-research/faculty/dave-ulrich.

62   "Rating the Management Gurus," *Bloomberg Businessweek* / October 14, 2001, www.bloomberg.com/news/articles/2001-10-14/rating-the-management-gurus.

63   Interview with Jeroen Wels, Unilever, 2020.

64   "What's Trending in Jobs and Skills," Boston Consulting Group / Rainer Strack et al., September 12, 2019, www.bcg.com/publications/2019/what-is-trending-jobs-skills.

65   "Hybrid Jobs," Burning Glass Technologies / 2019, www.burning-glass.com/research-project/hybrid-jobs/.

66   Interview with Jeroen Wels, Unilever, 2021.

67   "Zappos Killed the Job Posting – Should You?," *Harvard Business Review* / John Boudreau, May 28, 2014, https://hbr.org/2014/05/zappos-killed-the-job-posting-should-you.

68   "Introduction: The social enterprise in a world disrupted," in *2021 Global Human Capital Trends*, Deloitte LLP / Erica Volini et al., December 9, 2020, https://www2.deloitte.com/us/en/insights/focus/human-capital-trends/2021/social-enterprise-survive-to-thrive.html.

69   *The Definitive Guide: Employee Experience*, The Josh Bersin Company, 2021.

70   "Four ways to include 'gig workers' in your company culture," Lattice / Andy Przystanski, February 10, 2020, https://lattice.com/library/4-ways-to-include-gig-workers-in-your-company-culture.

71   The Josh Bersin Company research on leadership and development best practices, November 2021.

72   "Z-Work is a new SPAC with an unusual target: gig workers," *Fortune* / Shawn Tully, February 15, 2021, https://fortune.com/2021/02/15/spacs-z-work-gig-economy-startups-work-from-home/.

73   "Skills of the Future: Building Professional Development in a Flexible Workplace," Betterworks / March 25, 2021, www.betterworks.com/skills-of-the-future-building-professional-development-in-a-flexible-workplace/.

74   "2019 Population Estimates by Age, Sex, Race and Hispanic Origin," U.S. Census Bureau / June 25, 2020, www.census.gov/newsroom/press-kits/2020/population-estimates-detailed.html.

75   "The Age Premium: Retaining Older Workers," *New York Times* / Steven Greenhouse, May 14, 2014, www.nytimes.com/2014/05/15/business/retirementspecial/the-age-premium-retaining-older-workers.html.

76   "How BMW Deals with an Aging Workforce," CBS News / Richard Roth, September 5, 2010, www.cbsnews.com/news/how-bmw-deals-with-an-aging-workforce/.

77   "Only skin deep? Re-examining the business case for diversity," Deloitte LLP / September 2011, www.ced.org/pdf/Deloitte_-_Only_Skin_Deep.pdf.

78   "The Best Job Candidates Don't Always Have College Degrees," *The Atlantic* / Bourree Lam, September 24, 2015, www.theatlantic.com/business/archive/2015/09/ernest-young-degree-recruitment-hiring-credentialism/406576/.

79   *The Science of Fit*, Bersin by Deloitte / Josh Bersin, 2014.

80   Proprietary interview, 2017.

81   "Facebook's head of recruiting explains the company's top 3 approaches to finding exceptional employees," *Business Insider* / Richard Feloni, February 17, 2016, www.businessinsider.com/how-facebook-finds-exceptional-employees-2016-2.

82   Interview with Leena Nair, Unilever, 2017.

83   "Credit Analytics Case Study: The Bon-Ton Stores, Inc," S&P Global / Jim Elder and Elijah Harden, July 24, 2018, www.spglobal.com/marketintelligence/en/news-insights/blog/credit-analytics-case-study-the-bon-ton-stores-inc.

84   *The Science of Fit*, Bersin by Deloitte / Josh Bersin, 2014.

85   *The Science of Fit*, Bersin by Deloitte.

86   "Southwest Airlines Is Dead Serious about Employee Fun," Eric Chester / Eric Chester, October 31, 2017, https://ericchester.com/southwest-airlines-is-dead-serious-about-employee-fun/.

87   "When Goal Setting Goes Bad," Harvard Business School / Sean Silverthorne, March 2, 2009, https://hbswk.hbs.edu/item/when-goal-setting-goes-bad.

88   "Wells Fargo's 17-month nightmare," CNN Business / Jackie Wattles, Ben Geier, and Matt Egan, February 5, 2018, https://money.cnn.com/2018/02/05/news/companies/wells-fargo-timeline/index.html.

89 "The Five Elements Of A 'Simply Irresistible' Organization," Forbes.com / Josh Bersin, April 4, 2014, www.forbes.com/sites/joshbersin/2014/04/04/the-five-elements-of-a-simply-irresistible-organization/?sh=31aec36d51b1.

90 "A Formula for Perfect Productivity: Work for 52 Minutes, Break for 17," *The Atlantic* / Derek Thompson, September 17, 2014, www.theatlantic.com/business/archive/2014/09/science-tells-you-how-many-minutes-should-you-take-a-break-for-work-17/380369/.

91 *The Good Jobs Strategy: How the Smartest Companies Invest in Employees to Lower Costs and Boost Profits*, Zeynep Ton / New Harvest, January 14, 2014.

92 *Business Resilience: The Global COVID-19 Pandemic Response Study*, The Josh Bersin Company, 2020.

93 Interviews with executives, Anheuser-Busch, 2020.

94 "2020 Training Industry Report," *Training* / Lori Freifeld, November 17, 2020, https://trainingmag.com/2020-training-industry-report/.

95 *Case Study: Visa Enables a Culture of Learning in the Face of Industry Disruption*, Bersin by Deloitte / Jeff Mike and Emily Sanders, 2018.

96 Interviews with employees, Cummins, 2017.

97 Interview with Maria Neuhold, Erste Group, 2019.

98 Interview with senior vice president of HR, Cisco, 2016.

99 *What Makes a Great CEO?*, Glassdoor / Andrew Chamberlain and Ruoyan Huang, August 2016, www.glassdoor.com/research/app/uploads/sites/2/2016/08/FULL-STUDY_WhatMakesGreatCEO_Glassdoor-2.pdf.

100 "Quotations from Chairman Powell: A Leadership Primer," GovLeaders.org / Oren Harari, 1996, https://govleaders.org/powell.htm.

101 Proprietary interview, 2017.

102 *Jack Welch & The G.E. Way: Management Insights and Leadership Secrets of the Legendary CEO*, Robert Slater / McGraw-Hill, July 31, 1998.

103 *High-Impact Performance Management*, Bersin & Associates / 2006.

104 *High-Impact Performance Management*, Bersin by Deloitte / 2015.

105 Interview with Edgar Schein, 2017.

106   *Work Rules! Insights from inside Google That Will Transform How You Live and Lead*, Laszlo Bock / Twelve Books, April 1, 2015.

107   "Using a Pulse Survey Approach to Drive Organizational Change," *Organization Development Review* / Julian Allen, Sachin Jain, and Allan H. Church, October 2020, www.researchgate.net/publication/344785639_ Using_a_Pulse_Survey_Approach_to_Drive_Organizational_Change.

108   "IBM Is Blowing Up Its Annual Performance Review," *Fortune* / Claire Zillman, February 1, 2016, http://fortune.com/2016/02/01/ ibm-employee-performance-reviews/.

109   "How Millennials Forced GE to Scrap Performance Reviews," *The Atlantic* / Max Nisen, August 18, 2015, www.theatlantic.com/politics/archive/2015/08/ how-millennials-forced-ge-to-scrap-performance-reviews/432585/.

110   "$26.7 Billion Growth in Corporate Leadership Training Market 2020- 2024 | Includes Insights on Key Products Offered by Major Vendors | Technavio," Cision / Technavio, March 4, 2021, www.prnewswire.com/ news-releases/-26-7-billion-growth-in-corporate-leadership-training- market-2020-2024--includes-insights-on-key-products-offered-by-major- vendors--technavio-301240344.html.

111   "The New Best-Practices of a High-Impact Learning Organization," The Josh Bersin Company, September 3, 2012.

112   "Classic Performance Management System A Barrier to Disruptive Innovation," Juniper Networks / 2012, https://cdn2.hubspot.net/ hubfs/3820722/Downloads/CEB%20Juniper%20Case%20Profile.pdf.

113   Interview with P.V. Ramana Murthy, Indian Hotels Company Limited, September 20, 2020.

114   "Donna Morris, Senior Vice President of Global People and Places, Adobe," SHRM / www.shrm.org/hr-today/news/hr-magazine/pages/donna-morris- senior-vice-president-of-global-people-and-places-adobe.aspx.

115   Proprietary interviews.

116   *High-Impact Total Rewards*, Bersin by Deloitte / Pete DeBellis and Anna Steinhage, 2018.

117   *environmental + social initiatives,* Patagonia / 2015, www.patagonia.com/on/ demandware.static/Sites-patagonia-us-Site/Library-Sites-PatagoniaShared/ en_US/PDF-US/patagonia-enviro-initiatives-2015.pdf.

118   *2021 Global Human Capital Trends*, Deloitte LLP / Erica Volini et al., December 9, 2020, https://www2.deloitte.com/us/en/insights/focus/human-capital-trends/2021.html.

119   *Engagement and the Global Workplace*, Steelcase / 2016, https://info.steelcase.com/global-employee-engagement-workplace-comparison?hsCtaTracking=1fbd9f96-e99e-40b0-b2cc-22c61ab752cc%7C804cc58f-5e34-4793-9bb2-49272c845f1d#compare-about-the-report.

120   "How the Coronavirus Outbreak Has – and Hasn't – Changed the Way Americans Work," Pew Research Center / Kim Parker, Juliana Menasce Horowitz, and Rachel Minkin, December 9, 2020, www.pewresearch.org/social-trends/2020/12/09/how-the-coronavirus-outbreak-has-and-hasnt-changed-the-way-americans-work/.

121   Interview with Joe Whittinghill, Microsoft, 2021.

122   "The hybrid office is here to stay. The shift could be more disruptive than the move to all-remote work.," *The Washington Post* / Jena McGregor, March 30, 2021, www.washingtonpost.com/business/2021/03/30/hybrid-office-remote-work-citigroup-ford-target/.

123   *The Definitive Guide: Employee Experience*, The Josh Bersin Company, September 2021.

124   *The Definitive Guide: Employee Experience*, The Josh Bersin Company.

125   *2021 Global Human Capital Trends*, Deloitte LLP.

126   "Wellbeing," LinkedIn search / April 2021, www.linkedin.com/jobs/search/?currentJobId=2493155972&keywords=wellbeing.

127   Human Performance Institute / Johnson & Johnson, www.humanperformanceinstitute.com.

128   "Making Distance Work," Steelcase / www.steelcase.com/research/remote-work-making-distance-work/.

129   "Navigating What's Next: The Post-COVID Workplace," Steelcase / April 2020, https://info.steelcase.com/hubfs/Steelcase_ThePostCOVIDWorkplace.pdf.

130   "Deloitte Canada's New National Office Redefines 'Work' for Employees and Clients," GlobeNewswire / Deloitte LLP, October 5, 2016, www.globenewswire.com/fr/news-release/2016/10/05/1085138/0/en/Deloitte-Canada-s-New-National-Office-Redefines-Work-for-Employees-and-Clients.html.

131 "Deloitte Canada's New National Office Redefines 'Work' for Employees and Clients," GlobeNewswire.

132 *Adaptive Space: How GM and Other Companies Are Positively Disrupting Themselves and Transforming into Agile Organizations*, Michael J. Arena / McGraw-Hill Education, June 12, 2018.

133 "Current Understandings of Microaggressions: Impacts on Individuals and Society," Association for Psychological Science / September 13, 2021, www.psychologicalscience.org/news/releases/2021-sept-microaggressions.html.

134 "How To Shut Down 'Microaggressions' At Work," Fast Company / Lydia Dishman, March 7, 2017, www.fastcompany.com/3068670/how-to-shut-down-microagressions-at-work.

135 "Salesforce just spent another $3 million to close its pay gap," CNN Business / Julia Horowitz, April 4, 2017, money.cnn.com/2017/04/04/news/companies/salesforce-equal-pay-women/index.html.

136 *Waiter, is that inclusion in my soup?* Deloitte LLP / May 2013, https://www2.deloitte.com/content/dam/Deloitte/au/Documents/human-capital/deloitte-au-hc-diversity-inclusion-soup-0513.pdf.

137 *Elevating Equity and Diversity: The Challenge Of The Decade*, Bersin & Associates / Josh Bersin, February 11, 2011.

138 *Firms of Endearment: How World-Class Companies Profit from Passion and Purpose, Second Edition*, Rajendra Sisodia, David Wolfe, and Jagdish Sheth / Pearson FT Press, January 17, 2014.

139 "Fighting Workplace Discrimination: A Commitment to Building Businesses Beyond Bias," SAP / Jill Popelka, July 16, 2020, https://news.sap.com/2020/07/fighting-workplace-discrimination-a-commitment-to-building-business-beyond-bias/.

140 "Diversity and Inclusion," SAP / www.sap.com/africa/about/company/diversity.html.

141 "Diversity Training Doesn't Work," *Harvard Business Review* / Peter Bregman, March 12, 2012, https://hbr.org/2012/03/diversity-training-doesnt-work.

142 "Diversity Management in Corporate America," *Contexts* / Frank Dobbin, Alexandra Kalev, and Erin Kelly, Fall 2007, https://scholar.harvard.edu/dobbin/files/2007_contexts_dobbin_kalev_kelly.pdf.

143 "enabling human progress," Chevron / www.chevron.com/sustainability/ social/diversity-inclusion.

144 "our purpose & history," Target / https://corporate.target.com/about/ purpose-history.

145 "A Business and Its Beliefs," IBM / Sam Palmisano, www.ibm.com/ibm/ history/ibm100/us/en/icons/bizbeliefs/.

146 "All You Need Is Love, Gratitude, and Oxytocin," *Greater Good Magazine* / Lauren Klein, February 11, 2014, https://greatergood.berkeley.edu/article/ item/love_gratitude_oxytocin.

147 "InnovationJam," IBM / www.collaborationjam.com.

148 "To Thrive in Hybrid Work, Build a Culture of Trust and Flexibility," Microsoft / September 9, 2021, www.microsoft.com/en-us/worklab/ work-trend-index/support-flexibility-in-work-styles.

149 Interview with Dawn Klinghoffer, Microsoft, 2021.

150 *Work Rules! Insights from inside Google That Will Transform How You Live and Lead*, Laszlo Bock / Twelve Books, April 1, 2015.

151 "Survey: Fewer than 4 in 10 Americans could pay a surprise $1,000 bill from savings," Bankrate.com / Jeff Ostrowski, January 11, 2021, www.bankrate.com /banking/savings/financial-security-january-2021/.

152 "Average Credit Card Debt in America: 2021," ValuePenguin / Joe Resendiz, July 9, 2021, www.valuepenguin.com/average-credit-card-debt.

153 "More than half of older millennials with student debt say their loans weren't worth it," CNBC Make It / Abigail Johnson Hess, April 8, 2021, www.cnbc.com/2021/04/08/older-millennials-with-student-debt-say-their-loans-werent-worth-it.html.

154 *Insights from IMPACT 2018*, Bersin by Deloitte / Bersin Insights Team, 2018.

155 "enabling human progress," Chevron / www.chevron.com/sustainability/ social/diversity-inclusion.

156 "Anka Wittenberg," Convening Leaders PCMA / https://conveningleaders. org/anka-wittenberg/.

157   "Women in Leadership at SAP: The Journey to 25%," SAP / Sue Sutton,
       July 21, 2017, https://news.sap.com/2017/07/women-leadership-sap-
       journey-to-twenty-five-percent/.

158   "Autism at Work Program," SAP / www.sap.com/about/careers/your-career/
       autism-at-work-program.html.

159   "The Smartest Building in the World," Bloomberg Businessweek / Tom
       Randall, September 23, 2015, www.bloomberg.com/features/2015-the-
       edge-the-worlds-greenest-building/.

160   The Josh Bersin Company research on pay equity, 2020, 2021.

161   "Cayenne pepper ginger shots, homemade lemon tarts, and Michelin-starred
       chefs — here's what employees at Silicon Valley's biggest tech companies
       are offered for free," *Business Insider* / Katie Canales, July 31, 2018,
       www.businessinsider.com/free-food-silicon-valley-tech-employees-apple-
       google-facebook-2018-7#salesforce-intentionally-didnt-build-a-cafeteria-in-
       its-new-tower-but-it-does-have-some-free-snacks-8.

162   "A Day in the Life of a Pivotal Engineer," VMware / Bebe Peng,
       March 20, 2018, https://tanzu.vmware.com/content/blog/a-day-in-the-
       life-of-a-pivotal-engineer.

163   "Employee Benefits Survey," U.S. Bureau of Labor Statistics / September 23,
       2021, www.bls.gov/ncs/ebs/factsheet/paid-vacations.htm.

164   "Americans Waste 662 Million Vacation Days at Work," American
       Automobile Association / January 16, 2018, www.projecttimeoff.com/issue.

165   "Turn Your Career Into A Vacation | Jay Jay Maniquis (Jaycation) | DH113,"
       Digital Hospitality Podcast / Cali BBQ, September 9, 2021, https://calibbq.
       media/jaycation-career-interview-jay-jay-maniquis-dh113/.

166   "Turn Your Career Into A Vacation | Jay Jay Maniquis (Jaycation) | DH113,"
       Digital Hospitality Podcast.

167   "A company that profits as it pampers workers," *The Washington Post* / Brigid
       Schulte, October 25, 2014, www.washingtonpost.com/business/a-company-
       that-profits-as-it-pampers-workers/2014/10/22/d3321b34-4818-11e4-b72e-
       d60a9229cc10_story.html.

168   "How to squeeze those steps into busy days," Aetna / www.aetna.com/
       microsites/attainbyaetna/articles-attain/how-to-squeeze-those-steps-into-
       busy-days.html.

169   *Work Rules! Insights from inside Google That Will Transform How You Live and Lead*, Laszlo Bock / Twelve Books, April 1, 2015.

170   "6 Dog-Friendly Companies to Work For," *Dogster* / Sassafras Lowrey, February 26, 2018, www.dogster.com/lifestyle/dog-friendly-companies-to-work-for.

171   "The government's 'karoshi' report," *The Japan Times* / October 12, 2016, www.japantimes.co.jp/opinion/2016/10/12/editorials/governments-karoshi-report/#.WZ3yJz6GPRY.

172   Interview with Alex Badenoch, Telstra, 2021.

173   "Hybrid Jobs," Burning Glass Technologies / 2021, www.burning-glass.com/research-project/hybrid-jobs/.

174   *2019 Workplace Learning Report*, LinkedIn Learning / 2019, https://learning.linkedin.com/content/dam/me/business/en-us/amp/learning-solutions/images/workplace-learning-report-2019/pdf/workplace-learning-report-2019.pdf.

175   *2018 Workplace Learning Report*, LinkedIn Learning / 2018, https://learning.linkedin.com/resources/workplace-learning-report-2018.

176   *2021 Workplace Learning Report*, LinkedIn Learning / 2021, https://learning.linkedin.com/resources/workplace-learning-report.

177   "Amid the pandemic, a rising share of older U.S. adults are now retired," Pew Research Center / Richard Fry, November 4, 2021, www.pewresearch.org/fact-tank/2021/11/04/amid-the-pandemic-a-rising-share-of-older-u-s-adults-are-now-retired.

178   "The Connection Between Retiring Early and Living Longer," *The New York Times* / Austin Frakt, January 29, 2018, www.nytimes.com/2018/01/29/upshot/early-retirement-longevity-health-wellness.html.

179   "Tackling loneliness in retirement," *The Times of India* / Ashutosh Garg, July 17, 2019, https://timesofindia.indiatimes.com/blogs/the-brand-called-you/tackling-loneliness-in-retirement/.

180   "Corporate Training Market to Reach $417.21 Billion, Globally, by 2027 at 9.4% CAGR: Allied Market Research," Cision / Allied Market Research, December 8, 2020, www.prnewswire.com/news-releases/corporate-training-market-to-reach-417-21-billion-globally-by-2027-at-9-4-cagr-allied-market-research-301188115.html.

181 "Farmers Insurance piloting human-like VR training," Institute for Immersive Learning / April 7, 2020, www.immersivelearning.news/2020/04/07/farmers-insurance-piloting-human-like-vr-training/

182 "Walmart Revolutionizes Its Training with Virtual Reality," SHRM / Nicole Lewis, July 22, 2019, www.shrm.org/resourcesandtools/hr-topics/technology/pages/virtual-reality-revolutionizes-walmart-training.aspx

183 "How HP is Transforming Learning with Brain Candy," Human Capital Institute (HCI) / Francine Rosca and Mike Jordan, www.hci.org/session/how-hp-transforming-learning-brain-candy.

184 *The Hybrid Job Economy: How New Skills Are Rewriting the DNA of the Job Market*, Burning Glass Technologies / Matthew Sigelman, Scott Bittle, Will Markow, and Benjamin Francis, January 2019, www.burning-glass.com/research-project/hybrid-jobs/.

185 *The Enterprise Learning Framework*, Bersin by Deloitte / 2017.

186 "AT&T's Talent Overhaul," *Harvard Business Review* / John Donovan and Cathy Benko, October 2016, https://hbr.org/2016/10/atts-talent-overhaul.

187 Interview with Frank Anderson, Defense Acquisition University, 1998.

188 Interview with Jenny Dearborn, SAP, 2017, 2018.

189 "Interview: Microsoft's HR chief on the company's changing culture and new 'growth mindset,'" GeekWire / Todd Bishop, June 25, 2015, www.geekwire.com/2015/interview-microsofts-hr-chief-on-the-companys-changing-culture-and-new-growth-mindset/.

190 "Exclusive: Satya Nadella reveals Microsoft's new mission statement, sees 'tough choices' ahead," GeekWire / Todd Bishop, June 25, 2015, www.geekwire.com/2015/exclusive-satya-nadella-reveals-microsofts-new-mission-statement-sees-more-tough-choices-ahead/.

191 Interview with Satya Nadella, Microsoft, 2020.

192 *High-Impact Learning Culture*, Bersin by Deloitte / Josh Bersin, 2016.

193 "Why Jeff Bezos says Amazon is 'the best place in the world to fail,'" *The Washington Post* / Jena McGregor, April 6, 2016, www.washingtonpost.com/news/on-leadership/wp/2016/04/06/why-jeff-bezos-says-amazon-is-the-best-place-in-the-world-to-fail/.

194 "Agility and Curiosity: Two Crucial Characteristics Found In Businesses Best Positioned To Survive the Pandemic," Momentive / September 15, 2020, www.momentive.ai/en/newsroom/agility-and-curiosity-found-in-businesses-best-positioned-to-survive-pandemic/.

195 *High-Impact Learning Culture*, Bersin by Deloitte / Josh Bersin, 2016.

196 "Hybrid Jobs," Burning Glass Technologies / 2021, www.burning-glass.com/research-project/hybrid-jobs/.

197 "New LinkedIn Research: Upskill Your Employees with the Skills Companies Need Most in 2020," LinkedIn Learning / Amanda Van Nuys, December 28, 2019, www.linkedin.com/business/learning/blog/learning-and-development/most-in-demand-skills-2020.

198 "Census Bureau's 2018 County Business Patterns Provides Data on Over 1,200 Industries," United States Census Bureau / Earlene K. P. Dowell, October 14, 2020, www.census.gov/library/stories/2020/10/health-care-still-largest-united-states-employer.html.

199 "Nurse Salaries Rise as Demand for Their Services Soars During Covid-19 Pandemic," *The Wall Street Journal* / Melanie Evans, November 22, 2021, www.wsj.com/articles/nurse-salaries-rise-as-demand-for-their-services-soars-during-covid-19-pandemic-11637145000.

200 "The Fourth Industrial Revolution: What it means, how to respond," World Economic Forum / Klaus Schwab, January 14, 2016, www.weforum.org/agenda/2016/01/the-fourth-industrial-revolution-what-it-means-and-how-to-respond/.

201 "New Research Shows Top Soft Skills Are Requested Four Times More than Top Hard Skills," Industry Dive / America Succeeds, April 14, 2021, www.hrdive.com/press-release/20210413-new-research-shows-top-soft-skills-are-requested-four-times-more-than-top-h/.

202 Interview with James Rush, Marsh McLennan, 2015.

203 "Rethinking career paths in the digital age: Career Ladder to Lattice," NASSCOM Insights / Reema Aswani, March 12, 2020, https://community.nasscom.in/communities/talent/rethinking-career-paths-in-the-digital-age-career-ladder-to-lattice.html.

204 "Skill up for the future," Salesforce / https://trailhead.salesforce.com.

205 Interviews with Credit Suisse, MetLife, UnitedHealth Group, Allstate, and NetApp leaders, 2019, 2020, 2021.

206 "The Capability Academy: Where Corporate Training Is Going," The Josh Bersin Company, October 5, 2019.

207 "The Overwhelmed Employee," Deloitte LLP / Josh Bersin, 2018, hr.com/en/ webcasts_events/webcasts/archived_webcasts_podcasts/the-overwhelmed-employee--what-hr-should-do_jdd8w2qy.html.

208 "Top 10 Corporate Universities," Chief Learning Officer Exchange / CLN, February 26–28, https://view.ceros.com/iqpc/top-ten-corp-u/p/1.

209 "Top 10 Corporate Universities," Chief Learning Officer Exchange.

210 "40 Best Practices for Creating an Empowered Enterprise," Bersin by Deloitte / October 2017.

211 *High-Impact Learning Culture*, Bersin & Associates / Josh Bersin, September 2010, https://joshbersin.com/wp-content/uploads/2016/11/2010_ LEARNING_CULTURE.pdf.

212 "Overview," xAPI.com / https://xapi.com/overview/?utm_source =google&utm_medium=natural_search.

213 "1920 – 1929," Unilever / July 25, 2015, https://web.archive.org/ web/20150725211548/http://www.unilever.com/about/who-we-are/our-history/1920-1929.html.

214 Interviews with Leena Nair, Unilever, annual since 2014.

215 "Leena Nair on How to Build a Purpose Cycle – Then Build a Better World," Thrive Global / Leena Nair, October 19, 2017, https://thriveglobal.com/ stories/leena-nair-on-how-to-build-a-purpose-cycle-then-build-a-better-world/.

216 Interview with Leena Nair, Unilever, 2021; interview with Jeroen Wels, Unilever, 2021.

217 Interview with Jeroen Wels, Unilever, 2021.

218 Interview with BV Pradeep, Unilever, 2018.

219 *Glassdoor Workplace Trends 2021*, Glassdoor / Andrew Chamberlain, November 19, 2020, www.glassdoor.com/research/app/uploads/ sites/2/2020/11/Workplace_Trends_2021_Glassdoor_Final.pdf.

220   *Glassdoor Workplace Trends 2021*, Glassdoor.

221   Interviews with senior banking executives, 2019, 2020, 2021.

222   Interview with Kiera Fernandez, Target, 2021.

223   "About Philips Lighting," Philips / www.slc.philips.com/support/connect/ about-us.

224   *The Wealth of Nations*, Adam Smith / W. Strahan and T. Cadell, 1776.

225   "Looking ahead to 2050, Americans are pessimistic about many aspects of life in U.S.," Pew Research Center / John Gramlich, March 21, 2019, www.pewresearch.org/fact-tank/2019/03/21/looking-ahead-to-2050- americans-are-pessimistic-about-many-aspects-of-life-in-u-s/.

226   "2020 Edelman Trust Barometer," Edelman / January 19, 2020, www.edelman.com/trust/2020-trust-barometer.

227   "2020 Edelman Trust Barometer," Edelman.

228   "Our Credo," Johnson & Johnson / www.jnj.com/credo/.

229   "Our Credo," Johnson & Johnson.

230   *The Responsible Company*, George Goyder / Oxford: Blackwell, January 1, 1961.

231   "Consumer Bill of Rights," Encyclopedia.com / www.encyclopedia.com/ finance/encyclopedias-almanacs-transcripts-and-maps/consumer-bill-rights.

232   "What We Do," Ben & Jerry's Foundation / https://benandjerrysfoundation.org /about/what-we-do/.

233   "Record-breaking Black Friday Sales to Benefit the Planet," Patagonia / Rose Marcario, www.patagonia.com/stories/record-breaking-black-friday-sales- to-benefit-the-planet/story-31140.html.

234   *2021 Target Corporate Responsibility Report*, Target / August 2021, https:// corporate.target.com/corporate-responsibility/reporting-progress.

235   "citizenship," Dictionary.com / www.dictionary.com/browse/citizenship.

236   "Benjamin Graham Value Investing History," Columbia Business School / https://www8.gsb.columbia.edu/valueinvesting/about/history.

237 *Deloitte Global Millennial Survey 2020*, Deloitte LLP / 2020, www2.deloitte.com /content/dam/Deloitte/global/Documents/About-Deloitte/deloitte-2020-millennial-survey.pdf.

238 *World Happiness Report 2020*, World Happiness Report / 2020, https:// worldhappiness.report/ed/2020/.

239 "Work and Well-being during COVID-19: Impact, Inequalities, Resilience, and the Future of Work," in *World Happiness Report 2021*, World Happiness Report / March 20, 2021, https://worldhappiness.report/ed/2021/work-and-well-being-during-covid-19-impact-inequalities-resilience-and-the-future-of-work/.

240 "The History of Salesforce," Salesforce / September 2021, www.salesforce.com /news/stories/the-history-of-salesforce/.

241 "Salesforce Hits Record-Setting Milestone with $10 Billion Run Rate," Subscription Insider / Dana E. Neuts, August 29, 2017, www.subscriptioninsider.com/monetization/auto-renew-subscription/ salesforce-hits-record-setting-milestone-with-10-billion-run-rate.

242 "Salesforce Employee Reviews about 'long hours,'" Glassdoor search / www.glassdoor.com/Reviews/Salesforce-long-hours-Reviews-EI_ IE11159.0,10_KH11,21.htm.

243 Interview with head of employee experience, Salesforce, 2019.

244 "Salesforce CEO Marc Benioff: We're Erasing Our Gender Pay Gap—Again," *Fortune* / Claire Zillman, January 20, 2017, http://fortune.com/2017/01/20/ salesforce-marc-benioff-gender-pay-gap-davos/.

245 "UCSF Children's Hospital Receives $100 Million Gift From Marc and Lynne Benioff," PND by Candid / June 18, 2010, https://philanthropynewsdigest. org/news/ucsf-children-s-hospital-receives-100-million-gift-from-marc-and-lynne-benioff.

246 "2021 Best Places to Work," Glassdoor / www.glassdoor.com/Award/Best-Places-to-Work-LST_KQ0,19.htm.

247 "Glassdoor's Best Places to Work 2021 Announced: Bain & Company Wins #1," Glassdoor / Glassdoor Team, January 12, 2021, www.glassdoor.com/ employers/blog/best-places-to-work-2021/.

248 "Many companies take 90-day no-layoff pledge," *The Times of India* / Shilpa Phadnis, April 4, 2020, https://timesofindia.indiatimes.com/business/india-business/global-companies-pledge-not-to-lay-off-staff/articleshow/74976303.cms.

249 "The Case Against Layoffs: They Often Backfire," *Newsweek* / Newsweek Staff, February 4, 2010, www.newsweek.com/case-against-layoffs-they-often-backfire-75039.

250 "Companies Adjust Executive Pay Amid COVID-19," Equilar / Amit Batish, May 7, 2020, www.equilar.com/blogs/452-companies-adjust-executive-pay-amid-covid-19.html.

251 "BlackRock tops $9 trillion on record inflows," Pensions & Investments / Christine Williamson, April 19, 2021, www.pionline.com/money-management/blackrock-tops-9-trillion-record-inflows.

252 "BlackRock's Message: Contribute to Society, or Risk Losing Our Support," *New York Times* / Andrew Ross Sorkin, January 15, 2018, www.nytimes.com/2018/01/15/business/dealbook/blackrock-laurence-fink-letter.html.

253 "Larry Fink's 2021 Letter to CEOs," BlackRock / Larry Fink, 2021, www.blackrock.com/corporate/investor-relations/larry-fink-ceo-letter.

254 "Deutsche Telekom," Forbes.com / May 13, 2021, www.forbes.com/companies/deutsche-telekom/?sh=e4207496ddd1.

255 "Design thinking, digitalization, and you," Deutsche Telekom / Lisa Machnig, October 27, 2017, www.telekom.com/en/company/details/design-thinking-digitization-and-you-507370.

256 "Design Thinking in HR: Deutsch Telekom Case Study," The Josh Bersin Academy / Josh Bersin, May 9, 2021.

257 Interview with Reza Moussavian, Deutsche Telekom, November 2021.

258 "Compare Deutsche Telekom vs Telstra," Glassdoor search / Glassdoor, 2021, www.glassdoor.com/Compare/Deutsche-Telekom-vs-Telstra-EI_IE4092-E6563.htm.

259 "SAP speeds past BMW and Daimler, to be crowned the most desirable business to work for in Germany, according to LinkedIn," CNBC Make It / Alexandra Gibbs, April 3, 2019, www.cnbc.com/2019/04/03/linkedin-top-companies-to-work-for-in-germany-2019.html.

260 *Employee Experience: The Definitive Guide*, The Josh Bersin Company, 2021.

261 "August Reflections: Four Big Lessons From The Pandemic," The Josh Bersin Company, November 18, 2020.

262 Interview with Guy Martin, Autodesk, 2018.

263 Proprietary research.

264 "AI operators will play a critical role as bots redefine the workplace," VentureBeat / Albert Tomer Naveh, December 29, 2017, https://venturebeat. com/2017/12/29/ai-operators-will-play-a-critical-role-as-bots-redefine-the-workplace/.

265 "Wendy's Is Going to Install Self-Ordering Machines in 1,000 Stores," *Fortune* / Tara John, February 27, 2017, https://fortune.com/2017/02/27/wendys-self-ordering-kiosks/.

266 Interviews with executives, S&P Global, 2020.

267 "How Technology is Hijacking Your Mind — From a Magician and Google Design Ethicist," Thrive Global / Tristan Harris, May 18, 2016, https://medium.com/thrive-global/how-technology-hijacks-peoples-minds-from-a-magician-and-google-s-design-ethicist-56d62ef5edf3.

268 "Here's how many hours American workers spend on email each day," CNBC / Abigail Johnson Hess, September 22, 2019, www.cnbc.com/2019/09/22/heres-how-many-hours-american-workers-spend-on-email-each-day.html.

269 "Is your inbox making you ill? Reading work emails causes your blood pressure and heart rate to soar," *DailyMail.com* / Emma Innes, June 4, 2013, www.dailymail.co.uk/health/article-2335699/Is-inbox-making-ill-Reading-work-emails-causes-blood-pressure-heart-rate-soar.html.

270 "Texting remains a very popular means of communication, but 5G's rollout is stalled," TechRepublic / N.F. Mendoza, February 10, 2021, www.techrepublic.com /article/texting-remains-a-very-popular-means-of-communication-but-5gs-rollout-is-stalled/.

271 *Sierra-Cedar 2019–2020 HR Systems Survey White Paper, 22nd Annual Edition*, Sierra-Cedar / October 2, 2019, www.sierra-cedar.com/2019/10/02/pr-2019-hrss-white-paper-release/.

272   "UKG Unveils Life-Work Technology Vision at Annual Connections Conference," Ultimate Kronos Group (UKG) / April 30, 2021, www.ukg.com/about-us/newsroom/ukg-unveils-life-work-technology-vision-annual-connections-conference.

273   "The Massive Market Impact of Microsoft Viva," The Josh Bersin Company, August 28, 2021.

274   Interview with Reza Moussavian, Deutsche Telekom, 2021.

275   *The Definitive Guide: Employee Experience*, The Josh Bersin Company, September 2021.

276   "Which Parts Of Employee Experience Really Matter Most?," The Josh Bersin Company, November 6, 2019.

277   "Our Credo," Johnson & Johnson / www.jnj.com/credo/.

278   "The IKEA vision and values," IKEA / www.ikea.com/us/en/this-is-ikea/about-us/vision-and-business-idea-pub7767c393.

279   "HR Lessons from: Patagonia," PeopleGoal / Henry Watson, June 18, 2019, www.peoplegoal.com/blog/hr-lessons-from-patagonia.

280   Interviews with Dean Carter, Patagonia, 2016, 2017.

281   "The Progress Principle: Using Small Wins to Ignite Joy, Engagement, and Creativity at Work," Teresa Amabile / Harvard Business Review Press, http://progressprinciple.com/books/single/the_progress_principle.

282   "New Research Shows 'Heavy Learners' More Confident, Successful, and Happy at Work," LinkedIn / Josh Bersin, November 9, 2018, www.linkedin.com/pulse/want-happy-work-spend-time-learning-josh-bersin/.

283   "Global Productivity Growth Remains Weak, Extending Slowing Trend," The Conference Board / Joseph DiBlasi and Jonathan Liu, April 21, 2021, www.conference-board.org/press/global-productivity-2021#:~:text=Globally%2C%20growth%20in%20output%20per,reopening%20amid%20a%20waning%20pandemic.

284   "U.S. Employee Engagement Rises Following Wild 2020," Gallup / Jim Harter, February 26, 2021, www.gallup.com/workplace/330017/employee-engagement-rises-following-wild-2020.aspx.

285   "Can Mission Trump Earnings?," NewCo / May 22, 2018, https://shift.newco.co/can-mission-trump-earnings-a08f27c4d984.

286 "Happiness Report: World shows resilience in face of COVID-19," AP
     News / David Keyton, March 2021, https://apnews.com/article/2021-
     world-happiness-report-covid-resilience-79b5b8d1a2367e69df05ae68b5
     8aa435.

287 "2020 Edelman Trust Barometer," Edelman / January 19, 2020,
     www.edelman.com/trust/2020-trust-barometer.

288 "Income Inequality by Country 2021," World Population Review
     / 2021, https://worldpopulationreview.com/country-rankings/
     income-inequality-by-country.

289 "2021 Poverty Projections," Urban Institute / Linda Giannarelli, Laura
     Wheaton, and Katie Shantz, February 2021, www.urban.org/sites/default/
     files/publication/103656/2021-poverty-projections.pdf.

290 *Bowling Alone: The Collapse and Revival of American Community*, Robert D.
     Putnam / Touchstone Books, August 7, 2021.

index

* **Boldface** is used for figures and tables.

A

Abe, Shinzo, 136

Ability, diversity in, 132

Abundance mindset, 86

Acquisitions, 59

Acton, Lord, on power as corrupting, 102

Actuarial economics, 158

Adaptive learning, 161

Adaptive space, need for, 118–121

Adaptive Space (Arena), 121

Adobe

check-ins at, 89, 97, 99

performance management at, 87

physical space at, 118

study of work by, 192

ADP

acquisition of Global Cash Card, 60

acquisition of WorkMarket, 59

Chelsea Design Center, 120

wages at, 127

Advertising

revenue from, 190

targeting in, 55

Aetna

culture at, 107

talent production at, 92

Agile teams, 18, 24, 30, 31, 33

Agility, 9

coaches in, 39

groupings in, 13–14

models in, 13–14, 39–41, 80

principles in, 21–24, **23**

at Spotify, 80

AI-based technologies, 154. *See also* Artificial intelligence (AI)

Airbnb, 19, 88

Airline industry, levels of engagement in, 83–85

Alignment, intersection with autonomy, **37**, 37–38

Allianz

job rotation at, 149

value of internal experience, 64

Allstate

building of academies for actuarial economics, claims management, and other strategies, 158

value of internal experience, 64

Amabile, Teresa, 205

Amazon, 9, 31, 167
  bringing pets to work, 135
  development of sense of purpose, 27
  as forward-looking, 11
  need for experimentation and, 151
  teams at, 10

Amazon Web Services, 27, 121

AMC, select-to-fit approach at, 66–67

American Airlines, 201

American Automobile Association (AAA), calculation of vacation days, 134

American Express, 72

Anheuser-Busch InBev, 71

AnitaB.org, 63

Annual performance reviews, comparison with check-ins, **98**

ANZ Bank
  as product-focused, 40
  training program at, 12

Apollo, 20

Apple
  adaptive space at, 121
  competition and, 72
  hiring policy at, 63, 71
  improving work experience at, 191
  as million dollar company, 9
  as product-focused company, 34, 43
  reinvention of corporate learning platform, 157

Apprenticeships, 144

Arena, Michael, 27, 33–34, 121

Artificial intelligence (AI), 188
  impact of, 189
  Legion's use of, 60
  leverage data and, 161–162

Asana, 36

Ascending jobs, 148

AskMayoExpert, 189

Assessments, bias in, 121

AstraZeneca, 196

Atkins, Doug, 60

Atlassian, 19
  culture tools at, 99
  design team at, 39
  growth at, 40
  objectives-and-key-results approach at, 88
  physical space at, 118
  ShipIt hackathons at, 14
  Team Playbook at, 14

AT&T, 186
  ascending jobs at, 148
  career-coaching services at, 74
  learning environment at, 148

Attention to detail, 89

Autodesk, development of 3D-engineering design and manufacturing software at, 187–188

Automation, 189–190
  in creating work, 53, 55–57

Autonomy
  instilling, 25
  intersection of alignment with, **37**, 37–38

B

Badenoch, Alex, 30–31, 137

Bad work behaviors, 195

Bain & Company, as a best place to work, 181

Bank of America
  learning experience platforms at, 162
  no-layoff policy of, 181
  online learning platforms at, 146

Bank of Montreal, online learning platforms at, 146

Banks, purpose of, 168

Barra, Mary, 33–34, 185

Basecamp, 70

B Corps, 173

Benioff, Marc, 122, 178–179

Ben & Jerry's, 165, 173

Bersin & Associates, 211
  management roles at, 138–139

Bersin by Deloitte, 211

Best practices in a learning culture, 159, **160**

BetterUp guide managers, 159

Bezos, Jeff, 31, 78

Bias

in assessments, 121

in education, 63–64

elimination of experience, 64–65

pedigree, 63–64

in recruitment, promotion, and pay, 122

software in identifying gender, 132

BlackRock, 182

Blind, website of, 130

Blockchain technology, 72

BMW, use of redesigned workplaces, 62

Bock, Laszlo, 135

Bon-Ton Stores, 65–66

Boot camps, 144

Boss, shift to coach, 200

Boston Consulting Group, 10, 53

Bourke, Juliet, 122

Bowling Alone (Putman), 209

Brooks, Fred, 20–21

Brown, John, 8

Buffett, Warren

addiction to Coca-Cola and See's Candy, 175

enthusiasm for Geico, 175

strategy of, 175

Burnout tech firms, 92

Business

delivery models for, 8

digital transformation of, 141

rules of, 4

Business drivers, 9

Business outlook, 212

Business sustainability, productivity and, 205–206

Business unit teams, 9

C

Calibration meetings, 96

California, University of, at Berkeley, 63

Capability academy model, 158–159

Capital, 199

Capitalism, conscious, 174

Capital One

building of cloud technology academy by, 158

self-directed strategies in job training at, 145–146

teaching of soft skills at, 146

Careers

advisors on, 80

coaching, 74

differentiating between project manager and, 90

creating framework and giving clear guidance to employees and managers, 154–155

options in, 47

pathways in, 53

radical changes in, 143–144

urgent need to reinvent, 141–142

Carter, Dean, 101, 128

Cascio, Wayne, 182

Cemex, building of supply chain academy, 158

Certified B Corporations, 173

Chapters, 13, 39

Chat and conversational systems, 188

Check-ins, 87, 89

comparison with annual performance reviews, 98

encouraging feedback through, 97, 99

Chevron

DE&I surveys at, 122

diversity and inclusion at, 123

diversity committee at, 131

Chouinard, Yvon, 204

Christensen, Clayton, 77

Cisco
  benchmark studies on pay at, 100–101
  check-ins at, 97, 99
  leaders at, 78
  teamwork at, 15, 193–194
  training program at, 12, 15, 78
  wages at, 128
Citigroup, shift to hybrid work model, 113
Citizenship
  defined, 175
  holistic definition of, 179
  responsible, 182
  valuing companies by, 174–176
Clarity, 26
Cleveland Clinic, 11, 34–35, 69
Climate change, 182–183
  economic impact of, 171
Coaches
  shifting from bosses to, 200
  turning managers into, 91–93
Coaching, 37, 71–105
  and development, 88
  platforms, 159, 161
  smart software in enhancing, 105
  teams, 14
Coca-Cola, Warren Buffett's addiction to, 175
Collaboration, 155
Collective thinking, 93
Columbia University, research at, 121
Command and control management, 10
Companies
  aligning rewards to future needs, 155–157
  learning from mistakes, 159
  valuing by citizenship, 174–176
Compaq, 19
Compensation reviews, 88
Conjoint analysis, in building an efficient frontier or pay and benefits, 129
Conscious capitalism, 174

Consumer Bill of Rights, 173
Continuous performance management, 87–90
Continuous skills development, 24
Coordination, network effect of, 33
Corporate culture, 87, 118, 124, 130
Corporate learning, four Es of, 159, **160**
Corporate university, building a, 157–158
Costco, 71
  check-ins at, 89
Coursera, 159
COVID-19, 29, 38, 176–177, 186, 201
  vaccines and treatment for, 34
COVID-19 S protein, 34
Cracker Barrel, 182
Cross-functional teams, 9
Cross-generational diversity, 131
Cross-squad movement, 37
Cross-training, 72
Crotonville, 90
Culture, 107–136
  alignment in, 64
  aspects of irresistible, 109–110
  building inclusive, 131–132
  corporate, 87, 118, 124, 130
  diversity in, 131–132
  employee listening as value in, 180
  shift from rules to, 200
Culture of recognition and listening, embracing, 124–127
Cummins
  DE&I surveys at, 122
  talent mobility at, 73
Customer relationship management (CRM) platforms, 53
CVS
  development of Snowbird program, 62
  tenured employees at, 144
Cybersecurity, 141, 158

D

Data
finding irresistible companies using,
211–212
leveraging in management decisions,
103–105
product management approach to, 196
role of, 195
state of people-related, 196
Data-driven recruitment program, 63–64
Data science, 158
Dearborn, Jenny, 149–150
Dell, 19, 34
Deloitte, 59, 187
appraisals at, 86
check-ins at, 97, 99
forced retirement from, 143
*Deloitte Global Human Capital Trends
Report* (2021), 10, 55–56, 108, 115
Deloitte Global Millennial Survey (2020),
176–178
goal management system at, 86
job levels at, 48–49
performance management at, 85–86
positions for gig workers, 59
study of diversity and inclusion, 122
Deloitte University, building around design
thinking, 158
Dependability, 26
Descending jobs, 148
Design-centered engineering, 24
Design teams, 9
Design thinking, 185–186
application of, 189–190
building university around, 158
use of, in creating inclusive workspaces,
132–133
Deutsche Telekom
agile coaches at, 39
focus on design thinking, 185–186
Glassdoor ratings of, 186
leadership-in-crisis program at, 115
segment ion of workforce at, 197
stake in T-Mobile and Sprint, 185
WhatsApp groups at, 71
work-life balance at, 194
Development, rethinking in a network,
138–139
DeVita, company focus of, 169
Digital currency fluency, 72
Digital cryptocurrencies, 72
Digital Equipment, 20
Digital marketing, 158
Digital-marketing analytics, 55
Digital reskilling, 146
Discussion forums, 71
Diversity
equity, and inclusion (DE&I), 122, 168
new forms of, 123
taking ownership for, 121–124
training in, 123
Doctors and nurses, demand for, 152
Document and calendar synchronization,
114
DoorDash, 60, 194
Doubling down on wellbeing, 117–118
Dove, 165
Drive (Pink), 25
Dropbox
objectives-and-key-results approach at, 88
perks at, 133–134
Dunbar, Robin, 31–32
Dunbar number, 31–32
Durable skills, 153
Dynamic shifting of resources, 24

E

Earth Day, 173
Ecolab, pulse survey results at, 104
Economic growth, and job lookers, 138–139
Economics, actuarial, 158
Edelman's Trust Barometer, 172

Education bias, 63–64

Elevating Equity and Diversity research, 122

Elliott, Shayne, 40

Email content management, 152

Employee-centric systems, 186

Employee-focused tools, 187–190

Employee listening as cultural value, 180

Employee performance management system, 198

Employees

  creating a career framework and giving clear guidance to managers and, 154–155

  engagement of, 207

  experiences of, 4, 185–198

  listening to, 126–127

  productivity of, 204–206

  tenured, 144

Employment, productivity and, 205

Empowerment, 9

Emsi Burning Glass, 52–53, 141

  single-function jobs at, 146

Energy, hiring for, 69

Engagement, 9, 206–207

  levels of, in the airline industry, 83–85

Environment, elements of, 109–110

Equilar, 182

Equinix, growth at, 104

Equinix Business School, creation of, 104

Equity, pay, 100, 171–172, 178, 195

Erste Group, 77

ESG factors, 182

ESG-focused programs, 167

Evaluation, purpose of, 96

Execution, natural stress between learning and, 139

Executive compensation, reducing, 182

Experience API (xAPI), 162

Experience bias, elimination of, 64–65

Exxon

  appraisals at, 86

  management and, 45

  promotion at, 140–141

  training regime at, 149

  wages at, 127–128

EY, 30

F

Facebook, 9, 41. *See also* Meta

  on managing people, 103

Face-to-face, working, 29–31

Facial recognition, 188

Fairness, 208–209

  taking ownership for, 121–124

Fairygodboss, website of, 129–130

Farmers Insurance, job training at, 145

Feedback

  creating culture of, 27

  encouraging through check-ins, 97, 99

  negative connotation with, 89

  tools for, 37

Feedback and goal reviews, 88

Fernandez, Kiera, 124, 168–169

Fieldglass, SAP acquisition of, 59

Fink, Larry, 182

Firms of Endearment, 123

Fitbit, improving work experience at, 191

Fiverr, 58

Flatley, Jay, 134

Flexibility, 109

Followership, 11

Ford, shift to hybrid work model, 113

Formal training, importance of, 145

Fourth Industrial Revolution, 153

Freelancer, 58

Freelance work, 44

Frontline worker platforms, 186

Fuel50, 155

FullContact, 134–135

Functional hierarchy, 7

Furniture flexibility, 119

G

Gallup, development of first employee-engagement survey by, 206

Gandara, Amelia, 43

GE Fuse, 43

Gender bias, software in identifying, 132

Gender diversity, 131

Gender pay equity, 178, 195

Gender pay inequities, 195

Genentech, 207

General Assembly, 65, 159

General Electric (GE)
agile methods at, 40
check-ins at, 97
ending of "rank and yank" at, 90
insights at, 89, 90
job networks at, 74
MVP at, 24
reinvention of corporate learning platform, 157
sourcing of external talent at, 43
succession management at, 45

General managers, building, 79

General Mills
DE&I surveys at, 122
job rotation at, 149
local brands, flavors, and products of, 167
talent production at, 92, 149

General Motors (GM), 27, 33–34, 185
as forward-looking company, 11, 27
looking at skills of the future, 155
performance of, 175
succession management and, 45

Generation Zs, 176

Genpact, 59
training of gig workers, 59

Gherson, Diane, 25

Gig work, 58–61

Gini index, 208

Glassdoor, 124–125, 142, 205, 211–212
analysis of, 181
bringing pets to work, 135
data in, 168
leadership at, 130
pay in, 100, 127, 133
ratings, 16, 71, 81, 93, 122, 178
website of, 129–130
Workplace Trends 2021, 168

GlaxoSmithKline, 34

Glint, 194

Global awareness, 155

Global Cash Card, ADP acquisition of, 60

Global coronavirus pandemic, 11

GM2020, 33

Goals
embracing clear, transparent, 69–71
sharing of, 114

Goal-setting, 70–71, 87, 88
traditional versus new techniques in, **95**

Golden State Warriors, 10–11

Goler, Lori, 18, 40–41, 103

Good Jobs Institute, 71

Google
adaptive space at, 121
Adwords system of, 142
check-ins at, 99
coaching teams at, 14
committee of peers at, 102
competition and, 72
culture in, 24
data-driven recruitment program of, 63–64
hiring focus at, 63
HR apprenticeship program at, 51
job swaps with, 47–48
as million-dollar company, 9
pay at, 100, 128, 133
Project Oxygen team at, 26
reliance on objectives-and-key-results approach at, 88

snack program at, 135
   tapping into human desire and, 9
   use of psychological tricks and, 191
Google Workspace, resolving issues of productivity and, 193
Goyder, George, 173
GPA, correlation between job success and, 63
Graham, Benjamin, 175, 176
Greenpeace, 173
Growth, 137–163
   mindset for, 68, 71–72, 150–151
   versus promotion, 140–141
   shift to, 200
Groysberg, Boris, 27
Guilds, 13–14

H

Hagel, John, 8
Happiness, 208–209
Harris, Tristan, 191–192
Harvard University, 25
Headspace, 194
Hewlett-Packard
   Brain Candy program at, 145
   as product-focused, 34
   workforce transformations at, 153
Hewlett Packard Enterprise (HPE), 49
Hierarchical career ladders, 144
Hierarchical career model, 47, 144
Hierarchical organizational charts, 45
Hierarchical structure, 45
   top-down, 19–20
Hierarchy
   effect of network of teams, 14
   reducing, 19–21
   shift to teams, 200
   teams as opposed to, 7–41
Hierarchy of needs (Maslow), 124, **125**, 127
HipChat, 37

Hiring
   getting right, 68–75
   new ways of, 62–65
Hogan, Kathleen, 31
Hog-butchering model, 21
Holistic approach
   taking a, 159–161
   taking to wellbeing, 134–135
Hourly workers, financial insecurity and, 128
Hubspot, 142
Hulu, job training at, 145
Human capital management (HCM), 193–194
Human-centered leadership, 81, 115–116, **116**
Human relations
   age of, 196
   apprenticeship programs in, 51
   IBM use of agile in, 25
Human resources, work of, 114–115, 194
Human spirit
   power of, 201
   unleashing the power of the, 199
Hybridization, 53
Hybrid jobs, 146
   importance of, 152–153
Hybrid work model, shifting to, 113–114
Hybrid workspaces, 31
Hyperwinning companies, 4
Hyphen, website of, 130

I

IBM, 19–20, 34, 45, 59, 86, 89
   check-ins at, 97
   checkpoint system at, 89
   cognitive career advisors powered by Watson at, 147–148
   job rotation at, 144
   looking at skills of the future, 155
   physical space at, 118
   promotion at, 140–141

reducing hierarchy at, 19–21

reinvention of corporate learning platform, 157

on respect for the individual, 124

respect for the individual and, 124

tenured employees at, 144

training of gig workers, 59

training regime at, 149

use of agile in human relations, 25

value of internal experience, 64

wages at, 127–128

workforce transformations at, 153

IKEA

collective thinking at, 93

hiring by, 69

mission of, 204

retention rate at, 69

Inclusion, 108, 155

need for, in culture, 131–132

taking ownership for, 121–124

Inclusive workspaces, use of design thinking in creating, 132–133

Income inequality, 208

economic impact of, 171

Indeed

need for communications, 152

pay review at, 100

Indian Hotels Company Limited, 97

Industrial Revolution, 7

Industry 4.0, 153

Infrastructure investment, lack of, 206

ING Bank, 35, 38–39, 40

physical space at, 118

Ingersoll Rand, 49

success profiles at, 154–155

talent mobility at, 74

ING Group

as forward-looking company, 11

tribes at, 13

Initial public offerings (IPOs), 59

Inner work life, 25

Innovation, 155

Integrated CRM, 55

Intel, 19

OKR model pioneered at, 70

Internal mobility, 48

Intuit, 60–61

check-ins at, 99

Invisible hand theory, 171

Irresistible, 5

Irresistible companies

career models, 144–149

finding using data, 211–212

J

Jack Welch & The G.E. Way (Slater), 85

Jain, Sachin, 29

Jaycations, 134

JetBlue, 84

Jira, 70

Jobs

ascending, 148

correlation between GPA and success in, 63

crafting of, 26

deletion of descriptions, 57–58

descending, 148

economic growth and, 138–139

evolution of hybrid, 53, **54**

old architecture as problem, 52, **54**

recrafting of, 67

rotation of, 51–52, 144

shift to work, 52–53, 200

swaps in, 47–48

training programs for, 144

Jobs, Steve, 43, 78

John Deere, 40

Johnson & Johnson

credo of, 172–173

mission of, 204

Johnson & Johnson Human Performance Institute (HPI), employee wellbeing at, 117

Jordan, Mike, 145

Josh Bersin Company, 211

Juniper Networks, 93

   wages at, 128

K

Karoshi, 136

Kennedy, John F., establishment of Consumer Bill of Rights by, 173

Kern, John, 21

Knowledge, including deep, of the organization, 27

Kununu, website of, 129–130

L

Labor, 199

Layoffs

   costs of, 182

   move away from, 181–182

Leaders

   development of, 91–92

   embracement of growth mindset, 68

   need for, 80

   purpose of, 79–80

   successful, 81

   training, 93

Leadership, 78

   failures in, 195

   focusing on, 162–163

   human-centered, 81, 115–116, **116**

   involvement with learning culture, 149–150

   in a network, 79–83

   recognizing importance of, 136

   updating models of, 155

Lean Startup (Ries), 24

Learning

   adaptive, 161

   on the job, 72

   natural stress between execution and learning, 139

   personalized, 161

Learning culture

   best practices in, 159, **160**

building, 151

   need for a, 149–151

Learning curve, 141

Learning platforms

   reinvention of corporate, 157

   use of, 162

Legendary Entertainment, 71

Legion, use of AI, 60

Leverage data, AI and, 161–162

Lever Brothers, merger with Margarine Unie, 165

Liberty Management System (LMS), 14

Liberty Mutual, 14

   building of academies, 158

   learning management system at, 99

Life-work technology, 193

Lincoln, Abraham, 199, 200

LinkedIn, 159, 194

   hiring focus at, 63

   need for communications, 152

   objectives-and-key results approach at, 88

   pay at, 100, 127, 133

   productivity and, 205

   skills at, 142

Lipton, 165

Listening to employees, 126–127

Longevity, 61–62

M

Machine learning, 141

Mackey, John, 107

Macrolearning, 149

Management

   command and control, 10

   continuous performance, 87–90

   customer relationship, 53

   focusing on, 162–163

   goal, 86

   growth, 178–179

   human capital, 193–194

   human-centered approach to, 115–116, **116**

leveraging data in decisions, 103–105
past and present archetypes, **82**
performance, 87, 198
potential in, 46
product, 196
succession, 45
talent, 29
Managers
creating a career framework and giving clear guidance to employees and, 154–155
need for, 80
reducing power and level of, 102–103
role of, 80, 118
turning into coaches, 91–93
Manifesto for Agile Software Development, 21, **23**
Manufacturing teams, 9
Margarine Unie, merger with Lever Brothers, 165
Market demand, paying people based on, 99–101
Marketing analytics, 152
Marketing managers, job of, 141–142
Marketo, 142
Marsh McLennan, 155
Martin, Guy, 188
Maslow, Abraham, 137
hierarchy of needs, 124, **125**, 127
Massachusetts Institute of Technology (MIT), 63, 159
research at, 121
Massive open online courses (MOOCs), 159
Mastercard, 72
use of learning experience platforms by, 162
Mastery, instilling, 25
Mayo Clinic, 35, 189
McChrystal, Stanley, 15
Meeting overload, 135
Mercadona, 71
Mercer workplace flexibility study, 30
Messaging, 192

Meta, 189. *See also* Facebook
data-driven recruitment program at, 63–64
gig workers at, 58
pay equity at, 100
teamwork at, 15, 18, 37, 40–41
as trillion dollar company, 9
MGM Resorts, 201
Michelin, older workers at, 62
Microlearning, 149
Microsoft, 11, 19, 53, 58, 121
flexible work opportunities at, 113
inclusive, growth mindset at, 150–151
mission of, 204
pay equity at, 100
tapping technology as perk, 135
teams at, 16, 37
tools at, 104
Microsoft 365, 194
Microsoft Teams
meetings of, 187
resolving issues of productivity and, 193
Microsoft Viva, 194
Microtasks, managing, 36–37
Militello, Joe, 22
Millennial, student debt of, 129
Millennials, 176
Mindsets
abundance, 86
growth, 68, 71–72, 150–151
Mission, 204
hiring for, 69
Mission Bell Winery, 40
Mission statement, need for up-to-date, 179
Mobile messaging applications, 114
Monster, 44
Morality (Sacks), 4
Morgan Stanley, no-layoff policy of, 181
Morris, Donna, 99
Moussavian, Reza, 185–186
Murphy, Barry, 19
Murthy, Ramana, 97

MVP (minimum viable product), 24

The Mythical Man-Month (Brooks), 20–21

N

Nadella, Satya, 58, 150–151

Nair, Leena, 165–166

Nap time, as perk, 135

NASSCOM, building of career framework for the future of IT, 156

National Basketball Association, 11

National Public Radio, 40

Nestlé

  DE&I surveys at, 122

  job rotation at, 144–145

  local brands, flavors, and products of, 167

  talent production at, 92

Netflix, 43

  job training at, 145

Network

  leading in a, 79–83

  rethinking development in a, 138–139

  of teams, 9, 12, 41

Network effect of coordination, 33

New York Life, check-ins at, 97

Nine-box grid, 45–46, **46**, 47, 85

99designs, 58

Nooyi, Indra, 165

O

Objectives-and-key-results (OKR) approach to goal-setting, 15, 70, 87, 88

  putting into practice, 93–94

Officium, 110

Ohana Book project, 178

Online training programs, 187

Open career marketplace, 48

Open-plan formats, 119

Oracle, 70

  tapping technology as perk, 135

Organizational culture, 207

  developing that supports performance, 27

Organizational endurance, 203–209

Organizational learning, forms of, 139

Organizational network analysis (ONA), 195

Organization charts, hierarchical, 45

Output, shift to employee experience, 200

Outsourcing firms, 59

Overwork, 188

Overwork death, 136

Ownership, taking, for inclusion, diversity, and fairness, 121–124

P

Pandora, transparency at, 130

Partners, 49

Passion, hiring for, 69

Patagonia

  collective thinking at, 93

  goal-setting and performance at, 101–102

  mission of, 204

  products of, 173–174

  staff meeting at, 135

  wages at, 128

Pay

  bias in, 122

  equity in, 100, 171–172, 178, 195

  fairness of, 133

  personalizing, 129

PayPal, 49,

  competition and, 72

  no-layoff policy of, 181

Payscale, wages at, 127

Pedigree bias, 63–64

Peer-review process, 49

Peet's Coffee, 60

People

  human-centered approach to management of, 115–116, **116**

  paying competitive wage to, 127–129

  right role for, 49–52

People with Purpose program, Unilever, 165

PepsiCo, 11, 89, 165

  HP apprenticeship program at, 51

performance appraisals at, 97
talent management at, 29
PepsiCo Process Shredder, 197–198
Performance
developing organizational culture that supports, 27
evaluating in new way, 94, 96–97
impact of recognition on, 125
reviews of, 88
Performance management, 85–87
continuous, 87–90
Perks, finding, 133–134
Personalized learning, 161
Personal reinvention, 142
Pets, bringing to work, as perk, 135
Pfizer, as wellness company, 168
Philips Lighting
mission of, 170
purpose of, 169–170
Philz Coffee, 60
Physical pods, 37
Pink, Daniel, 25
Pivotal Labs (now part of VMware), 22
perks at, 134
Planning, replacement, 45
Pluralsight, 159
Potential, defining, 46
Powell, Colin, 81
Price, Dom, 19
Procter & Gamble (P&G), 47, 49
Productivity, 204–206
resolving issues of, 193
Product management approach to data, 196
Profits, importance of, 166
Progress, providing ability to see, 25–26
The Progress Principle (Amabile), 205
Project leaders, 80
Project manager, differentiating between career coach and, 90
Project: Time Off, calculation of vacation days, 134

Promotion
bias in, 122
growth versus, 140–141
shift to growth, 200
Proximity, physical and virtual, 29–31
Psychological tricks, use of, 191
Psychological safety, 26
Purpose
focusing on, 165–183
instilling, 25
providing ability to see, 25–26
Putman, Robert D., 209

Q
Quit rate, 44

R
Rainforest Alliance, 165
Rallyteam, 59
Workday acquisition of, 59
Rapid iteration, 24
Ratings, competing for, 96
Recessions, problem of, 171
Recognition, 109
impact on performance, 125
Recruitment, bias in, 122
Regenerative performance, 102
Relationships, respecting and rewarding the value of, 163
Reliance's My Voice, 71
Remote work, 113
hybrid as successful approach to, 114–115
Replacement list, 45
Replacement planning, 45
Reskilling programs, 144
Responsible citizenship, 182
The Responsible Company (Goyder), 173
Responsible Restructuring (Cascio), 182
Reward expertise, 162
Rewards, 109
aligning to the company's future needs, 155–157

Reward systems, as problem, 52, **54**
Ries, Eric, 24
Rigby, Darrell, 40
Ritz Carlton, 16
Robinson, C. H., 40
Robotics, impact of, 189
Routine work, disappearance of, 188–189
Royal Bank of Canada, 169
    purpose of, 169
Rules, shift to culture, 200

S

Sacks, Jonathan, 4
Safety
    creating environment of, 26
    psychology, 26
Sainsbury's, 169, 201
Salary.com, wages at, 127
Salesforce, 142, 178–179
    gender bias study by, 122
    growth management at, 178–179
    launch of Trailhead by, 156
    volunteer time off (VTO) of, 135, 178
Sales teams, 9
Samsung, 34
Sanofi S.A., 34
    as wellness company, 168
Santander Bank, purpose of, 169
SAP, 34
    acquisition of Fieldglass, 59
    Autism at Work program at, 132
    diversity and inclusion at, 131–132
    tapping technology as perk, 135
    teamwork at, 15
    willingness to invest in learning, 150
SAP Academy for Sales and Presales, 150
Scalable learning, 8
Scale
    industrial concept of, 20
    organizing teams at, 35–39
Schein, Edgar, 87

Schneider Electric, 196
    use of gig workers, 60
Search engine optimization, 55, 141–142, 152
Select-to-fit model, 68
SellMax, 58
Semper, Janice, 10
Sendmail, 19
Services-team approach, 16
Shahid, Humera, 60–61
Shared space, 119
Shell Oil Company, employee learning at, 146
Shift, 44–62
ShipIt hackathons, 14
Sierra-Cedar's 2020 global study of technology, 193
Signet Jewelers, 182
Silicon Graphics, 20
The Silo Effect (Tett), 32
Silos, removing between teams, 32
SimplrFlex, 58
Skills
    changing nature of, 52–53
    development of, 56
Skillsoft, 159, 194
"Skunk works" approach, 32
Slack, 16, 27, 37
    allowing time for, 71
    resolving issues of productivity and, 193
Slack channels, 187
Smith, Adam, invisible hand theory of, 171
Snacks, as perk, 135
Snyder, Kieran, 121–122
Social cohesion, 209
Social-distancing mandates, 190
Social feedback, 192
Social-influencer marketing, 142
Socially conscious companies, performance of, 122–123
Social media, 55
Social networking, 191

Social tools, 125–126

Sodexo, DE&I surveys at, 122

Soft skills, 153

  teaching of, 146

Software, in identifying gender bias, 132

Southwest Airlines, 16, 182

  customer experience net promoter scores at, 84–85

  hiring by, 69

Speed, 9

S&P Global, design thinking and, 190

Spotify, 35–36, 88

  agile model at, 80

  objectives-and-key-results approach at, 88

  physical space at, 118

Sprint, 36, 185

Squads, 13, 38

Square, competition and, 72

Standup meetings, 36

Stanford, online courses offered by, 159

Starbucks, 168

  AI-driven platform at, 60

  no-layoff policy of, 181

  pay at, 133

  teaching of baristas and, 161

State of Texting 2021 report, 192

Steelcase

  workplace design at, 110

  workplace satisfaction at, 118–119

Stripe, 50

Strong Vocational Interest Blank, 143

Structure, 26

SuccessFactors, 70

  tapping technology as perk, 135

Succession management, 45

Success profiles, 154–155

Sun, 20

Surgical team model, 21

Sutherland, Jeff, 40

Swift feedback, 24

Sybase, 78

  promotion at, 140–141

Systemic racism, 195, 208

T

Taj Hotels, 11

Takeuchi, Hirotaka, 40

Talent marketplace, 59

  model of, 47

Talent mobility, 48

  facilitating and supporting, 72–75

Talent production, 92

Talent reviews, 96

Target

  achievements of, 174

  diversity and inclusion strategy at, 124

  mission of, 124, 168–169

Teachers Insurance and Annuity Association of America (TIAA), shift to hybrid work model, 113

Teams, 16

  agile, 24, 30, 31, 33

  building clear sense of purpose, 27

  characteristics of effective, 25–27

  combination into squads, tribes, and chapters, 13

  creating culture of feedback, 27

  creating environment of safety and trust, 26

  defined, 12

  developing organizational culture that supports performance, 27

  empowering, 84

  forming own work practices, 26–27

  including deep knowledge of the organization, 27

  instilling autonomy, mastery, and purpose, 25

  intelligence systems of, 16

  network of, 9, 12, 41

  as opposed to hierarchy, 7–41

  organizing and networking, 32–35